Authoring a PhD

Palgrave Study Guides

Authoring a PhD
Career Skills
Critical Thinking Skills
e-Learning Skills
Effective Communication for
  Arts and Humanities Students
Effective Communication for
  Science and Technology
The Foundations of Research
The Good Supervisor
How to Manage your Arts, Humanities and
  Social Science Degree
How to Manage your Distance and
  Open Learning Course
How to Manage your Postgraduate Course
How to Manage your Science and
  Technology Degree
How to Study Foreign Languages
How to Write Better Essays
IT Skills for Successful Study
Making Sense of Statistics
The Mature Student's Guide to Writing
The Palgrave Student Planner
The Postgraduate Research Handbook

Presentation Skills for Students
The Principles of Writing in Psychology
Professional Writing
Research Using IT
Skills for Success
The Student Life Handbook
The Student's Guide to Writing (2nd edn)
The Study Skills Handbook (2nd edn)
Study Skills for Speakers of English as
  a Second Language
Studying the Built Environment
Studying Economics
Studying History (2nd edn)
Studying Law
Studying Mathematics and its Applications
Studying Modern Drama (2nd edn)
Studying Physics
Studying Programming
Studying Psychology
Teaching Study Skills and Supporting Learning
Work Placements – A Survival Guide for Students
Write it Right
Writing for Engineers (3rd edn)

Palgrave Study Guides: Literature

General Editors: John Peck and Martin Coyle

How to Begin Studying English Literature
  (3rd edn)
How to Study a Jane Austen Novel (2nd edn)
How to Study a Charles Dickens Novel
How to Study Chaucer (2nd edn)
How to Study an E. M. Forster Novel
How to Study James Joyce
How to Study Linguistics (2nd edn)

How to Study Modern Poetry
How to Study a Novel (2nd edn)
How to Study a Poet
How to Study a Renaissance Play
How to Study Romantic Poetry (2nd edn)
How to Study a Shakespeare Play (2nd edn)
How to Study Television
Practical Criticism

Authoring a PhD

*How to plan, draft, write and finish
a doctoral thesis or dissertation*

Patrick Dunleavy

First published 2003 by
PALGRAVE MACMILLAN
Houndmills, Basingstoke, Hampshire RG21 6XS and
175 Fifth Avenue, New York, N. Y. 10010
Companies and representatives throughout the world

PALGRAVE MACMILLAN is the global academic imprint of the Palgrave
Macmillan division of St. Martin's Press, LLC and of Palgrave Macmillan Ltd.
Macmillan® is a registered trademark in the United States, United Kingdom
and other countries. Palgrave is a registered trademark in the European
Union and other countries.

ISBN–13: 978–1–4039–1191–9 hardback
ISBN–10: 1–4039–1191–6 hardback
ISBN–13: 978–1–4039–0584–0 paperback
ISBN–10: 1–4039–0584–3 paperback

This book is printed on paper suitable for recycling and made from fully
managed and sustained forest sources.

A catalogue record for this book is available from the British Library.

Library of Congress Cataloging-in-Publication Data
Dunleavy, Patrick.
    Authoring a PhD : how to plan, draft, write, and finish a doctoral
thesis or dissertation / Patrick Dunleavy.
        p. cm.
    Includes bibliographical references and index.
    ISBN 1–4039–1191–6 – ISBN 1–4039–0584–3 (pbk.)
        1. Dissertations, Academic–Authorship–Handbooks, manuals, etc.
    2. Academic writing–Handbooks, manuals, etc. I. Title: Authoring a Ph. D.
II. Title.
    LB2369 .D85 2003
        808'.02–dc21   2002042453

10   9   8   7
10 09 08 07 06

Printed in China

For Sheila and Rosemary

Thanks for the encouragement

All rules for study are summed up in this one: learn only in order to create.
Friedrich Schelling

Contents

List of Figures and Tables

Figures

Tables

Preface

The conservative political philosopher Michael Oakeshott once argued that:

> A university is an association of persons, locally situated, engaged in caring for and attending to the whole intellectual capital which composes a civilization. It is concerned not merely to keep an intellectual inheritance intact, but to be continuously recovering what has been lost, restoring what has been neglected, collecting together what has been dissipated, repairing what has been corrupted, reconsidering, reshaping, reorganizing, making more intelligible, reissuing and reinvesting. [1]

Even if we leave aside Oakeshott's evident antiquarian bias against any genuine or substantive innovation here, this 'mission statement' is extensive enough. Indeed it is far too large to be credible in the era of a 'knowledge society', when so many other people (working in professions, companies, cultural and media organizations, governments, civil society groups or as independent writers and researchers) also attend to 'the intellectual capital [of] a civilization'.

This book is written in the hope of somewhat assisting any of these people who produce longer creative non-fiction texts. It is especially directed to research students and their advisers or supervisors in universities. In undertaking or fostering the doctorate they still pursue the most demanding ideal of original research. 'Nothing was ever yet done that someone was not the first to do,' said John Stuart Mill, and that is what the doctoral ideal always has celebrated and always should.[2] Each doctoral dissertation or thesis is to a large extent *sui generis*. But this book reflects a conviction that in the humanities, arts and social sciences research students also need to acquire a core of generic authoring skills that are substantially similar across diverse disciplines and topics. While research skills training has been formalized a great deal in the last two decades, these 'craft' skills of authoring have been relatively neglected and left unsystematized.

For Oakeshott and other traditionalists my enterprise here will seem no more than another brick in the wall, a further step towards the bureaucratization of modern society foreseen by Max Weber.[3] But I believe that learning the craft of how to plan, draft, write, develop, revise and rethink a thesis, and to finish it on time and to the standard required, is too important and too often mishandled a set of tasks to be left to the somewhat erratic and tangential models of induction and training that have prevailed in the past. There is a long and honourable tradition now of scholarship reflecting upon itself. It stretches back through Friedrich Schelling's idealist vision in *On University Studies*, to Francis Bacon's musings in *The Advancement of Learning*, and before him to some significant reflective writings of the medieval thinkers and the ancient Greek philosophers.[4] Now, as in those earlier times, scholars and students are not (cannot be) immune to external influences and rationalization processes. In modern conditions universities can privilege their existing modes of generating and transmitting knowledge only so long as they are demonstrably the best of available alternatives.

Of course, completing a doctoral dissertation is also too personal and too subtle a process, too dependent upon students and supervisors or advisers, too variable across thesis topics, disciplines and university contexts, for any generic advice to encompass more than a tiny proportion of what a given doctoral student needs to help her develop as an author. But covering this fraction in a systematic way can still be very valuable, time-saving and perhaps inspiring. PhD students know their own situation better than anyone else in the world. They can build on a small amount of 'ready-made knowledge' (as Schelling termed it),[5] picking and choosing those elements of this text that are relevant for their problems. I hope that this book may also help thesis advisers (with knowledge of a range of doctoral projects in their own discipline) to extend and systematize their thinking and guidance to students about authoring issues. So this book is written as a foil for students and their supervisors, as a grid or a framework which they can set against their own situations and experiences.

I have written up this advice in a modest but not a tentative way, because I know no other style that will seem honest or convincing. For some readers there is a risk that my suggestions may come across as overly slick or didactic, as if I am seeking to dictate what squads of PhD students should do. But I am acutely aware that readers always will and always should construct their own personalized versions of this text, adapting and domesticating what works for them, and setting to one side what does not fit. I have written like someone devising a menu for a restaurant, wanting to offer a treatment that is challenging and convincing, and an experience which is consistent and as complete as possible. But I am conscious that no one (in their right frame of mind) will pick up and consume more than a fraction of this menu at a time.

Lastly let me stress that this book is to a large extent a conduit for the ideas of many student and staff colleagues, whose wisdom and suggestions I have jotted down, adopted, tried out and probably shamelessly purloined over the years. I owe my heaviest debt to some 30 people who have worked with me on their own doctorates across two and a bit decades. They have taught me so much as they developed their ideas, not just about their thesis topics but also about our joint profession.[6] In different ways, each of them will know the frailties and limitations of supervisors all too well, and I can only ask their tolerance of any gloss on their experience which this volume inadvertently gives. My next biggest debt is to colleagues at the London School of Economics and Political Science who have co-supervised PhDs with me or co-taught the School-wide seminar on PhD writing.[7] From their very different styles of teaching and encouraging, I have learned much. I am grateful also to a wide range of other colleagues, who may recognize their own ideas and inputs scattered across these pages. Lastly I would like to thank the students from 18 disciplines who attended my PhD writing course at LSE over more than a decade. Their questions, challenges and innovations have consistently stretched my knowledge, and convinced me that we could do more to help.

I hope that the enterprise of gathering these ideas together in one volume will seem justified for most readers, and that if it does you will contribute to the book by e-mailing me your comments, criticisms and suggestions for changes or additions. For me, even in our rationalized times, the doctorate still remains a crucial vehicle for developing new and original thought in the humanities and social sciences, especially amongst young people, who (as Plato said) are 'closer to ideas'.[8] If this book strikes even a few positive chords among new generations of scholars and supervisors, then writing it will have been worthwhile.

Patrick Dunleavy   January 2003

London School of Economics and Political Science
London
p.dunleavy@lse.ac.uk

1

Becoming an Author

> In writing a problem down or airing it in
> conversation we let its essential aspects emerge.
> And by knowing its character, we remove, if not
> the problem itself, then its secondary, aggravating
> characteristics: confusion, displacement, surprise.
> *Alain de Botton* [1]

The authoring process involves all the component parts of producing a finished piece of text, that is: envisaging what to write, planning it in outline, drafting passages, writing the whole thing, revising and rewriting it, and finishing it in an appropriate form, together with publishing all or parts of your text. At every stage a complex mix of intellectual and logistical issues can crop up. As de Botton suggests of problems in general, often there are genuine (permanent) dilemmas surrounded by more resolvable delaying or distracting factors. Neither the fundamental problems nor their penumbra of aggravations may be straightforward to resolve, but we can often make progress on the latter by making the issues involved more explicit. My aim here is to shed light on common authoring problems and to point out solutions which others have found helpful and that may also work for you.

I begin by discussing the importance of authoring as a generic set of skills at the doctoral level. A thesis or a long dissertation (I use these words interchangeably from here on) forms a critical element in all the main models of PhD education. Some key authoring principles have important application across many

1

humanities and social science disciplines. The second section considers the varying authoring tasks involved in the 'classical' model of PhD and newer 'taught PhD' models. The third section looks at a foundation skill for becoming a good author, which is to actively manage your readers' expectations.

Authoring is more than just writing

> To write is to raise a claim to be read, but by whom?
> C. Wright Mills   [2]

To do authoring at doctoral level is to become a qualified (and hopefully published) academic writer. It involves acquiring a complete set of 'craft' skills, a body of practical knowledge that has traditionally been passed on by personal contacts within university departments from supervisors to students. A basic theme of this book is that authoring skills are a crucial element to completing a successful doctorate. They are fundamental in achieving a coherent, joined-up argument for your thesis. Proficiency in authoring can also help you meet the requirements of 'originality' and making a substantive contribution to the development of a discipline, which are still key criteria for awarding a doctorate in good universities. And acquiring authoring capabilities is very important in finishing a doctorate on time and avoiding the long delays for which PhD students were once notorious.

Yet PhD students are only rarely taught authoring skills in an explicit way in universities. The knowledge involved has not often been codified or written down. Great effort is normally put into communicating to students the substantive knowledge of each discipline, with an intense socialization and training in its research methods. By comparison the teaching or training of students in authoring has been given little attention. Partly this reflects a widespread conviction amongst academic staff that at the PhD level becoming an effective writer is completely bound up with becoming a good researcher, and with mastering the subject matter of one individual academic discipline. Authoring a doctorate has often been seen as too diffuse an activity to be legitimately or usefully studied in universities. Many, perhaps most, working academics might doubt that much useful can be said about the generic skills involved in authoring – outside the context of each particular discipline. Hence in offering advice about authoring to their students most university teachers and supervisors have had few credible resources to hand. Many advisers must draw largely on their own experience, of supervising earlier students, or perhaps of being a PhD student themselves up to three decades ago. This neglect of authoring skills is not universal. The editors of academic journals and most publishers of university-level books can and do draw a distinction between people's prowess in a discipline and their proficiency as writers. They recognize that good researchers can be bad writers, and that uninspiring researchers can still be good writers, interpreters and communicators. But the thrust of much doctoral education none the less remains that if you get the research right then the writing aspect will somehow just fall naturally into place.

This conventional approach assumes that beginning PhD students will be sustained by discipline-specific study skills inculcated in their earlier education, at first degree or masters level. As their research goes on they will presumably learn how to produce good (or at least acceptable) writing in the style of their discipline via a process of trial and error, 'learning by doing' over successive drafts – first of papers, then of chapters, and ultimately of a complete thesis. Doctoral students are mentored intensively and hence should get detailed criticisms and individual advice from their supervisors and perhaps other colleagues. This advice is always text-specific and discipline-specific, focusing on this or that substantive argument or piece of research, on whether a particular point has been proved sufficiently, or whether a given way of expressing an argument is legitimate or appropriate in its context, and so on. From many repeated instances of these comments and interactions the hope is that students will progressively build up their own sense of what can and cannot be said, how it may be said, and how other professionals in their subject will interpret and react to their text.

In undertaking research and in developing disciplinary knowledge the craft approach to PhD education still works well, even though it has been extensively supplemented in modern times by much more formalized, extensive and lengthier processes of advanced instruction. And on authoring issues, many students will perhaps be lucky and have sympathetic staff as their supervisors, people who are themselves skilled and experienced authors and who are also prepared to devote a lot of time and effort to inculcating similar authoring skills via individual working with students. In these circumstances the by-product approach can still deliver outstanding results.

But normally the by-product model of how students learn and develop is far more problematic in relation to authoring skills. In modern universities the pressures of teaching, research, publishing and administration on qualified staff frequently cause this model to break down in one or several respects. Doctoral instruction via individual supervision is costly and time-consuming. One of the reasons for a more formal and col-lective trend in doctoral education has been to reduce the amount of individual teaching needed, with peer group semi-nars used more to help students to develop their ideas and com-munication skills. Even in the most traditional view of PhD education, which still stresses one-to-one induction of each stu-dent by a single supervisor, the transmission of authoring skills is vulnerable. Some supervisors may be indifferent writers, or not very interested in or proficient in developing other people's authoring capabilities. Their students can find themselves with-out any fall-back source of guidance. Above all, the by-product way of doing things can be very time-consuming and erratic, hence worrying and psychologically taxing for students. Informal or 'trial and error' methods may unnecessarily stretch out the period people take to complete a doctorate. And it may make the process of becoming a competent and talented author in your own right more problematic than it need be.

Here is where this book aims to be useful, in helping PhD stu-dents and their advisers to think more systematically about authoring skills. On the basis of supervising my own students over the years, and of teaching a large and intensive course on PhD drafting and writing at my university for more than a decade, I take what might be labelled an 'extreme' view by more conventional colleagues. I believe that in most of the social sciences and all of the humanities disciplines, a set of general authoring skills determine around 40 to 50 per cent of anyone's success in completing a doctorate. Of course, your ability to complete doctoral-level work will be primarily conditioned by your own research ideas and 'native' originality, and your hard work, application and skill in acquiring specific knowledge of your discipline and competence in its methods. But unless you simultaneously grow and enhance your authoring abilities, there are strong risks that your ideas may not develop sufficiently far or fast enough to sustain you through to finishing your thesis at the right level and in a reasonable time. Doing good research and becoming an effective author are not separate processes, but closely related aspects of intellectual development that need to work in parallel. I also believe that authoring skills are relatively generic ones, applicable in a broadly similar way across a range of disciplines at doctoral level. Hence this book draws on a wide range of previous writings and insights by earlier generations of university scholars.

Different models of PhD and the tasks of authoring

In contemporary universities there are a number of different models of what a doctorate consists of. The way in which you

Model of PhD	Supervision	Thesis requirement	Found in
Classical model focuses on thesis writing throughout, with only preliminary training or coursework	Either one or two supervisors (UK); or a small supervisory committee (Europe)	**Big book thesis:** an integrated set of chapters usually around 80,000 to 100,000 words long	British-influenced and European-influenced university systems, and more text-based disciplines
Taught PhD model The first stage involves coursework assessed by a general examination. The second stage is a dissertation	Main adviser, plus minor adviser, plus rest of dissertation committee	**Papers model dissertation:** four or five publishable quality papers, around 60,000 words	American-influenced university systems, and more technical social sciences elsewhere

need to develop authoring skills will vary somewhat across each of these models, as well as across different humanities and social sciences disciplines to some extent. There are two main types of PhD education: the 'classical' model associated closely with a 'big book' type of thesis; and the more modern 'taught PhD model', normally associated with a shorter 'papers model dissertation'. I show how the advice given here and in the rest of this book can be adjusted to match the model of doctorate that you are completing.

The classical model of PhD developed over centuries in Europe and is still dominant in university systems influenced by European and British or Commonwealth practices across most of the humanities and social sciences. The most traditional version of this approach conforms closely to the 'sorcerer's apprentice' tradition where students come to sit at the feet of an individual supervisor, a great man or woman in their field who long ago wrote a big book. Now the supervisor will inculcate the right spirit in the doctoral candidate in a hand-crafted way, passing on the accumulated wisdom of the discipline orally, and commenting at length on the student's successive writing efforts, so as to help her work them up over several years into a big book of her own. Socialization into the discipline used to be very informal in this approach. The relationship between supervisor and supervisee is a very strong bond, and one that is critical for the student's progress. In the British and Commonwealth model the supervisor is concerned only with developing the doctorate and assisting the doctoral candidate, and *not* with examining the final thesis. This separate task is usually undertaken by two (sometimes three) people not previously involved with the student's work. The examiners have a brief to maintain a consistent professional standard for awarding the doctorate across all universities (see Chapter 8).

However, in many places and disciplines coursework now plays a much more important role even in the classical model of PhD education. In Europe the single supervisor is also often replaced by a three- or four-person supervising committee, backed up by more active departmental tutelage of all their PhD students as a group. Here socialization into the discipline is semi-formalized and more collectively organized. And learning how to become a professional author is somewhat more a matter of sitting in repeated research seminars, interacting with lots of different staff members, getting reactions to trial papers from seminar colleagues, and again receiving oral and written comments on draft chapters from the supervisory committee. Normally in European universities the several supervisors are also examiners in its final stages, with the job of deciding whether the student's final thesis should be accepted as a doctorate. They thus have an advisory/supportive role but also a regulatory/evaluative role. It can be hard for them to reconcile and manage the two roles together.

The different versions of the classical doctorate model work fine when everything aligns the right way, but badly if they do not. In the older, individualized version the transmission of ideas can take place speedily and smoothly if the supervisor and her student get along well at a personal level, sharing pretty much the same interests amicably. But things can often go wrong. Relations between the two can degenerate, with the supervisor becoming neurotic about a younger rival encroaching on her terrain, or the student discovering that her supervisor has feet of clay. Or they can become too close, with the supervisor being so dominant in the relationship that the student becomes a mere disciple, repeating or replicating rather than creating anew. Or student and supervisor can fail to connect, with the student's focus and interests diverging from the supervisor's expertise, while changing supervisors is difficult. Often busy supervisors are distracted by many other academic obligations, and may well be wholly absent on sabbatical or research leave at crucial times. Periods with 'fill-in' supervisors are often problematic.

The newer, more collective supervision variant of the classical model is generally more flexible and resilient, and so has tended to become more common over time, even in British or Commonwealth university systems. Having multiple supervisors and more formalized PhD training provided by departments means that students have their eggs in several baskets, some of which will tend to work well much of the time. Students are less dependent on their personal relations with just one person. If relations with one member of their committee go awry, they can often compensate by developing more reliance on their most sympathetic supervisor. Students are also usually better covered for absences by one of their supervisors. But a supervisory committee can cause other problems. Students may well get conflicting advice from different advisers, between which they have to pick a difficult path for their own work. They may also have to invest quite a few personal resources in steering their supervisors towards some agreement and consensus on the way forward. And where senior people play roles in both supervising and examining the thesis, students may find it harder to handle their relationship with them.

However supervision is organized, the classical model of PhD always culminates in the production of a 'big book' thesis, usually limited to a length of 100,000 words. It must be presented in a conventional book format, with a succession of linked chapters and an integrated overall argument. A very high level of authoring skills is needed to produce and to structure this amount of closely ordered text. There is often a considerable mismatch between the way that authoring skills are developed in both versions of the classical model sketched above and the level of proficiency in producing and developing text that is needed for a big book thesis. Some parts of this book, such as Chapter 2, are very tailored to students producing this kind of thesis, and every chapter will be relevant for them.

The taught PhD model has two key elements. The first is an extensive and demanding programme of coursework usually lasting two or three years and assessed at the end, by a General Examination in the USA. The second element is a medium-length *papers model dissertation* undertaken for a further two to four years and assessed by a dissertation committee. The American PhD committee always includes the student's advisers plus two or three other senior staff who do not work closely with the student. The 'main adviser' is the staff member who principally guides a student in completing their dissertation (similar to the principal supervisor in the classical model PhD). The 'minor adviser' works with the student but less intensively. Some universities stipulate that the minor adviser should not be a specialist in the same area that the student's dissertation is in. The committee members may read the student's work at several stages, but especially when the dissertation is complete, and they conduct the 'dissertation defence', or final oral examination (see Chapter 8). Normally a dissertation cannot be accepted without either all members of the committee agreeing, or without all bar one member agreeing, including the student's main adviser and three or four other senior staff.

The 'big book' thesis is not appropriate in the taught PhD model, given the amount and the demanding level of coursework covered for the general examination. In this version of the doctorate, it is often not seen as sensible to make doctoral students plough through the chore of writing a single coherent mega-text, incorporating elements such as comprehensive literature reviews or other introductory materials that may not count for much in professional terms. The papers model dissertation asks students to write a smaller amount of text, certainly less than 60,000 words, and in a less joined-up form. The dissertation essentially comprises four or five papers written at a good research standard. The papers may not have to be very closely connected to each other, although there will normally be some short introduction and possibly a brief closing discussion of interconnections in the research or the joint implications of the chapters. What really matters is that each of the four or five papers should be of 'publishable quality'. That is, they should be assessed by the dissertation committee as new work that makes a scholarly contribution and hence is capable of publication in a professional journal (whether or not the papers actually have been published at this stage).

This approach has generally developed furthest away from the older 'big book' thesis in the more technical and mathematical social sciences. Here the main way of advancing knowledge is a relatively short article (of 8000 words or less) in a refereed professional journal. Writing whole books has long been very uncommon in mathematical and technically based disciplines, and it is less important in terms of communicating new research than authoring journal articles. In these disciplines research books have tended to decrease in numbers while journals have boomed. And book authoring has become more of a mid-life and later years professional activity, rather than being associated with the doctorate. Even in British- and European-influenced university systems, therefore, a papers model PhD thesis has become common in the more technical social sciences.

For students doing a papers model dissertation or thesis, Chapter 2 here (about the macro-structure of a thesis as a whole) is not necessarily relevant. If your four or five papers are not in fact closely connected then the overall sequencing of materials through your text is not an important issue. However, if your materials are more connected than this, then the advice in Chapter 2 may still be helpful in maximizing the impact and development of your arguments. Also there may still be issues about achieving a consistent style and presentation across your papers that are worth following up. And if later on in your career you should set out to write a book, then this chapter could be useful to revisit. All of the other chapters are still fully relevant in the papers model dissertation. Perhaps if your work is very technical or mathematical and raises few issues of literary feel you might want to skip the first part of Chapter 5, covering style issues. But there are some important principles for professional communication in here, which apply equally well to technical information.

Not all taught PhDs culminate in a papers model dissertation. Humanities faculties in many more traditional American universities may require a major, book-like dissertation as well as the completion of a general examination in order to award the PhD – making a very demanding overall standard. If this 'mix and match' format fits the situation in your university, then again the whole of this book should be relevant for the second half of your doctoral studies.

There is one other model, called a *'professional' doctorate*, that has previously been rare but which may develop further in future. It basically extends the two or three years of coursework in the taught PhD model into a full four or five years. At a limit this approach may dispense with a final PhD dissertation altogether in favour of more assessment and the production of a number of smaller papers or the completion of a project or other non-written piece of practice. In other cases a very stripped-down dissertation is retained, perhaps 30,000 words long, without the clear originality or publishability requirements of the models above. Given the demanding amounts of years of extra coursework that students face in this approach, completing even a short dissertation at the right level may not be straightforward. Instead you may find yourself under considerable pressure from other project and course work on tight deadlines, which eats into your time for authoring and developing research. At the same time the very short theses or long essays completed under this model (and possibly some of the assessed papers also) will still have to operate at more advanced levels than those which are produced by masters (MA or MSc) students. Again students doing a professional doctorate might skip Chapter 2. But they should find that the rest of the book is highly relevant to their situation, especially for producing advanced text at a good scholarly level but written under acute time and workload constraints.

Managing readers' expectations

> The book speaks only to those who know already the kind of thing to expect from it and consequently how to interpret it.
> *Michael Oakeshott, about cookery books*   [3]

> A book, like a landscape, is a state of consciousness varying with readers.
> *Ernest Dimnet*   [4]

Producing a PhD is normally a longer piece of writing than anything you have ever done before. If you have to tackle a 'big book' thesis then it may easily be the longest text you ever complete, even assuming you enter an academic career and keep writing for another several decades. As a university teacher you will rarely get three or four years again to work full time on a single research project. Perhaps you will publish books, but most academic books have to stay between 60,000 and 80,000 words long, while 'big book' theses can be up to 100,000 words – with students typically taking it to the limit. Even where your doctorate has a papers model dissertation, this will normally be because your discipline's dominant type of academic publication is journal articles. And so your dissertation will still be four, five or even six times more text than a full paper. It may be equivalent in length to four years' academic research output in your later career, but all wrapped up together in a single pair of covers. So the simplest reason why it is important to think systematically about how to author a doctorate is that producing this much joined-up text for the first time is unavoidably difficult. The longer the text the more taxing it becomes for you as an author to understand your own arguments and to keep them marshalled effectively.

It is also harder for your readers to follow your thoughts as the text grows in size. Readers' difficulties will increase the more unfamiliar is the material they are asked to grapple with – a substantial problem for thesis authors who are supposed to be undertaking original research. Almost by definition, much of a new thesis may be unfamiliar even to experienced professional readers. The epigraph from Oakeshott, above, stresses that even the apparently simplest text (like a cookery book) rests on a shared set of conventions between an author and her readers about how that kind of book should be written. Knowing your discipline's conventions inside out will help you do authoring more reliably. Yet as the Dimnet epigraph also points out, different readers may still code the same text in different ways. Trying to think consistently about how readers will understand your text, writing with readers in mind, is a fundamental aspect of becoming a good author. It is not something that is external to the process of producing and understanding your arguments, but rather an integral stage in helping you be most effective in organizing and expressing your thought.

In one way or another all authoring involves you in constantly managing readers' expectations and recognizing that different people in the readership will have different perspectives on your text. Writing your thesis to be accessible to the widest feasible readership can help you in becoming a better author, by developing your own ideas and improving the clarity and direction of your research design and finished thought. Most doctoral dissertations may never get published, but many others do see the light of day, as complete books in some cases but more generally in the form of one or several journal articles (see Chapter 9). Writing with readers in mind will hugely help the quality of your text, and maximize your chance to be one of the published group, and hence to feed into the development of scholarly thought. The alternative outcome is to produce only a 'shelf-bending' thesis, one which after submission goes into a library and over the next two decades slowly bends a shelf. A thesis that is never published in whole or in part may be read at most by one or two later scholars in your own institution. Or perhaps some very diligent researchers elsewhere may be sufficiently interested in exactly your topic to find and borrow your work. But, equally likely, it could remain unread by anyone else beyond your supervisors and examiners, like Thomas Gray's roses 'born to blush unseen'.[5]

Seeing things from a reader's perspective is not an easy task. Academic authors typically spend so long in developing their research, clarifying their theories, and expressing their arguments in a close-joined way, that they can find it very hard to see how their text will be received and interpreted. For PhD students this problem is especially acute because the thesis is their first extended piece of writing, and usually has a limited audience whose reactions are difficult to ascertain in advance. In addition (as I discuss in Chapter 2), PhD projects usually become closely bound up with people's identities as a beginning scholar and apprentice researcher, making it hard for students to be self-aware or critical about their work.

All these features mean that some students can write obsessively with only two or three readers in mind, namely their supervisors or advisers, and perhaps the examiners. Since advisers, supervisors and examiners all get paid for their roles, students often picture them as incapable of being bored. They are assumed to be so committed to absorbing the text that they are unconcerned about how (un)interesting it is. And since examiners are senior figures at the height of their profession, they are also often pictured as completely unconcerned about the readability or accessibility of the thesis. They are presumed capable of mastering any level of difficulty. Sometimes they are also seen as pedantically obsessed about the details of research methods and about scholarly referencing for every proposition. Adopting anything like this kind of orientation can have a very poor effect on the quality of the text that you produce. In publishing circles PhD theses are often a byword for unreadable arguments, pompous and excessively complex expression of ideas, and an overkill in referencing, literature reviews, and theoretical and methodological detailing.

Like other forms of mild paranoia, research students' defensive mind-set bears little relation to the facts. Rational PhD supervisors, advisers and examiners do not carry out their role for the money, still less for the dubious academic kudos involved. Instead most professors and other senior figures undertake supervision and examining for three reasons: they hope to encounter or foster fresh and original work; they want to induct promising young scholars into the disciplines to which they have devoted their lives; and they see it as a duty to colleagues in their department and in the wider profession. So providing them with a clear and accessible text is only the most basic politeness which they can expect. Writing to be understood by the widest possible audience of informed, professional readers will help ensure that your advisers and examiners form the best impression of your work and can carry out their tricky task in the speediest and easiest way. By contrast, a complex or obscure text, written in a crabbed and inaccessible way, makes working with you more off-putting. In the end-game of finishing and submitting the dissertation it may even raise fundamental doubts in advisers' or examiners' minds about your ability to carry on professional activities essential for a later academic career, such as effectively teaching students or publishing regularly in journals (see Chapters 8 and 9).

There are many different ways in which your writing will generate readers' expectations. Any accessible piece of text longer than a few pages must include 'orientating devices', ways of giving advance notice of what is to come (discussed in detail in Chapters 3 and 4). In addition academic dissertations usually require a very developed apparatus for situating the particular work undertaken in a wider context of scholarly endeavour. In a 'big book' thesis the most important signalling elements are a review of the previous literature, and one or more theoretical chapters. In any research dissertation or paper readers look very carefully at the author's own statements of what their study will accomplish. Readers become disappointed when authors do not give any indications of what is to come in later chapters, sections or paragraphs; or signal that something will arrive and then it never does; or deliver something different from what was signalled; or draw them into spending time on a project which turns out differently from what they thought. Each of these outcomes makes readers worry: perhaps the author does not know what she thinks, does not understand the topic she has set out to tackle? The implication soon follows: perhaps this book or article is not worth my time or attention? For thesis examiners or a dissertation committee this feeling may very easily spill over into: maybe this thesis does not meet the standard that a doctorate should? Hence for PhD students, more than for most authors, these are dangerous thoughts to engender.

Authors can often create readers' expectations inadvertently, without intending to do so. Doctoral theses and academic research papers commonly start with some level of literature review. It is quite common for beginning students to wax lyrical in these sections about the limits or inadequacies of previous research in their field. Most people write literature reviews early on, often before fully appreciating the difficulties of grappling with research materials and extracting useful or interesting information from them. Hence it is easy to get carried away by a conviction that using different methods or a new theoretical approach will generate much more illuminating results. But if you make some strong criticisms of earlier work, what impact does this have on readers? It tends to generate an expectation that your own research will be much better than what has gone before. After you have searchingly exposed what was wrong in previous studies, readers must believe that you are confident of being able to transcend those limitations. Hence every criticism you make can build a difficult threshold for your own research to surmount. Cumulatively the effects of overenthusiastic critique can be disabling.

Similarly, academic readers will pick up dozens of small pointers from the way that you write text, which will engender expectations about what you are trying to do. For instance, how you label schools of thought in your discipline, and how you then describe your own work, will cue readers to where you stand in the subject's intellectual currents, who you are aligned with and who you are opposed to. Many commentators have detected tribalist tendencies amongst academics, such that they must cluster into schools of thought and create possibly fake factional conflicts amongst themselves. Others lament a proprietorial instinct that leads to a constant differentiation of positions. Charles Caleb Colton observed wryly: 'Professors in every branch of knowledge prefer their own theories to the truth; the reason is that their theories are private property, but the truth is common stock.'[6]

Yet some aspects of academic differentiation and cue-giving are not just extraneous elements. Labels and jargon are great time-saving devices in academic life, just as they are in ordinary existence. If I can say to you, 'Dolly Parton is a *country and western singer*' then this four-word label sums up a lot of different features – dressing up in fake cowboy clothes with fringes on them, singing in a yodelling fashion with a slide guitar accompaniment, and favouring songs about rural backwoods themes, the trials of married love and American patriotism. If I have to spell out these features every time it will take a lot longer than three words to explain. Similarly, academic jargon is an essential element of maintaining a professional conversation (in person and in print) where meanings are precise and specialist topics can be handled flexibly and economically. If your PhD thesis is to be interesting at all then it is inevitable that it will focus to a great extent on some kind of controversy in your discipline, some nexus of debate between different theories, or thematic interpretations, or methodological positions, or empirical standpoints. You will thus have to discuss positions, register criticisms, affirm some loyalties – in short take sides. Beginning students often underestimate the importance and pervasiveness of the side-taking cues which their text conveys. They pick up and use 'loaded' terminology or concepts without appreciating how some readers will decode its presence. So to manage readers' expectations effectively requires that you carefully judge all elements of your presentation, the explicit promises and the implicit signals which you give to readers about the intentions of your work and its relationship to the discipline.

Conclusions

Starting work on a PhD dissertation inaugurates an apprenticeship not just in your chosen academic discipline and its research skills, but also in authoring. This aspect of your new role can easily attract too little attention, both from your supervisors or advisers and in terms of your own priorities. But the craft skills of authoring are an important aspect of your role, critical for your success in progressing and finishing the thesis. It is an area where you can make solid and cumulative progress that will stand you in good stead throughout a professional career. The most fundamental aspect of authoring is to manage readers' expectations successfully, ensuring that they see the text as coherent, well paced and organized, and delivering upon your promises in a credible way. And for new PhD students, a critical step in beginning to manage readers' expectations is to define clearly the intended overall thrust of their thesis – its central research question.

2

Envisioning the Thesis as a Whole

> In dreams begin responsibility.
> *W. B. Yeats* [1]

What is your dissertation about? And what contribution do you aim to achieve? What will be new or different about your work? How would you justify the time and resources that you will devote to it? These fundamental questions will seem very pressing in the beginning stages of your research, as Yeats' intangible process of locking you into a long-run project begins. But they do not go away later on. You can often push such issues into the background in the central stages of the thesis, during field visits, case studies or the hard slog of library or archive work or data collection and analysis. But they tend to return during the 'mid-term slump' in morale that often afflicts dissertation authors. And they invariably crop up again when you have a first draft of your complete thesis, and have to fashion it into a polished and defensible final version. This chapter is about the importance of thinking through some reasonable answers before you invest too heavily in a particular research topic and approach. I consider first how to define one or several questions that will inform your project as a whole. The second section looks at the demands of doing 'original' and interesting research.

Defining the central research questions

> Certain books seem to have been written, not in order to afford us any instruction, but merely for

> the purpose of letting us know that their authors
> knew something.
> *Johanne Wolfgang von Goethe* ²

At the most fundamental level any doctorate is a contract, of a rather peculiar kind. For a 'big book' thesis the specific nature of the contract is that the author develops and communicates a question, and then proffers an answer to it. For a papers model dissertation there will rarely be one big central question, but instead a set of more loosely related and more specific or detailed research issues. Then the examiners or dissertation committee determine if the research text produced actually answers the questions posed. If there is a close fit between the question and answer, either at the whole-thesis level or within each 'paper', then the dissertation passes successfully. But students must not offer a mushy set of materials undirected to a clear question. They must not promise what they cannot deliver, or claim to achieve what they have not established. An equally common problem is that the question asked in a dissertation and the answer provided may not connect in any discernible way. The author may be convinced that they are doing X, but to the readers it seems as if they are doing Y, a significantly different enterprise. Or the question may be so broad that the answer the student provides relates to it in only the haziest way. Alternatively the question may be specific but the answer given may be too vague or ill defined to relate closely to it. Finally if some of the answer does not fit with the question asked, or if part of the question is left unaddressed or unanswered, the thesis may seem problematic. Hence the thesis contract is a demanding and constraining one both for students and for those assessing their work.

But equally the contract provides students with a great deal of protection and additional certainty. The examiners or dissertation committee are not allowed to invent their own questions, nor to demand that the doctoral candidate address a different question from the one she has chosen. The assessors *have* to take the candidate's question as the basis for assessment, within certain minimal conditions. These tests essentially require that the PhD author should establish a clear question, whether for the whole thesis or for each of its component 'papers'. She must show that the question is a serious one and a legitimate focus for academic enquiry, which is to say that it must relate to the existing literature and debates in some sustained way. But once these conditions are established, the interrelationship of the question and the answer has to be the touchstone for accepting or failing the work undertaken.

You define the question: you deliver the answer. The unique features of this situation are often hard to appreciate. Throughout all our earlier careers in education someone else defines the question. At first degree and masters levels we can concentrate solely on delivering an answer that satisfies this external agenda. So it can be quite hard to understand the implications of instead defining and then answering your own question. Beginning PhD students often believe that they must tackle much bigger or hard-to-research questions than could possibly be answered in a PhD, just because this is the way that questions are framed in the research literature that they read. But professional researchers in universities will typically have many more resources for tackling big issues (such as large budgets, sophisticated research technologies at their disposal, large cooperative research teams, or squads of people to assist them). What is a good question for professional researchers to address is not usually a good question for someone doing a PhD thesis in lone-scholar, no-budget mode.

If attempting an unmanageable or overscaled question for a doctorate is one danger to be wary of, then veering to the other end of the spectrum carries opposite dangers. Here PhD students choose topics of perverse dullness or minuteness, thinking not about a whole readership for their thesis but only about the reactions of a few examiners or members of their dissertation committee. A topic is chosen not to illuminate a worthwhile field of study but just to provide a high certainty route to an academic meal ticket. Such defensively minded theses focus on tiny chunks of the discipline. They may cover a very short historical period, a single not very important author or source, a small discrete mechanism or process, one narrow locality explored in-depth, or a particular method taken just a little further in some aspect. The titles for such research dissertations are usually descriptive, without theoretical themes, and often circumscribed by deprecatory or restrictive labels ('An exploratory study of ...' or 'Some topics in ...').

A closely related syndrome is the gap-filling thesis, designed solely to cover an uninhabited niche in the literature rather than to advance a wider intellectual purpose. Such projects can exactly replicate an existing established analysis in a new area, or fill in a small lacuna in knowledge between a set of already studied points. There are two problems with empty regions, however. The first is that gaps often exist for a good reason; for instance, because the topic has little intrinsic interest or is too difficult to undertake. The second problem is that the most obvious holes in the literature that are worth studying may easily attract other researchers. Hence someone else may publish research or complete a PhD on the topic over the three or four years that it will take you to produce a finished thesis. Potential competition from other people's doctorates or from well-funded research projects is a serious risk for any gap-filling thesis. A study whose chief rationale is that it is the first treatment of something may be substantially devalued by becoming the second or third such analysis.

There are longer-term problems with picking a defensive or an overcautious topic just to get finished. Once your PhD is completed its title will have to be cited on your résumé or curriculum vitae for many years to come. Your doctoral subject will only cease to matter professionally when you have built up quite a body of later work to succeed it, especially a later book. So while a completed PhD is a fine thing, a very dull, off-putting, or unfashionable subject is not a good foundation for getting hired into your first academic job. Especially at the short-listing stage, most university search committees operate with only a small amount of paper information. Unless you have a set of different publications already in print, they naturally tend to read a lot into your PhD subject, seeing it as expressive of your character and temperament. In addition, it may be very hard to spin off any worthwhile publications from a completely dull PhD.

> It's no good running a pig farm for thirty years
> while saying 'I was meant to be a ballet dancer'.
> By that time pigs are your style.
> *Quentin Crisp*   [3]

These considerations can be magnified by the psychological effects of fixing on a boring or tiny subject for 'manageability' reasons. Most doctoral students experience some form of mid-term slump in their morale, one or more periods when they lose confidence in their project and wonder if it is worth continuing. If your topic is inauthentic for you, if you are not genuinely interested in your thesis question and committed to finding an answer to it, then it will be all the harder for you to sustain your confidence and momentum through such periods. It is also pretty demotivating at this stage to become aware that you have picked an uninteresting or uninspiring topic that is unlikely to maximize your later career prospects. So it is important to take seriously the scope to configure what your research will be about, avoiding both overreaching topics and underambition. Your own personal commitments and interests count first here, of course. But other people's views do as well.

The challenge posed by having to explain your thesis topic can also be a salutary stimulant to clarifying your own thinking. During the course of your doctorate there will be gruesome occasions, at dinner parties or drinks with strangers, when someone turns to you and asks what it is you do. Once you admit to working on a doctorate, your conversation partner's inevitable follow-through is to ask about your subject. From this point on you have typically about two minutes to convince your normally sceptical inquisitor that you know what you are doing and that it is a worthwhile thing to be at. As a PhD student you are often assumed to be highly committed to and closely bound up with the subject you have chosen. Both insiders and outsiders to university life may think of your personality as reflected in (even defined by) your research topic. People doing doctorates are invariably seen as more committed to (even obsessed by) their particular subject than would be true of professional academics doing research later in their careers. So the 'dinner party test' is always a frustrating experience to undergo, and many students feel that it is an impossible one for them to pass. To expect them to be able to capture the essence of their sophisticated and specialized topic, and to convey it in a few lines to a complete stranger, is just absurdly to underestimate what they are about. Yet in my view the test is a good one. If you cannot give a synoptic, ordinary language explanation in two or three minutes of what you are focusing on and what you hope to achieve, the chances are very high that in a very fundamental way you do not yet understand your thesis topic.

You define the question: you deliver the answer. This proposition means that every effective PhD thesis should be genuinely personalized in some way. You should take a manageable part of the existing literature's questions or concerns, and then tailor or modify that topic so as to shape it so that it can be feasibly answered. The way that the question is shaped should be reasonably distinctive, coming at a subject from a personally chosen angle. If you have such a personalized (even mildly idiosyncratic) perspective then it is less likely to be adopted by other researchers during the course of your studies.

It is best to try and frame your thesis around an intellectual problem or a paradox, not around a gap. It needs to focus on a set of phenomena that ask for explanation, which you can express as a non-obvious puzzle and for which you can formulate an interesting and effective answer. The philosopher Robert Nozick recently asked, 'What is an intellectual problem?' and concluded that it had five components.[4] The first is a goal or objective which can tell us how to judge outcomes, how to see that an improvement has been achieved. The second is an initial state, the starting situation and the resources available to be used, in this case usually the existing literature. A set of operations that can be used to change the initial state and resources forms the third component of an intellectual problem, perhaps new data and a toolkit of research methods. Constraints are the fourth element, designating certain kinds of operations as inadmissible. The final element is an outcome. A problem has been solved or ameliorated somewhat if a sequence of admissible operations has been carried out so as to change the initial state into an outcome that meets the goal without breaching the constraints in doing so. In French doctoral education this broad approach to defining a topic is often characterized as a search for 'une problématique'. The synonymous English word 'a problematic' is too ambiguous with the adjectival 'problematic' (meaning 'difficult') to play an equivalent role. However, if you think of 'problematizing' your thesis question – setting the answer you hope to give within a framework which will show its intellectual significance – then you will get near to what the French term means.

> Father Brown laid down his cigar and said
> carefully, 'It isn't that they can't see the solution.
> It is that they can't see the problem.'
> *G. K. Chesterton* [5]

> Most problems people face cannot be specified with
> such exactness. And often people do not simply
> *face* given problems; their task is to *make* a problem,
> to *find* one in the inchoate situation they face.
> *Robert Nozick* [6]

Many PhD students from countries or disciplines with more empiricist approaches, or placing more emphasis on intellectual or social consensus, find the idea of problematizing their thesis topic difficult and odd. They often regard their chosen topic as obviously worthy of study or intrinsically interesting and important in common-sense terms alone. They see no puzzle or enigma in front of them, merely an empirical landscape only partially painted by previous authors, which is their opportunity. This is a dangerous state of mind to be in at the start of a doctorate. It is often associated with people picking overly derivative topics important at some previous levels of education, or taking on very conventionally framed subjects from the existing literature which are too large or difficult to resolve in a PhD. Above all, an 'unproblematized' thesis topic normally provides students with no worthwhile intellectual focus or protection at the examination stage. It leaves open too many questions along the lines of: what is this thesis for?

You define the question: you deliver the answer. The proposition is symmetric, with equal scope for you to intervene on both parts. The quickest way to get a great fit between the question asked and the answer delivered in a thesis is to try and work out what you will be able to say, or hope to be able to say. *Then* frame your research question so as to fit closely around it. You must find legitimate ways to leave out bits of the research literature's questions or concerns that you are not going to be able to answer or will not feel comfortable tackling. That means you must think about the practicalities of research and your capabilities and resources from the word go, 'guesstimating' results and outcomes at the same time as you formulate a topic.

In a sense this exercise is like turning to the answer pages at the back of a maths textbook before you work out how to derive the right result. It is no use formulating a great topic that depends on your achieving a theoretical breakthrough that has eluded previous scholars, or turns completely on your empirical analysis producing results of a particularly clear or convenient kind.

It is fine to be hopeful and to think about a best possible case: what would you be able to say if everything went just as you hope that it will? But you also need to build in some insurance outcomes, things you can do or say if high-risk elements of your plan do not turn out as hoped. For instance, if you initially believe that you can achieve a theory advance, there is still a risk that it will prove more elusive than you anticipate. In this case, can you fall back on something more reliable and predictable, such as the exegesis of and commentary on an important author's thought in the same area? Or if you hope to establish a strong relationship between variables A and B in an empirical analysis, what will be gained from finding that this linkage does not exist or is only marginally present? These considerations mean that you must structure your question robustly, with a measure of redundancy in your research plan, so as to cover what you will do in your thesis even if some elements of the plan do not turn out as intended. Above all, you need to shape the thesis question to showcase your findings, to bring out their interest and importance and to give a sense of completeness to the whole.

These things are not easily accomplished. They are not tasks to be finished in a single effort at the outset of your thesis and with a high level of determinacy. Instead they mostly have to be discovered a bit at a time, and then worked up in successive attempts. Shaping your question to fit around your answer involves repeated iterations where you define a plan and formulate some ambitions. Then you do some lengthy research and painfully produce some text expressing your understanding of the results. After that you consider how far the thesis plan requires alteration (perhaps including wholesale redesign) as your ideas and level of information have changed. Your early ideas on what your thesis will look like, in your first six months or first year, will be like those of a sculptor choosing a block of stone and marking the crudest 'rough form' concept on it, before embarking on the long job of chiselling out a finished piece.

Doing original work

> All good things which exist are the fruits of originality.
> *John Stuart Mill*   7

> We never think entirely alone: we think in company, in a vast collaboration; we work with the workers of the past and of the present. [In] the whole intellectual world ... each one finds in those about him [or her] the initiation, help, verification, information, encouragement, that he [or she] needs.
> *A. G. Sertillanges*   8

Authoring and thinking go together. You will very rarely work out what you think first, and then just write it down. Normally the act of committing words to screen (or pen to paper) will make an important contribution to your working out what it is that you do think. In other words, the act of writing may often be *constitutive* of your thinking. Left to ourselves we can all of us keep conflicting ideas in play almost indefinitely, selectively paying attention to what fits our needs of the moment and ignoring the tensions with what we said or thought yesterday, or the day before that. Writing things down in a systematic way is an act of commitment, a decision to firm up and crystallize what we think, to prevent this constant reprocessing and reconfiguring. Like all such resolutions of uncertainty, making this commitment is psychologically difficult, possibly forcing each of us to confront the feebleness or inadequacy of our own thought. This potential for disappointment can in turn create incentives for us to postpone starting to write, a chain of reactions which may culminate in 'writer's block' even for very experienced authors (see Chapter 6).

For beginning doctoral students, however, the most characteristic source of uncertainty closely associated with a choice of topic is whether their work will fit the normal 'original work' requirement. All good universities in either the classical or the taught PhD models still demand that the thesis or dissertation should be novel research making some form of distinctive contribution to the development of knowledge in a discipline. What kind of work meets this criterion is famously difficult to pin down. Most European universities' doctoral rules (or rubrics) are almost silent on how originality is to be determined. Instead they concentrate on process, requiring only that suitably qualified examiners be recruited to sign off on the presence of original work (whatever that is). The University of London has a much more explicit specification than most, but even this tells examiners only that a doctoral thesis can show originality in two ways. Either it will report 'the discovery of new facts', or it will display 'the exercise of independent critical power', or both.[9] 'New facts' are the result of empirical researches, and can be established by undertaking an investigation of something not hitherto available. For instance, this could include reading and commenting on little-analysed documents; exploring unreported or unpublished parts of an archive; conducting a case study in a locality or organization not previously or recently studied; running a survey, or collating together published quantitative information, and then statistically analysing the data; and so on. 'Independent critical power' is almost as vague a criterion as 'originality'. But presumably the idea here is that the thesis author shows that she can marshal some significant theoretical or thematic arguments in an ordered and coherent way, and can explore already analysed issues from some reasonably distinctive angle or perspective of her own.

The notion of 'independence' is an important one at the doctoral level. A candidate for PhD is supposed to speak with their own distinctive professional 'voice' on major issues in their discipline. This aspect may be less visible in those countries where PhD students are expected either to generally assist their supervisors in their work, or to be apprentices labouring in their department's vineyard on a designated topic (while also undertaking activities like teaching). It can be disconcerting for these students to appreciate the importance of the 'independent work' criterion for awarding the doctorate. Newly PhD-ed people cannot be clones of their supervisors, nor even just walk in their footsteps. Often this realization dawns on students quite late, sometimes in the run-up to a final draft, or perhaps in the final oral examination itself. For highly insulated PhD students it may even come much later, when their attempts to publish papers or a book from their doctorate are rebuffed, or when appointments at other universities prove elusive.

Framing your own view while still grounding your work in an established academic tradition and some part of the contemporary discourse of your discipline, is a knack that takes time to develop. There are two common ways in which beginning students may go wrong: either being overly derivative from the existing literature on the one hand, or overclaiming about the novelty or value of their own contribution on the other. The first excess is to structure your opening chapter or chapters exclusively or extensively around summaries of a succession of previous books and articles. Here references and quotations are obvious crutches, used to limp along from one point to the next. A telltale sign of this syndrome is a long succession of paragraphs where the opening words of *every* paragraph are somebody else's name and reference: 'Smith (1989) argues...' or 'According to Jones (1997)...'. Writing in this manner simply signals to readers an unintended message: 'Here comes yet another derivative passage.'

> If you speak of nothing but what you have read, no one will read you.
> *Arthur Schopenhauer*   [10]

> Do not read, think!
> *Arthur Schopenhauer*   [11]

Especially for students doing 'big book' theses, the scale of the research literature's questions often suggests that they should begin their own work by writing long literature reviews in an effort to try and somehow absorb it within their covers. This exercise can produce many thousands of words in exegesis. But surveying other people's contributions typically yields only superficial coverage or criticisms of earlier studies. It does not necessarily get you any closer to finding your own distinctive question. And it can accentuate an inability to cut down or personalize your thesis topic. Perverse effects here are often serious. It can be very depressing to set out trying to answer someone else's question, and progressively discover that with the limited time and resources at your disposal it cannot be done. An overextended literature review can also consume vast amounts of time, often leading students to postpone doing any creative work of their own for a year or 18 months. Even so, less confident supervisors and advisers often encourage this pattern of behaviour. If they are unfamiliar with your precise topic, a literature review can seem functional for their needs, providing them with a quick potted education about it.

The experience of doing a literature review may also subconsciously foster in you an illusion that is the occupational hazard of text-orientated intellectuals – the idea that the solution to conflicting theoretical positions, and to identifying a particular position of your own, can be found in conducting a super-extended trawl. Somehow the lure of the hunt or the quest often persuades people that with a bit more effort they can turn up 'the answer'. But a solution to your theoretical, methodological or empirical problems does not necessarily lie out there in the literature. Reviewing more and more of other people's work will not in itself throw up the insight or angle you need.

> The world does not contain any information. It is as it is. Information about it is created in the organism [a human being] through its interaction with the world. To speak about the storage of information is to fall into a semantic trap. Books or computers are parts of the world. They can yield information when they are looked upon. We move the problem of learning and cognition nicely into the blind spot of our intellectual vision if we confuse vehicles for potential information with information itself.
> *Ivan Illich* [12]

Of course, it is still always a sensible precaution to undertake some form of systematic documentation and bibliographic search at the outset of any PhD, so long as you assign it a strictly limited time frame. A speedy but comprehensive review of previous work on your topic is especially easy now that Web systems and computerized bibliographic tools are available. They offer much more sophisticated search facilities and far faster access to source materials than was state-of-the-art even five years ago. Electronic journal archives should mean that you can now instantly download the abstracts and full text of potentially relevant academic papers. These tools have also extended the reach of searches to include possible rival PhDs already ongoing or just starting in your own or other countries. A search for closely similar PhDs is a worthwhile precaution to take before committing to a topic. But again do not fall into the trap of thinking that the originality of your work hangs on your 'owning' a PhD topic exclusively. Your best defence against being trumped by other people's ongoing research lies in a distinctive and personalized framing of your thesis question and approach, not in having a deserted niche or a 'gap' topic all to yourself.

A second frequent mistake is overdoing things. Beginning students often overclaim about the novelty of their ideas or approach. They make rash promises of theoretical or empirical breakthroughs that do not materialize. Or they adopt and promote various innovations at the start of their theses that do not seem to be justified by actually doing any useful work later on. Academic readers are especially resistant to 'neologisms' (the invention of new terms and vocabulary). They also will hate your interpreting established terms with a different meaning from those already in use. And many will resist the introduction into your analysis of novel 'conceptual frameworks' or algebra or diagrams, *unless* these strategies seem to add significantly to your analysis. Any of these tactics may encourage readers to anticipate more from your work than is actually going to appear, and so risks a major failure in managing their expectations. The quickest and surest way to boost readers' resistance is to set out your views while denying *any* influence from earlier work in your discipline, or insisting that ideas already in common currency have somehow originated or re-originated with you alone.

> Somebody says: 'Of no school I am part,
> Never to living master lost my heart;
> No more can I be said

> To have learned anything from the dead'.
> That statement – subject to appeal –
> Means: 'I'm a self-made imbecile'.
> *Johanne Wolfgang von Goethe* [13]

> An artist who is self-taught is taught by a very
> ignorant person indeed.
> *John Constable* [14]

Steering a middle way between being a non-independent voice and overclaiming is a difficult course. One foundation is to recognize that any new work rests on an accumulation of previous and current literature, as the epigraph from Sertillanges at the start of this section makes clear. A useful device to bear in mind here is the 'value added' concept, which also links back to Nozick's issue of how you 'solve' or progress an intellectual problem (see pp. 23–4 above). A business 'adds value' when it pulls in resources at price X and then recombines or processes them to create an output which can be sold on for a higher price Y. The difference between X and Y is the 'value added'. Focusing on your own 'value added' means keeping a critical eye on the extent to which you have transformed or enhanced or differentiated the starting materials of your analysis. Then tailor your claiming behaviour to fit closely with that. It also means retaining a strong relational pattern of argument in which you appropriately acknowledge the extent to which you draw on the existing literature. But you can perhaps ensure that you seem on top of rather than overly dependent on previous work by treating these debates in a more organized way, as a competition between clearly labelled schools of thought, each of which has merits or insights but also limitations.

> A new theory, even when it appears most unitary
> and all-embracing, deals with some immediate
> element of novelty or paradox within the
> framework of far vaster, unanalysed, unarticulated
> reserves of knowledge, experience, faith and
> presupposition ... We neither can, nor need,
> rebuild the house of the mind very rapidly.
> *Robert Oppenheimer* [15]

The nature of academic debates is such that complete closure of many controversies is unlikely. More than four centuries ago Blaise Pascal remarked about the incomplete establishment and yet persistence of religious belief: 'We have an incapacity of proof, insurmountable by all dogmatism. We have an idea of truth, invincible to all scepticism.'[16] Something of the same condition is the best that can be hoped for of any academic viewpoint in contemporary debates. Participants often share a common vision of what disciplinary advance consists in, but disagree strongly on which contending position best meets these criteria. No one 'line' will ever sweep the field or be without its critics and dissenters. The normal 'resting state' of most academic disciplines is that there is a 'conventional wisdom' in J. K. Galbraith's sense of a mainstreamed, seen-as-unproblematic viewpoint.[17] This position usually controls the intellectual commanding heights, the councils of professional bodies and the editorial control of the (most) prestigious journals. However, there will also usually be one or more 'insurgent' critical views – new or previously minority positions that are attracting support. Often there are also one or more 'legacy' views critical of the orthodoxy as well. These are older positions now displaced in large part by the conventional wisdom but still staging rearguard actions or successful guerrilla attacks. The maintenance of continual academic debate means that you need to think through carefully the position that you expect to adopt. Bear in mind the likelihood that intellectual viewpoints will significantly change over the course of the three or four years it takes you to finish your doctorate. There may well be extensive jockeying for position or even a change of mainstream approach in your discipline during this period.

Once you have a good sense of where your interests lie, and can relate your question effectively to the research literature, the hard part is to sit down and try to contribute, that is to push ahead knowledge in some particular area or endeavour. A potent reason why we all tend to overextend literature reviews is that doing so postpones this psychologically taxing moment when we have to think through ideas for ourselves. Facing a blank sheet of paper and attempting to jot down new thoughts or make interesting connections can often seem threatening. In a university environment surrounded by the massed ranks of learning in the library, and by so many other people seemingly adept at the task, not all the influences to which you are exposed are necessarily supportive ones. For instance, being in an institution with a strong historical tradition of advanced study in your discipline can be encouraging for creative thought in some circumstances, as you seek to emulate previous generations of doctoral students. But such an apparently favourable context can also be intimidating and disabling in other ways, for instance suggesting that many of 'your own' ideas have already been devised by others.

> Most people would die sooner than think; in fact they do so.
> *Bertrand Russell* [18]

> Few people think more than two or three times a year; I have made an international reputation for myself by thinking once or twice a week.
> *George Bernard Shaw* [19]

Thinking on your own is also difficult because genuine learning has a kind of dialectical feel to it. Just as you cannot build up stronger muscles in a limb until you have in effect strained or torn the ones you already have by vigorous exercise, so you cannot really internalize new ideas without losing something of the previous mental framework you used to make sense of the world. Hence we all encounter a small dread that we will lose confidence in what we previously believed, yet without replacing that earlier, thoroughly familiar, and competently working model with a new set of ideas that we can use as effectively and felicitously. If that happened we would know that we did not know how to interpret some phenomena, and be worse off. Perhaps we would be aware of the set of ideas we really need now, but still be unable to thoroughly master or understand them. For PhD students, aspiring to operate on the frontiers of knowledge at a professional level, this outcome would be an especially disturbing one. This risk adds a further twist to the asymmetry noted by Jean-Baptiste Biot: 'There is nothing so easy as what was discovered yesterday, nor so difficult as what will be discovered tomorrow.'[20]

> You have learnt something. That always feels at
> first as if you had lost something.
> *George Bernard Shaw*   [21]

> I'm not afraid of failure ... If you are learning
> anything new, you have got to get through
> humiliation.
> *Eddie Izzard*   [22]

> One does not set out in search of new lands
> without being willing to be alone on an
> empty sea.
> *André Gide*   [23]

So far, perhaps you feel, so depressing. But there are also definite routines and regimes which you can develop to help you do creative thinking more easily and frequently. Recognizing the difficulties in being original is a crucial first step, for it means that you can take appropriate encouragement from small forward steps, rather than setting your sights unrealistically high. As the quotations from Russell and Shaw above make clear, a key first step could simply be to set aside time so as to purposefully try and develop your own ideas. Make sure that these session times are sufficiently long to be worthwhile, usually at least an hour or two. On the other hand, there may also tend to be diminishing returns in much longer sessions. It may not be realistic to seek to be creative for hours on end. Develop the habit of thinking in a fairly disciplined way that works for you, splitting your think-time into separate stages where you try to do only one discrete operation at a time.

It is *always* best to begin by surfacing or 'brainstorming' ideas in a deliberately uncritical mode for at least 15 or 20 minutes. During this time jot down everything that occurs to you about or around a topic, without editing, evaluating or scrubbing out any of your ideas at all. When this period is over, you should have a full ideas sheet (covering one or several pages), littered with jottings and annotations and stray thoughts. Once this stage is over, you can move on to evaluation and organization, spending an equivalent amount of time thinking carefully about how each of the elements on your ideas sheet relates to your central question or problem. At this point cross through or marginalize jottings or possibilities on the ideas sheet which are not really relevant, or which will not work as you wish. (But since it's also easy to be too self-critical, cross things out lightly, so you can still read what's there.) Then think about how to organize or sequence the remaining ideas, using graphic devices (boxes, lines, arrows etc.) to structure your ideas sheet. As you make progress, take the skeleton of one subset of ideas and expand it onto further ideas sheets of its own, seeing if you can flesh out and expand what you have got.

Jotting thoughts down whenever you have them is a second seemingly obvious but actually crucial aspect of increasing your creativity. Nothing is so evanescent as your own good ideas, so fleetingly present and so easily lost. One of the most famous social psychology articles sheds light on this issue, focusing on 'the magical number seven, plus or minus two'.[24] Empirical research shows that on average we can all of us hold only about seven ideas at the forefront of our attention. Very clever people are perhaps able to focus on nine ideas at once, while less adept people (like me) may only be able to concentrate on five ideas at a time. When we are confronted by larger sets or longer lists of ideas we tend to react by *randomly* dropping some elements from the forefront of our attention. Hence if you think of a lot of ideas *without* jotting them down, you may appropriately be anxious that you will forget them.

> The best way to get a good idea is to get a lot of ideas.
> *Linus Pauling*   [25]

> There is no such thing as a logical method of having new ideas or a logical reconstruction of this process.
> *Karl Popper*   [26]

One way we normally counter this fear of forgetting is to keep recycling the same seven (or five or nine) things in the forefront of our attention, the repetitions serving to reassure us that the original notions are still there, still retrievable. The more stressed we get (often without noticing it) the more we may repeat this operation, squeezing out having any new ideas. To get new ideas you need to break out of this cycle of anxiety

and recycling. Jotting things down as notes in a regularly
maintained or filed notebook, or in a well-saved and cumulative file on your PC, is a key step. It creates what Montaigne
called a 'paper memory', which normally helps enormously to
give you the psychological security to move on and think of
additional ideas, secure in the knowledge that you will not
forget what was value-added or worthwhile in today's session.[27]

> Chance gives rise to thoughts, and chance removes
> them; no art can keep or acquire them.
> A thought has escaped me. I wanted to write it
> down. I write instead, that it has escaped me.
> *Blaise Pascale* [28]

> Creative research is a problem-generating activity.
> Problem discovery cannot be a scheduled
> activity. It can happen at any time.
> *Lewis Minkin* [29]

Jotting everything down also means keeping a notebook of
problems or questions or possible ideas for development with
you constantly – for use in seminars, during conversations with
friends and colleagues, when you are out and about, and even
perhaps by your bed at night. It is best to have a system for your
jottings that allows you to keep your records safely, but also
allows you to extract sheets for refiling in appropriate folders or
files. Using a PDA (personal digital assistant) may also let you
transfer ideas or jottings directly onto a PC-based filing system.
You cannot afford to have these materials floating around on
whatever scraps of paper are to hand, for then they may still get
lost again, undermining the psychological security you need to
stop recycling what you already have and to instead think of
new ideas. You can also use this notebook (or a PDA linkable to
the bibliography file on your PC) for securely capturing references to potentially relevant literature (see the second part of
Chapter 5).

If you assiduously jot things down you can also take full
advantage of the well-documented tendency for people satu-
rated in a field of study to get creative ideas or breakthrough
insights by chance associations, almost when they are not

looking for it. This pattern may reflect your subconscious helping out by processing difficult issues in the background over long periods. It may also reflect the fact that as your knowledge of an area builds up, so your anxieties about forgetting or not understanding tend to ease, as you gain the confidence and psychological security to think about things afresh rather than relying on other people's insights.

> In the field of observation, fortune favours only the prepared mind.
> *Louis Pasteur* [30]

> It is in our idleness, in our dreams, that the submerged truth sometimes comes to the top.
> *Virginia Woolf* [31]

Strengthening your motivation for doing original thinking is important too. Making a commitment of some kind – to an intellectual approach, a particular school of thought in your discipline, or a broad world view – all these can be helpful in suggesting an angle of attack for you, as the quote from Hamilton below suggests. Of course, you will always need to retain a capacity for relational argument. You must be able to recognize when a view you might want to hold is not credible or defensible. But so long as these conditions are met, the impetus provided by a reasoned commitment can be a helpful spur to ingenuity, encouraging you to look harder for particular ways of surmounting difficulties. Again some students who take an empiricist or 'common sense' view of what they are doing in their doctorates find this advice hard to apply to their work. But there is no worthwhile 'purely factual' research, even in the physical sciences.

> Those who stand for nothing, fall for anything.
> *Alexander Hamilton* [32]

Making a commitment does not entail *over*-theorizing your work, or linking it to unnecessarily high-flown ideas with little relevance to the value-added elements of the dissertation. Avoiding extraneous materials is an important part of keeping the thesis question in close sync with your research answers and appropriately managing readers' expectations. Your theoretical exposition should always be proportional to the value-added that you can credibly claim for your research. Nothing disrupts the fit between question and answer in a thesis more effectively than a theoretical framework which functions only as a heteronomous cog, a part of the analysis that turns and turns but never engages with anything else.

'It is relatively easy to build up a theory of the world', remarked the theologian Teilhard de Chardin.[33] But perhaps he was in an unusual category of persons. Doing genuinely new theory at PhD level is now very difficult in all of the humanities and social science disciplines. Their intellectual apparatuses have grown and extended a great deal in the last half century. The large empty spaces and opportunities for making major intellectual advances available earlier on have tended to be colonized. So relying on doing original theorizing should only form an integral part of your doctoral planning if you have very many confirming signals from your supervisors and colleagues that this is an area where you have some strong comparative advantage.

Still it is important to balance a reasoned scepticism about your ability to transcend some established limitations with the need to be a little bit ambitious, to stretch and push your capabilities in empirical analysis, or methodological work, or theoretical or thematic efforts. Until you try to do something a bit different or 'out of the box', how can you ever succeed? Unless you push yourself to do a bit more it will be hard to establish your genuine intellectual limits. There is now very good evidence that those people who do the most original work are generally less cautious than the ordinary run of scholars. Creative people tend to be more persistent and dedicated in their efforts, less put off by initial reverses or disappointments. They are also more sanguine or overoptimistic about their prospects of success than perhaps may seem 'rational'. They are more prone to dream of making big advances, which helps them to soldier on rather than be put off by barriers in their way (see Elster below). Creative people also find ways of underestimating the difficulties in their way. As Hirschman says, they mentally scale down the hurdles they need to surmount or the levels of effort associated with different elements of their work. Perhaps they also compress the time-scales involved.

> Creativity always comes as a surprise to us: we can never count on it and we dare not believe in it until it has happened. In other words, we would not consciously engage upon those tasks whose success clearly requires that creativity be forthcoming. Hence, the only way in which we can bring our creative resources into full play is by misjudging the nature of the task, by presenting it to ourselves as more routine, simple and undemanding of creativity than it will turn out to be.
> *Albert Hirschman* [34]

> In many cases, I submit, the belief that one will achieve much is a causal condition for achieving anything at all.
> *Jon Elster* [35]

These attributes of a positive mental outlook are much more characteristic of younger people than those in middle age. Life's disappointments often induce a progressively more cautious outlook in established scholars. They can subconsciously react to possible rejections or failures by renouncing difficult projects in advance. So it is no coincidence that in the most difficult or technically demanding subjects (like mathematics and highly mathematical physical and social sciences) genuine innovations or new insights are most associated with scholars in their twenties or early thirties. And in all disciplines journal articles publishing is most characteristically a young person's game. Older academics often retreat into editing journals or publishing chapters in edited collections put together by colleagues, rather than risk the rough and tumble of having their papers refereed, criticized and possibly rejected. This pattern also underpins the importance of the doctorate still as a key source of ideas and 'new blood' research in all the humanities and social science disciplines. And of course it sheds an interesting side-light on the folly of those governments and educational bureaucrats who in many countries have tried hard to routinize and de-skill the

PhD by making all students do only 'manageable' topics within very tight time limits.

> Experience takes more away than it adds: young
> people are nearer ideas than old men [and women].
> *Plato* [36]

For most students it is best to steer a compromise path between biting off more than you can chew in defining your doctorate and never pushing yourself enough to develop your own intellectual potential. You need to strive for a research design which encourages you to try out difficult things but also provides safeguards and insurance solutions if they do not work out. You should recognize also that being original in the modern social sciences and humanities is rarely about coming up with an entirely new way of looking at things. Instead it is mostly a more modest activity. Here originality involves encountering an established idea or viewpoint or method in one part of your discipline (or in a neighbouring discipline) and then taking that idea for a walk and putting it down somewhere else, applying it in a different context or for a different purpose. This characteristic also explains why the fringes of disciplines are often the most productive areas for new approaches. It is here that scholars are often most actively borrowing or adapting ideas developed in one discipline to do work in another.

> Someone accused him of stealing an idea from
> another composer and he shrugged and said, 'Yes,
> but what did he do with it?'
> *An anecdote about George Friedrich Handel, told by*
> *Robertson Davies* [37]

Originality should also be seen as most commonly a cumulative achievement. It rarely arises from a single-shot flash of insight or the Archimedean 'stroke of genius' of popular imagination. New ideas most often reflect the patient accumulation of layers of small insights and intuitions that only taken together allow an alternative view of a problem to crystallize. Sustained attention to a problem is almost always useful.

> My strength lies solely in my tenacity.
> *Louis Pasteur* [38]

> Creativity takes time.
> *T. Z. Tardif and Robert Sternberg* [39]

It may help your thinking also to formalize and even verbalize alternative interpretations of your problems and findings, and to express them as a debate between different positions. Lewis Minkin recommends adopting different roles or voices for short times as a useful device in interpretative writing. For instance, at different times you could try acting as 'detective' ferreting out hidden information, or 'pattern-maker' trying to systematize the information discovered, or 'juggler' trying to make apparently conflicting patterns fit together. The idea here is not to let your inner tensions and contradictions about your progress remain latent.[40] Instead try to surface explanatory problems more explicitly and it may help you to decide what weight to put on each interpretation. Minkin also mentions other possible positions. For instance, a fatalistic or 'awkward sod' view might be that events cannot be satisfactorily or plausibly explained. This position can function a little like a null hypothesis position ('there's nothing to find out here, only random connections'), and it may serve as a corrective to overelaborate explanation in some circumstances.

> The depth to which a sense of the difficulty, of the problem, sinks, determines the quality of the thinking which follows. Sometimes slowness and depth of response are connected [in] getting to the roots of the matter.
> *John Dewey* [41]

> Being puzzled, being unsure, being mistaken, and changing tack through trial and error, seem to be both integral and conducive to creative research.
> *Lewis Minkin* [42]

As your writings grow so many new issues will automatically arise. How can my theme or my findings in this chapter be dovetailed with those of another? If they seem distinct, can they be connected more strongly? Are they consistent, or conflicting, or simply at a tangent from each other? If they seem inconsistent, can they be reconciled? Academic value-added is mostly generated by two factors here. The first is being able to see clearly that these questions have arisen, which is determined partly by your own skill as a writer, codifier and communicator of ideas (to yourself as well as to everyone else). The second influence is your having the psychological courage and ingenuity to try and answer questions or tackle conflicts, rather than following a natural initial instinct to evade, suppress or disguise problems from readers. The most original people 'keep the faith' with uncomfortable research findings or disconcerting implications of their arguments, rather than just backing off from them or concluding that they must be wrong. Then they try to work these troubling findings back into a revised or adjusted framework of their intellectual commitments in some satisfactory way.

Conclusions

Karl Marx once remarked, 'Beginnings are difficult in all the sciences'.[43] For PhD students your first year or 18 months is always an acutely taxing time, involving multiple decisions and transitions. You are simultaneously setting out on an extended life-project, choosing and committing to an intellectual topic and an approach, which you then have to live with, and upgrading your normal work outputs to doctoral level. But the problems of defining what your dissertation argument is centrally about, and doing original and substantive work, are not just evanescent 'first-year PhD blues'. They are instead permanent aspects of becoming and remaining an independent and committed intellectual, someone who can effectively communicate her thoughts, and thus do more in the world than cause a library shelf to bend a little over a period of years.

Things do generally get easier though, as your materials accumulate and chunks of work get completed. How far and how fast you become more sanguine or assured depends on two things: on the one hand, the strength and clarity of your central research questions; and on the other, your ability to structure and organize the thesis materials as an effective whole, to which I now turn.

3

Planning an Integrated Thesis: the Macro-Structure

| The pattern of the thing precedes the thing.
| *Vladimir Nabokov* [1]

Any large text has to be broken up and arranged into a set of chapters. This task may seem unproblematic. First think about how many thousand words you want to write, and then how many chunks of text you need to split up this total effectively. Next settle on what topics to begin with, and where you want to end up. Then fix on some way to get from alpha to omega. So far, so straightforward. But there is a bit more to it than that. One of Neil Young's ironic songs has a record producer telling a rock artist that they have a 'perfect track', although they don't yet have either a vocal or a song. 'If we could get these things accomplished,' he says, 'nothin' else could go wrong.'[2] Planning a thesis from a blank-canvas requires a similar heroic optimism and there are multiple considerations to keep in mind.

Your structure has to be accessible for readers. They must see the sequence of chapters as logical, well organized and cumulative. At the same time, if you are to understand what you are about, the overall thesis plan has to sustain your progress as an author and researcher. It must keep your argument on track, motivate you to move on, and facilitate the development of your methods and approach. The succession of chapters has to be related in some definite and planned way to the timetable for your research. The vast majority of PhD students (around four-fifths at a guess) are 'serial' authors. They find it easiest to write chapters in a single sequence, starting chapter 5 only when chapters 1 to 4 are already pretty well defined. Generally speaking, writing chapter 5 when all you have to look at are disparate parts of (say) chapter 3 and chapter 6 is going to be a much more difficult proposition. But on the other hand, writing up your thesis so that its chapter sequence just records what research you did, in the order that you did it, can produce very incoherent structures, which cut across or obstruct the current organization of your argument and thought. Getting to a better, *designed* chapter structure often influences how good your doctorate is.

In this chapter I look at three different 'cuts' into the problem of organizing the component parts of your thesis into a storyline. The first way of looking at the issue focuses on the relationship of the whole and the core in your thesis, the core being the most value-added bits, the sections where you make a distinctive contribution to scholarship or research. The second cut looks at the choice between 'focusing down' or 'opening out' in the overall sequencing of materials. How you sequence elements often influences the weights which you give each component of your thesis, in terms both of text space and of research and writing time. The way that you make these decisions can affect readers' view of your work and your own effectiveness as an author and researcher. The third perspective focuses on choosing a strategy of explanation from a limited number of options. At the broadest level, there are actually only four possible ways of expounding your materials in creative non-fiction writing. Each of these options has its attendant advantages and disadvantages.

The whole and the core

> There are two things to be considered with regard to any scheme. In the first place, 'Is it good in itself?' In the second, 'Can it be easily put into practice?'
> *Jean-Jacques Rousseau* [3]

Anyone planning a long text needs to think logistically for a moment. Leave aside the intellectual issues of what substantive material to write and just ponder for a bit how much, what kind, in what order. A 'big book' thesis is a particularly fraught context in which to set out to write what is good or true before putting some numbers in the frame. In the first place universities now impose some important legal restrictions on what your doctoral dissertation can look like. In the past many people overwrote big book theses, greatly prolonging the time spent on them and creating long tomes that were excessively onerous to get examined. Nowadays any responsible university will limit the maximum time that you can spend on a PhD – usually allowing from five to eight years of full-time study, but more pro rata for part-time students. If the thought of (say) a six-year-long project makes you shudder, as it should, do not be fooled into thinking that this limit is purely notional. Every year there will be people who come up to the limit and some who overrun it.

Just as no one should go on and on as a permanent student, so doctoral theses are now normally limited to a maximum length, which may vary a little from one university or discipline to another. In Europe and Britain where the 'big book' thesis remains predominant in 'soft' disciplines, the upper limit can be safely thought of as 100,000 words – which is about 330 pages of A4 paper typed double-spaced. One A4 page is about 330 words, so that 1000 (or 1K) words cover three pages. (Obviously you should check the specific regulations applying to your discipline at your university and adjust my advice here to fit well inside your formal limit if it is less than 100K words.) You must take this constraint seriously from the start and make sure that you do not overwrite it. If you work away on your chapters in isolation, one at a time, it is very easy for hard-working people to write 125,000 or 150,000 (even 200,000) words of text without appreciating how the numbers are stacking up. At a late stage in your research to realize that you have 25 per cent or 50 per cent more text than you need or can submit is a very great shock. It can take weeks or months of painstaking work to make cuts of this magnitude in a complex text. And cutting out whole chapters at a late stage can be almost equally disruptive.

In fact the danger of overwriting is so acute that you need to make sure you come in well *within* the formal limit. A useful general rule is to produce a main text that is no more than four-fifths of the permitted length. A formal words target includes everything – all footnotes or endnotes, all appendices, data tables, figures and diagrams. The only thing normally excluded is the bibliography – an exhaustive alphabetical listing of every book, paper, document or other source cited, which every thesis must have in its closing pages. To be on the safe side, therefore, write no more than 80 per cent of the permitted number of words in your main text. An overall thesis constraint of 100,000 words means that your main chapters should not exceed 80,000 words. The 20,000-word difference here partly gives you some space for the notes, appendices and other supplementary materials. It also includes an insurance margin of around 10,000 words in case some of your chapters prove stubbornly longer than planned.

In terms of what happens to your research *after* it is finished, a main text of 80,000 words is also a lot better. At this length your thesis may be potentially publishable in cut-down form as a book, while one at the legal limit will be far too big (see Chapter 9). The average academic book is around 70,000 words long, and the closer you write to that kind of figure the less revising work will be entailed in converting your thesis into a monograph. Cutting (say) 100,000 words down to this length may not seem too difficult a task. In fact, it means losing a third of your work, and a cut of this magnitude could take several months work to achieve.

There are not usually formal rules about the *minimum* length for a doctoral thesis. But informal lower limits often do apply. Where universities follow the 'big book' thesis model, then academics generally interpret regulations specifying that a doctorate must make a 'substantive contribution to knowledge' to mean a pretty substantial tome. The one exception is dissertations using some condensed form of expression, such as mathematical exposition or a very formal, technical way of expressing arguments. But in these disciplines 'big book' theses are now rarely used and shorter 'papers model' dissertations are anyway the norm. Another consideration is that most universities in Europe and North America have a second-tier postgraduate thesis qualification below the PhD level, for which candidates do not need to undertake original research and which has a lower maximum word limit. In the UK, for instance, this non-doctoral research degree is called an M.Phil. (Master of Philosophy) and it requires people to write a satisfactorily presented thesis of no more than 60,000 words on a worthwhile topic. So there is a danger that PhD examiners presented with a short thesis of say 55,000 words may feel that it is too insubstantial to qualify for the doctorate, and perhaps operates more at the M.Phil. level. Wherever such second-tier research degrees exist, doctoral students not doing mathematical or formal work are well advised to write more text than the upper limit for the lower degree requirement. Your thesis should always look and feel like a doctorate to the examiners.

Once you have set the length of your main text, ideally at 80,000 words, you need to cut it up into chunks. A basic principle of organizing any piece of text is that it should be subdivided evenly, so far as possible, in this case into chapters. Regular chunking up of text fosters consistent expectations amongst readers: they know in advance how long chapters are. In addition, regular divisions always look better organized and controlled. To determine the number of subdivisions needed, bear in mind that a chapter has a practical maximum length of around 10,000 words. Chapters more extended than this length make it much harder for you to organize them internally and to control their argument effectively (see Chapter 4). Long chapters are also more difficult to convert into articles in academic journals, for which the optimum length is no more than 6000 to 8000 words. Conference papers should be even shorter, around 5000 to 6000 words long. A 10,000-word chapter can normally be edited down to form a decent 8000-word journal article. With a lot of surgery it is also feasible to recast most of it as a paper for an academic conference. But a chapter of 15,000 words will be effectively unpublishable in either form. At this length it will need radical rewriting if it is ever to see the light of day.

Chapters must also be of a certain minimum length if you are to fulfil your key mission as an author and successfully manage readers' expectations. A short chapter, one of less than about 6000 words, will be confusing for readers. It can easily seem insubstantial and disappointing. It may even appear as a 'fake' element that you have inserted on your contents page, to try and mask an otherwise obvious gap or unsuccessful patch in your research effort.

Of course, theses vary a great deal in how far they can be structured into similarly sized chunks. So these targets and limits are only indicative. There will be many occasions where you have to interpret them a bit flexibly. Yet it is a good idea to be very sceptical about writing chapters that are much longer or much shorter than 10,000 words. This central target length can be pushed up or down by 2000 words either way without doing any great harm. But chapter lengths should not go lower than about 8000 words or higher than about 12,000 words, except for the most pressing and exceptional reasons. Of course, it is often hard to predict at the planning stage how long chapters will turn out in the writing. If you end up with a substantially oversized chapter, say one that is 17,000 words long, the best strategy is to split it into two new, evenly sized chapters of around 8500 words each. Do not try to struggle along trying to organize so much text as a single unit. And do not ask your readers to cope with following an argument at the original monster length.

An overall text of around 80,000 words, evenly divided into chunks averaging 10,000 (or 10K) words each, implies that your thesis will need around eight chapters. The 8 × 10K format is a very potent one. It can usefully serve as a strong benchmark against which you should measure any different chapter structure. With eight chapters your contents page will easily meet the 'seven is a magic number' criterion (see p. 35 above). Your readers can hold the whole sequence in the forefront of their attention, and so can you. But if your structure has more than 10 or 11 chapters you will be unable to pay attention to it or envision it as a whole, and you may react by randomly 'forgetting' chapters or losing track of the sequence. Again what is true for you as author here will also be true for readers. Give them 14 chapters to keep in mind and you can be almost certain that the overall pattern of your argument will become less visible and harder to follow.

People often feel that the 8 × 10K norm is too restrictive and that they can handle many more chapters in their thesis by dividing it into parts, where each part is a set of connected chapters. For instance, a 15-chapter thesis may be too complex to envision clearly, but the idea is that it could be more manageable if divided into three parts of five chapters each. This use of parts, simply to manage an inflation of the number of chapters, should always be avoided. Your organizing problems will not go away, anyway, because the individual chapters will still become too small and fragmented. Conspicuously brief chapters will seem bitty and short-weight to readers whether they are linked together into parts or not.

A two-tier structure of parts sitting on top of chapters can also seem attractive as a way of signalling to readers that there are important continuities between chapters. For instance, it might be that chapters 1 to 4 deal with different aspects of one meta-topic, and chapters 5 to 8 are about a second, so that a two-part division will highlight this 'meta-structure' for readers. Similarly, different parts may use different methodologies, or be focused on different levels or aspects (for instance, national processes versus local processes). A part structure is more legitimate here, and may have something to recommend it in some circumstances. But a two-tier structure still requires careful management. For new authors it is a complication that is often mishandled, and so it is best avoided if possible. For instance, you can often indicate continuities between groups of chapters more simply by referring to the links between them in their titles. Ideally then you should pursue a clean and uncomplicated $8 \times 10K$ structure for your main text, without any other organizing devices above the chapter level.

So much then for the organization of the whole. But this section is also about the *core* of your thesis – which may be simply defined as all those sections with high research value-added. The core contributes to originality either by 'the discovery of new facts' or by 'the exercise of independent critical power'. This set of chapters contains all the most substantively new or different sections of your research, the ones that determine if you get a doctorate or not. In a 'big book' thesis not all of your doctorate can or should fall into the core. There will also be a certain irreducible amount of non-core materials, composed of:

♦ Lead-in material, which introduces and sets up core material for readers so that it is understandable and accessible. Sometimes dismissively labelled as 'throat-clearing' stuff, lead-in sections or chapters always require careful management. None the less they often loom much larger to students in terms of their length, and their writing and rewriting time, than their eventual role in the final thesis would justify. Readers often page through lead-in materials quite quickly, looking mainly for 'the beef' to be found later in the core sections.

◆ Lead-out materials do the 'book-closing' role for large theses, providing an integrating summation or restatement of what has been found, and setting it in a wider context.

When thinking about how to organize these three types of materials (lead-in, core and lead-out), it is vital that so far as possible they should form distinct blocks in this sequence, shown in Figure 3.1. They should not be split up and scattered around the thesis in little chunks. Readers must be able to clearly identify the core as a set of discrete, high value-added chapters. They should never have to search for smaller nuggets of originality dispersed in mixed chapters that also contain other kinds of material. The point of the lead-in materials is simply to frame, highlight and lead up to the core. In particular, they should ensure that readers can appreciate the originality and the usefulness of what you have done in your central research activities.

To get a doctorate (and to do a good thesis more broadly) the size of the core matters a great deal. You must make sure that there are enough core chapters, and that they are big enough in terms of the total wordage of your thesis, to colour the whole thing as an original piece of work. My suggested rule of thumb for 'big book' theses is that 50,000 out of the 80,000 words of main text must be core materials. That is, appreciably more

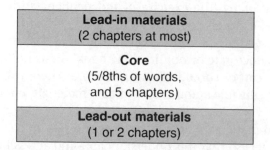

Lead-in materials
(2 chapters at most)
Core
(5/8ths of words,
and 5 chapters)
Lead-out materials
(1 or 2 chapters)

Figure 3.1   Interrelating the whole and the core

than half of your text should be original-ish stuff, reporting primary research that you have undertaken, or making new and distinctive arguments that you can plausibly claim to have originated or developed. This is a very demanding standard, but a therapeutic one. It throws into sharp focus the need to concentrate on your thesis's value-added elements. If you are doing a papers model dissertation then although your overall word length will be less, the ratio of core materials will be a good deal higher. Each of the four or five 'papers' chapters you need to write will have to be around 75 per cent original material to count as publishable, an even more demanding standard.

Do not end-load a 'big book' thesis, leaving all the good bits squeezed into the last third or quarter of the text, as many people do. A recurring problem in most humanities and social sciences disciplines is that students spend so much time and effort on writing lead-in materials that they create a long, dull, low-value sequence of chapters before readers come across anything original. To check your own plan, count the number of chapters and the number of pages that readers must scan through before they come to the core. Overextending the lead-in stuff will also squeeze out the time needed to do your core research and write it up properly. Long 'legacy' chapters (often literature reviews or methods descriptions inherited from your first one or two years of study) also restrict the text space you have available to set out the core properly.

Avoiding an end-loaded thesis is more difficult than it looks. When beginning students are doing text planning they often multiply introductory literature reviews, or insert unneeded theoretical or ground-clearing or methodological chapters. It is easy to become convinced that you must somehow discuss and explain everything about your project before actually doing it. To curb this tendency, try setting a maximum size limit for lead-in materials of two chapters. Obviously every 'big book' thesis needs at least one lead-in and one lead-out chapter, usually the first and last respectively. With only eight chapters overall, and a minimum size for the core of five chapters, that leaves you only one spare chapter that can hold additional lead-in materials – such as descriptive set-up materials or an account of your methods. Less commonly the 'spare' chapter might provide a second lead-out chapter, for instance where your research findings are very rich and require a lot of after-analysis. Note that if you schedule three chapters of lead-in material then you must either erode your core to half or less of your thesis (which is dangerous in meeting the doctoral level); or leave yourself no space for a proper lead-out chapter; or begin inflating the number of your chapters beyond what is ideal. Bear in mind the adverse impacts on professional readers of having to page through three whole chapters of secondary guff before they reach any worthwhile value-added elements. If you find that your initial thesis plan has four or more chapters of lead-in material, my advice would be scrap this schema at once and to rethink your approach from scratch.

Clearly identifying what is core in your thesis and what is not can be a psychologically taxing decision. You may tend to disguise from yourself that some chapters are not actually part of the core. Or you may enlarge your core inauthentically so as to include low value-added materials and get yourself up to having four or five apparently qualifying chapters. You need to guard against these tendencies, because being honest with yourself can be crucial for your research planning. For instance, what happens if you can only identify three chapters out of eight in your thesis plan that genuinely seem to be value-added material? You need to go back to the fundamental design of your project here, and see how you can produce one or two more core chapters. For instance, if you previously planned to undertake two case study or detailed analysis chapters, can you instead aim to undertake three or four case studies? Or if you previously were using just one method for generating results, should you think about employing another confirmatory method as well?

Being honest about your core is also vital to organizing your thesis effectively. Once you have the core firmly in focus you need to cue it and brand it heavily for readers. Your thesis title, your abstract, your chapter headings and the contents page, your preface and the introductory chapter – all these key organizers need to be mobilized so as to highlight, set up and frame the core materials in your thesis. The 'need to know' criterion should apply strongly here too. Ask of your lead-in chapter(s): 'What do readers *need to know* in order to appreciate the value-added elements to come in the core chapters?' At the start of your PhD studies cueing and branding the core is difficult, for you still will not have begun the key stages of your research. But these considerations need to come into even your early planning.

A key orientating device here is a rolling thesis synopsis of three or four pages. This document is for your own use and for your supervisors only. It greatly expands on your chapter plan or contents page by giving a paragraph of writing about what each chapter will say. The synopsis also expresses the main 'storyline' of your thesis. You should write your first synopsis as early as possible in your first year. Thereafter it is vital to keep revising it, so that it is permanently up to date and always captures your latest thinking. The whole point of a rolling synopsis is that you should never be writing or working into a vacuum. As you work on one chapter you always need to have a paragraph or so about what later unwritten chapters will cover, and an accessible summary also of the key points made in chapters already written. The rolling synopsis should always concentrate on summarizing your substantive arguments and conclusions – what you have claimed, what you have found out, and what you hope to discover.

Focusing down or opening out

> Thinking is a struggle for order and at the same time for comprehensiveness.
> *C. Wright Mills* [4]

> Thinking is a conversation with imaginary audiences.
> *Randall Collins* [5]

There are three basic sequences of chapters for a doctorate, which can be labelled the 'focus down' model, the 'opening out' model, and the 'compromise' model.

The focus down model

The most common, and most awful, sequence records four or five years' work, more or less in the order that it happened.

The contents page typically shows two, three or even four literature review chapters (sometimes even more); followed by a pretty boring or predictable methods chapter; then only three to four chapters of detailed substantive, applied or empirical work; and last a very brief concluding chapter. A rather cruel précis of the 'subtext' message this pattern conveys to readers would go like this:

Hi – this is the story of what I did during my doctorate. When I began I was a bit confused about what topic to pick. So I undertook a really big, broad literature review in order to bring myself and my supervisor up to speed on a field of possible topics. I wrote this up as a long chapter to get me through assessment by my department at the end of the first year. After that I narrowed the topic down a lot more and did an exhaustive literature review on a bit of the field where I thought I could do better than previous authors. Next I worked a great deal on my research methodology [or whatever 'techy' bits the research involved – for instance, I did a lot of searching for and accessing archives / I collected a lot of numbers / I translated a big text / I devised a framework for doing a content analysis / etc.].

At last, mid-way through my second or in my third year I went out into the field and got my hands dirty doing empirical research [or it may be, I went and sat in foreign libraries or an archive for a year / I analysed my numerical data over and over / I interviewed a lot of people / I did experiments in the labs]. At this point I discovered that things in the outside world [or, the archive documents / the library materials / the interview tapes / the computer databases / the test tubes] are pretty confusing and hard to make sense of. The results I got did not really support what I had expected to find, [or sometimes, did not seem to have any recognizable pattern at all]. Because I was puzzled, and a bit at a loss, I wrote several long chapters setting out in raw detail much of what I'd actually discovered, and trying to make preliminary sense of these findings.

By now I'd almost used up my word limit, my PhD finances were running low, and I was becoming jumpy that I'd never make it into the academic job market. So I pushed ahead to get things finished up somehow. My last chapter contains the little bit of *post hoc* rationalization of my results [or rethinking of my opening perspective] that I managed to scrape together during a very rushed final drafting stage.

There are multiple reasons why this kind of disappointingly familiar storyline recurs so frequently and predictably with doctorates. One of the most important of these influences is that many people in the humanities and social sciences regard the 'focus down' model of how a doctorate should be structured as either a natural or desirable or inevitable way to do things. Figure 3.2 shows the kind of sequence adopted by nine out of ten research students doing 'big book' theses in Europe in these disciplines, and often demanded by their supervisors. The order of material is shown along the horizontal axis from left to right, and the horizontal width of each block shows the weight of words assigned to that chunk of the thesis. The vertical size for each block shows the scope of the material or topics (the breadth of coverage) being considered at that stage.

The focus down model starts with a very broad literature review that progressively gets winnowed down as it goes on. A set of related big themes are raised initially, discussed superficially but then often set to the side one by one, or discarded

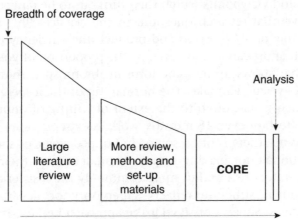

Figure 3.2   The focus down model

as unmanageable. Gradually a focus on something resembling the much narrower final topic is reached. At this point there is often an interregnum of methodological throat clearing, or a chapter discussing some underbrush of other 'confuser' topics. By now readers are often deep into the thesis, maybe three, four or five chapters in. At last the author moves on to presenting the substance of their own research, which normally concerns only a small part of their initially sketched topic. These core results sections come late on in the overall text. After the core chapters there is often little space or time for authors to do more than pull together a quick analysis chapter. Anyway most of the possible theoretical interpretations relevant to the findings have usually been exhaustively discussed already somewhere in the vast literature review zone at the beginning. So the final chapter is typically scanty, making only brief links from the author's own findings or substantive contribution back to the opening discussion of macro-themes.

The adverse effects of the focus down model on thesis authors are difficult to overstate. Research students typically spend far too long on their initial literature reviews or surveys, trawling previous work, and often becoming engrossed in collecting small argumentative angles or comprehensive references. People can waste a great deal of time on gathering and understanding information about subtopics which later get cut out of the core focus of their PhD, or on appreciating controversies and viewpoints which then turn out to be tangential to their eventual research question. In the classical PhD model, with a 'big book' thesis as end product, the efficiency of your research effort can be measured by the proportion of your total work that shows up in some form in the finished thesis. The focus down model makes the normal 'tip of the iceberg' problem much worse, often to the extent of writing off much of a year's effort, or even 18 months' work in extreme cases.

Of course there is often some kind of pedagogic or socialization rationale for making beginning students 'cut their teeth' on a literature review. But more commonly the insistence on a focus down structure reflects supervisory or departmental imperatives. Supervisors favour the approach because it allows them to 'read themselves in' on their student's new and different topic more gradually. This way of doing things also has 'safety first' appeal for bureaucratic reasons. Students who are made to do a big literature review in their first year almost always generate a reassuring bulk of text, which offers proof of their application and hard work. Composing it also gives them practice in writing skills, even if the text produced has (can have) little original content. This course also makes it easier for departments to assess beginning students' progress, following a maxim of: 'Never mind the content, feel the width of text.'

In the classical PhD model, where there was little or no formal research training via coursework, literature reviews historically helped socialize new researchers into the discipline. This past function is increasingly disappearing now, because virtually all PhD students have masters degrees and most PhD programmes have strong coursework elements. But what supervisors did in their youth still tends to influence their current expectations. Also completing a literature review is now something that students can conveniently be asked to do while they are being tied down to stay at the university by the new coursework demands.

But letting this period of your research go on much beyond your first four or five months will typically show sharply diminishing returns to effort. Students often become preoccupied with perfecting shallow, secondary criticisms of existing work. This pastime may have little scholarly value, but people get locked into it because they have not yet begun their substantive or field research, and hence they still imperfectly understand the practical difficulties of doing so. Students often write literature review chapters in a perfectionist tone, fastening terrier-like on smallish deficiencies of previous work without realizing the extent to which similar difficulties are likely to recur in their own research.

The alternative possibility to wasted effort is that once people have expended precious research time on extraneous elements, they may be unwilling to cut this material out. Instead they try to cram it in somewhere in their final thesis. Students are understandably reluctant to write off already completed chapters, even if this work has ceased to connect with their current research interests or central question. Instead they feel that they have to commit more time to keeping their early chapters integrated into the final thesis, even when the linkage is bogus, creates misleading expectations amongst readers, or imperils the intellectual coherence of their doctorate. Long early sections, written in their beginning years, are also frequently scattered with hostages to fortune, calculated to alienate examiners. Sloppy critical judgements or superficial treatments in these chapters are often not reappraised later on, partly because the student's own accumulating research experience and expertise may no longer relate to them closely.

The implications for readers are equally unfortunate. Experienced PhD examiners are inured to slow-starting theses. They will usually page through opening literature review chapters quite quickly, not expecting to see much that is not already thoroughly familiar. But if they get 80, 100 or 150 pages into the thesis (or even 200 pages in some instances) without meeting any value-added material at all, their patience will typically begin to wear thin. They may begin to question the originality of a thesis with so much secondary analysis included and to wonder if it really meets the standard for a doctorate. Students often imagine that readers will closely scrutinize their small critical comments and discussions in early chapters and ascribe them far more importance than they actually will. To get a more realistic view, think about how you approach books in your own field. Most of us are quite cynical and critical with new stuff, prepared to 'gut' books for their real value-added elements. We are also initially rather sceptical of accepting authors' judgements *until* they have established their credibility as original researchers. Readers of PhDs are no different. They will tend to see your secondary analysis commenting on other people's work as pretty lightweight or dispensable until you have established your own credentials as an original researcher. At an early stage in the thesis they still have no reason to take you seriously, or to believe that your criticisms are grounded in an awareness of research realities.

When readers do eventually reach the author's own research materials in the focus down model, their narrowness or detailed specificity may seem quite disappointing after the wide sweep of work and flashier intellectual themes initially discussed. And the speedy wrap-up ending to the thesis, inadequately linked back to the introductory themes, may leave readers asking 'so what?' and struggling to work out what they have learned from the thesis as a whole. The whole effect may be that the thesis ends 'not with a bang, but a whimper'.[6]

The opening out model

There are better ways of sequencing material in a long text. In the physical sciences the normal approach is the 'opening out' model shown in Figure 3.3, which works in an almost reversed manner. The first element in the sequence is a deliberately short and terse specification of the research question. It focuses tightly on the immediate issue to be tackled and gives only a brief discussion of the most recent relevant literature, plus a very compressed amount of essential set-up information. The second element, beginning within (say) 30 pages of the start, presents the author's key research findings and results. This is followed by a section of applied analysis, which tracks back and forth across what has been found out, and connects it up in detail with previous research and literature. Finally, once the author has convincingly established their research credentials the thesis 'opens out' into a discussion of the wider themes or theoretical implications arising from the research and discusses possible avenues for the next phase of work in the field.

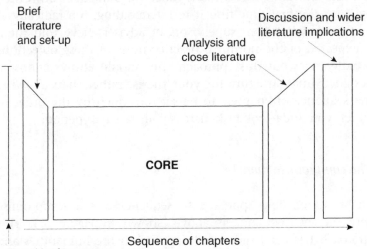

Figure 3.3   The opening out model

There are many advantages in the opening out model. Readers come into contact with your original work much sooner than in the focus down approach. They typically get far more analysis of your results and a better appreciation of how your results mesh with the immediately relevant previous research. Readers also encounter your views on other people's work after (and not before) you have established your credentials as a serious researcher. As a result your criticisms and suggestions should come across as much more grounded and authoritative than in the focus down model.

For authors the opening out model also has many substantial advantages. If you can cut short the usual long lead-in and acclimatization period at the beginning of your thesis, and get on with the key research tasks as early as possible, then you will have more time to thoroughly understand your findings later on. Analysing and writing up research results, moving from very detailed, often disorganized materials or complex outcomes to properly structured and well-presented findings, takes a surprising amount of time and intellectual effort. It cannot easily be rushed. The opening out model gives you a better chance to develop new interpretations and to let the implications of your results sink in.

Yet the opening out model is very little used in the social sciences or humanities. Many doctoral students confronted by it for the first time find it too demanding, too radically at odds with what their supervisors or advisers have told them is expected or the norm. In practice none of these objections actually rules out this approach. You should always choose a designed final structure for your thesis, rather than allowing the sequence of chapters to be set too much by the order in which you undertook tasks across your research period.

The compromise model

The third possible approach to sequencing is a compromise between the two models above, shown in Figure 3.4. This approach has been successfully applied in the humanities and social sciences. First you need to follow the advice above on keeping lead-in materials to a maximum of two chapters. That means

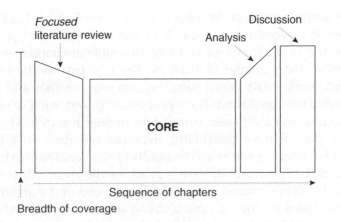

Figure 3.4 The compromise model

you should keep your original literature review down to just a single chapter, ideally one that is framed quite closely around your central research question from the start. Do not raise a lot of broader issues that you will never discuss again or where you have little or no value-added contribution to make. Instead try to focus on materials that readers 'need to know' to appreciate your research contribution, and no more. Next try to keep any set-up or background or methods materials down to just one further chapter, again following a strict judgement about what readers 'need to know' and avoiding long descriptive digressions. You should consider carefully whether you need to include a separate chapter on methodology in the main sequence of your argument at all. It is often best to write a special 'Research Methods Appendix' to come *after* the main set of chapters. It can be written as a reference material annex, which allows you to include very detailed information for examiners and fellow researchers, but without disrupting the development of your main argument.

Taking these steps should ensure that readers come into contact with your original research materials within (say) 50 or 60 pages of the start of your thesis. They are given an appropriate amount of time to 'warm up' on your themes and questions, and they get a very synoptic treatment of any background or set-up material that they really need to master. But readers no longer have to page through wads of filler material before beginning to appreciate your research contribution. Your core stuff thus comes across much earlier, leaving more space at the end of the thesis for you to do a couple of chapters or one decent, long chapter of analysis. The first part of these concluding materials might focus on bringing together and integrating the conclusions from your core chapters, each of which should cover a different component of your research. The second part of these concluding materials can then do a more limited opening out from the results of your analysis back into the wider literature. By saving much of the theory discussion and literature discussion to handle at the end of the argument, you should be able to form a strong theoretical or broad-view chapter. This way you can conclude your thesis on an upbeat, confident and professionally salient note.

Four patterns of explanation

> I have yet to see any problem, however complicated, which when you looked at it the right way did not become still more complicated.
> *Poul Anderson* [7]

When you try to communicate a set of connected information to someone else there are only a limited number of ways that you can do it. If your chosen way cuts across the other person's expectations then crossed wires may occur in the communication. This problem is made worse when your audience does not listen intently to every twist and turn of your account. For instance, people of different genders famously tend to choose incompatible modes of communication. Most women like to give and receive process-organized explanations, often running through the history of an event or an interaction from beginning to end in narrative succession. But most men prefer to receive 'bottom-line' information first. They want to know at the start what the key point of a story is, and only then will they be ready to listen much more selectively to the detail of how the story's outcome ended up as it did. Hence men easily get annoyed by what they code as women 'rabbiting on'. Equally, women often get turned off by men's overly terse and inaccessible explanations of complex phenomena. A variant of this particular contrast in modes of communication (serialistic rather than holistic) also runs through two of the alternative patterns discussed here. My thesis is that in the humanities and social sciences there are only four fundamental ways of handling long, text-based explanations, which I shall discuss in turn. These organizing patterns are: descriptive; analytic; argumentative; and a matrix pattern, combining elements of any two of the other three approaches.[8]

Descriptive explanations

Suppose that I am asked to give an account of the room where I am sitting and writing these words, which is my home study. Figure 3.5 shows the main features of the room, which are reasonably complex. A descriptive mode of explaining something is to take the way that things are organized *externally* or exogenously to me and to then use that pattern to structure the sequence of what I say. For instance, in explaining about my study I might start at some particular point, like the door, and then decide to sweep my arm around the room in a particular direction (clockwise in this case) listing everything that comes into my line of sight as I do so, as shown in Figure 3.5(a). Here I might say: 'First there is a white door, and next to it in a clockwise direction is a green painted wall, and a grey beaten-up sofa, and above it a noticeboard with papers pinned on it, a CD rack, then a series of long bookshelves with four-drawer filing cabinets underneath, and then a printer, an old desk-top PC, and a new laptop on a desk surrounded by papers, then a window with three frames...' and so on.

This listing account already illustrates some obvious deficiencies of a descriptive way of explaining things. The sequence of objects being named is united in only one way, namely proximity in the room. The things I list are next to each other. But in every other way the different objects described together are jumbled up randomly and unpredictably. The list may work OK if readers get to see Figure 3.5 (I certainly hope so). But without this visual support, the list could be very hard to take in and to visualize. The account I give of my study could also easily

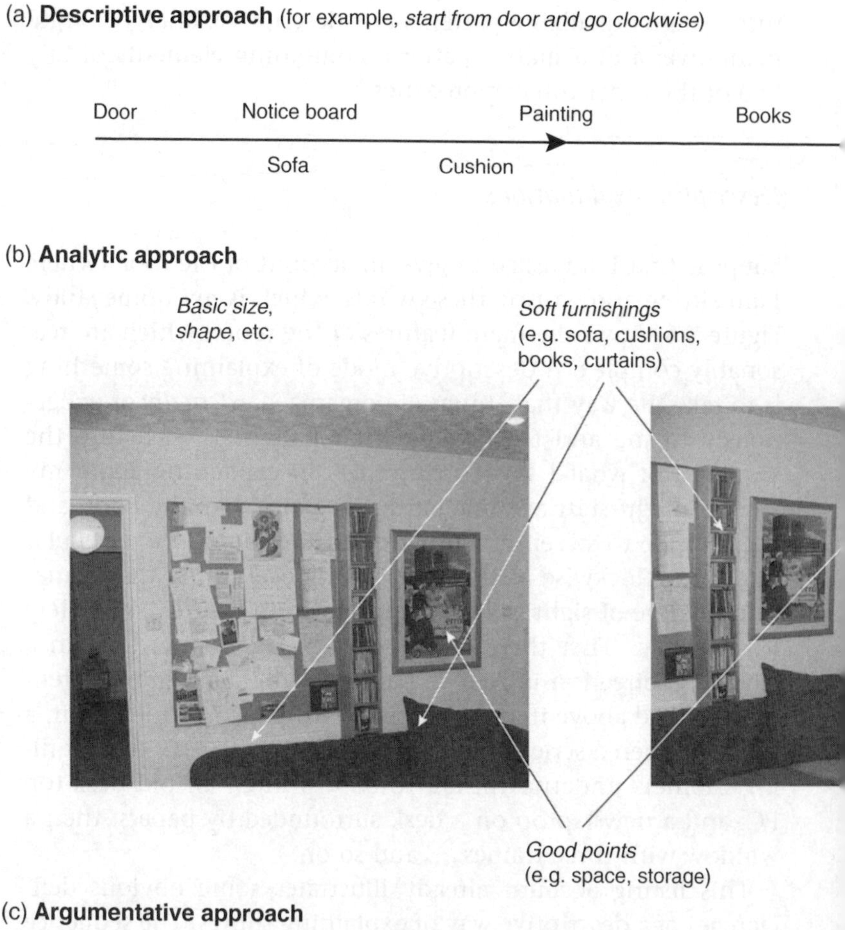

(a) **Descriptive approach** (for example, *start from door and go clockwise*)

Door	Notice board		Painting	Books
	Sofa	Cushion		

(b) **Analytic approach**

Basic size, shape, etc.

Soft furnishings (e.g. sofa, cushions, books, curtains)

Good points (e.g. space, storage)

(c) **Argumentative approach**

Figure 3.5   Three ways of viewing my home study

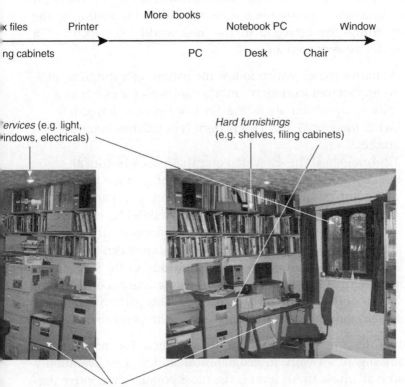

More books

x files   Printer   Notebook PC   Window

ng cabinets   PC   Desk   Chair

ervices (e.g. light,
*indows, electricals)

Hard furnishings
(e.g. shelves, filing cabinets)

Bad points
(e.g. eclectic furniture,
clutter overload)

become very long-winded and hard to organize mentally. These problems may perhaps lead you to think that I am setting up a straw person to knock down here, and that in practice in advanced humanities and social science research it would be very hard to find people utilizing this kind of pattern of explanation.

Think again. Most theses in these disciplines still follow a descriptive approach, in the sense defined above, in that their fundamental organization is set externally to the author, by the way things are arranged in the 'real world'. Key forms of a descriptive approach are:

◆ Narrative theses, which follow the pattern of a storyline set by an external work or by another author – for example, a critical exposition discussing Act 1 of a play, followed by Act 2, then Act 3, etc. This pattern is popular in literature studies.

◆ Chronological theses, which essentially let a historical sequence dictate their structure, beginning at the beginning and going on until they come to the end. This pattern is prevalent in historical studies and related fields.

◆ Institutional theses or those with a 'guidebook' structure – which replicate the pattern of an organization chart, or the relationships among different institutions, or the structure of a piece of legislation or a set of regulations, in order to trace out its working in loving detail. This pattern is popular in law, public administration, social policy, and so on.

Other descriptive patterns can be envisaged, for instance spatially organized work in geographical studies. Less commonly found at whole-thesis level is the most popular descriptive pattern in masters level or undergraduate essays, the 'random sequence of authors'. Here the order in which sources are discussed, and their relative weighting in the essay, are both determined by which sources students were able to access in the library that week in the time available to do the essay. So a lot is written about sources which were accessed first; rather less about sources which the student only had a short time to absorb; and least of all is said about sources which the student is only pretending to have read. But even the 'random sequence of authors' pattern often recurs over sections of a thesis.

In lower level university studies with exams as a key assessment method, and even for taught courses at PhD level, adopting a descriptive approach to organizing your ideas and sequencing your work is a popular but very damaging habit. It is prevalent because it seems a lazy way. You just pick up an already 'given' or perhaps 'obvious' structure existing 'out there', and organize your work around it. It is damaging because a descriptive approach demands a very high load of facts or other materials to make it work well, and yet it often becomes hard for authors to control and hence ends up looking very disorganized. Just as the things which sit next to each other in my study form an eclectic list, hard for readers to follow or understand, so things which sit next to each other in historical time or institutional space may be all jumbled up thematically or analytically.

But in 'big book' theses these difficulties are greatly ameliorated. The space and time constraints of lower level university studies are not so pressing at PhD level – indeed they may not seem to be present at all to beginning students. At doctoral level descriptive explanations can work better, because you can assemble the mass of facts and evidence needed to make the approach look comprehensive and non-naïve. In addition, some kinds of descriptive (externally structured) explanation are clearly popular with and accessible to a wide range of readers, especially historical and narrative writing. The most chronological of all A to Z storylines are biographies, which sell very widely.

Yet to make a descriptive structure work in most of the humanities and 'soft' social sciences in fact demands very high level authoring skills. In very subtle ways you need to first articulate and then weave into your meta-level descriptive account either analytic concepts or argumentative themes. This thematization of what seem to be just narrative, chronologies or 'guidebook' texts is an art that is harder than it looks. If you have not reached this high level of attainment then you should always examine carefully the three alternative approaches below before concluding that you can successfully make a descriptive structure work in your thesis. The danger is that your thesis argument flounders in a disorganized fashion, presenting a jumble of complexities in which a single not very important feature (like temporal proximity in historical accounts or institutional connectedness in guidebook arguments) is prioritized over everything else.

Such theses can often seem to be structured by no clear internal or intellectual pattern of organization.

Analytic explanations

It is not difficult to break up and reorganize a complex description into more analytic headings. The key step is to use organizing categories conjured out of your own brain rather than a sequence of ideas given to you externally. For instance, an analytic approach to describing my home study is shown in Figure 3.5(b), where I might structure my account around the following headings:

◆ the physical size, shape and features of the room (basically rectangular, with a little add-on bay window);
◆ the services in the room (the windows, ventilation, lights, central heating, plug points, etc.);
◆ the hard or fixed furnishings (shelves, bookcases, immovable heavy filing cabinets, etc.); and
◆ the soft or variable furnishings (curtains, carpets, movable furniture, PCs and electronic gear, books, CDs, etc.).

These different categories do not sit out there in the 'real world' for me to pick up ready-to-use: instead they are mental categories of my own choosing. But on the other hand they are not rocket science and they did not take ages to devise. I hope that these distinctions would not need a lot of explanation to be accepted as useful and reasonably familiar by most readers. But if I now run over what there is to see in my home study using these headings, I am pretty sure that most people will see this account as much clearer, as much better organized than the descriptive approach's almost random sequencing. As well as providing key principles for explaining why sets of things are treated together, the headings also capture clearly my value-added contribution and thus help to personalize the account.

Three main types of analytic structures are used in humanities and social sciences theses:

◆ Periodized historical or narrative accounts break away from a beginning-to-end chronology, and instead chunk up the storyline into a number of clear periods. The characteristics of each period can then be treated more synoptically. The crucial transitions are from one period to another. They are separated out for focused treatment, while the more ephemeral ebb and flow of less important events within each period is given less emphasis.

◆ Systematic accounts disaggregate complex processes into their component parts, as in my study example above. An overall set of phenomena (such as a change process or an intellectual problem) is split into different components and each aspect is treated using appropriate concepts, theories, methods and evidence for that category. For instance, you could split historical processes into separate economic, political, cultural and social changes, and develop different models of each, as well as an account of how they interconnect. Or you could analyse a novel or a play in terms of characters and their interactions, or identify different elements, myths or themes woven through a narrative.

◆ Causal analyses go further than simply handling different aspects under category headings. They seek to reconstruct complex multi-causation processes by grading and sifting how influences are patterned, weighting causes against each other, distinguishing long-term and short-term, or necessary and sufficient causes. Very sophisticated approaches here may trace out a complete algorithm, an analytic model of the processes that are being studied.

An analytic structure has many advantages, so long as the set of organizing categories being used is simple and robust, picking out clearly distinguishable sets of phenomena in very clear-cut ways. To organize a whole thesis, you need a fairly restricted structure of big, broad concepts. Fine-grain or subtle distinctions that take ages to explain are not suitable for this top-level organizing task, or indeed for providing an internal structure for chapters (see Chapter 4). Robust organizing categories should also be recognizable ideas, with which readers can easily connect. Both these requirements may seem to limit the scope for you to personalize your thesis organization.

They often seem restrictive for new authors who are convinced of the uniqueness of their individual approach. But it is perfectly feasible to impress clear views on your chapter plan without lurching off into idiosyncrasy or impenetrable distinctions.

Once you have an analytic structure of chapters it is also important *not* to follow through unquestioningly with a further analytic way of carving up material inside each chapter. Do not overdo the analysis. At its limit an ultra-analytic thesis can resemble a fairly unique (and awful) item of British cuisine, the canned 'fruit cocktail'. This dish consists of different kinds of tinned fruit (like peach, apricot, pear, apple, grapes, cherries and so on), all cut up into small cubes and mixed together, and then completely covered in a sugary syrup. When you eat a mouthful of canned fruit cocktail you may know intellectually that you are consuming different types of fruit, but the tastes are so effectively homogenized that you will have difficulty identifying what any given cube consists of. The analogous danger in academic life is that you wrench apart connected phenomena to such a detailed extent that your readers lose any grip on how the parts connect as a whole. For instance, if you analyse a chronological process into separate analytic components, and then analyse each of these in turn into subcomponents, readers may lose any working sense of how the processes being described operated over time, and hence find no clear narrative storyline at all. Overextended analytic arguments can also produce very formalistic patterns of organizing material, with multi-layered typologies or sets of categories being expounded which are very remote from 'ordinary knowledge' ways of looking at problems. In some technical or highly theoretical areas very formalized treatments may be acceptable, even expected, especially in the parts of social sciences and philosophy. But outside these areas, they can easily look off-putting or impenetrable, especially where an author uses unfamiliar organizing concepts.

Argumentative explanations

Organizing your account argumentatively is again easy to do. First you gather together all the points which might be made in one interpretation or intellectual position and express them coherently. Next you assemble an alternative or opposed interpretation, originating from a different intellectual position and seek to better explain the phenomena being focused on. The sequence of materials becomes one of 'pro' arguments then 'anti' arguments, of thesis and antithesis (and perhaps synthesis). Figure 3.5c shows how I might do this when giving an account of my home study. Here I could set out all the points that I like about my study, perhaps sequencing them in terms of their importance to me in evaluating the room. I like my study because it is spacious, conveniently shaped, equipped with lots of walls suitable for storage, newly set up, restfully decorated, well lit, quiet, set a bit apart from the rest of the house, and so on. Then I might consider all the problems I still have with the study, such as the amount of clutter I've managed to jam into it already, my inability to keep it neatly organized, or its patchwork feel. (The study was not equipped in one go, as 'real' offices are. Instead its current state represents a layered accumulation of different bits of kit that I've been able to afford at different stages of my career and never had the heart, or the finances, to scrap and start again from scratch.)

An argumentative approach will usually look well organized for readers, so long as you distinguish clear intellectual positions or sides in a controversy, using labels and schools of thought already recognized. By definition an argumentative approach focuses on a debate or disagreement and tends to project into sharp focus your value-added. It will also usually look personalized, especially where you have taken care to frame or configure your central thesis question in a way or from an angle which is particular to your work. This approach will also handle multiple theoretical positions or relational arguments explicitly, normally an important feature of humanities or social sciences research.

There are also some disadvantages of an argumentative approach at doctoral level. Pro- and anti- arguments, thesis and antithesis oppositions are usually pairs, and only rarely triples. So argumentative categories may not be enough to organize eight chapters. People sometimes react to this difficulty by trying to handle many more interpretations at once. Some students, especially those who have carried out overextended literature searches, somehow lapse into thinking that at doctoral level they must cover *all* possible interpretative positions, even if they are very numerous. In fact this option is neither feasible nor desirable in an argumentative approach. A doctorate is basically a monograph, treating a single subject intensively. It is not a textbook, still less a work of reference. Trying to show how four or five perspectives would handle a particular problem or interpret the same set of phenomena will quickly become very repetitive. Carried through at any decent level, such an enterprise can also consume a large amount of your wordage limit. You need to configure your thesis question, and set up any initial literature review which you do, so that you can legitimately restrict your work to considering only two, or at most three, main lines of argument.

Another problem with an argumentative approach is that it may not sit very comfortably in disciplines which adopt a 'normal science' approach, those with a hegemonic 'mainstream' view built up by the careful cumulation of work within a single, accepted paradigm. Argumentatively structured theses can be unattractive for students from more consensual societies (such as Japan), where overt disagreements can seem somewhat vulgar or wrong-headed. And since scholars often tend to self-select themselves into groupings of like-minded people, it will sometimes be hard to stand up and treat as credible a view considered 'deviant' by your local department's orthodoxy, perhaps even anathema to it. Finally it can be difficult to identify and develop an effective argumentative approach which is close-fitting around your thesis question at an early stage of your research. At the start of your effort you may tend to focus on disputes that are too broadly drawn or too conventionally specified, again a tendency that is exaggerated where people author long introductory literature reviews, rather than snappy focused ones.

Matrix patterns

To get more articulated organizational structures for neatly organizing eight or so chapters, you can combine any of the three approaches above. There are four pairs of possible combinations:

- analytic plus argumentative
- analytic plus descriptive
- argumentative plus analytic
- argumentative plus descriptive

In each pair, the first approach listed is the primary or top-level organizing principle, grouping together sets of chapters. The other part of the pair is the subsidiary or second-tier organizing principle, explaining the sequence of chapters within each of the top-tier groupings. Figure 3.6 shows this distinction in a diagrammatic way for the two matrix patterns combining analytic and argumentative approaches. If the analytic dimension is primary then arguments and interpretations are used in pairs of chapters pulled together by systematic or causal or functional criteria. If the argumentative dimension is primary, then each contrasting broad view is considered in turn, broken down into its component aspects.

Matrix patterns involving a second-tier descriptive organization of chapters are very common in doctoral theses. Here authors recognize that they cannot just pick up an external or 'real world' pattern of phenomena and use it to structure their thesis without risking a 'random shopping list' appearance. So analytic categories or a consideration of different argumentative positions are used to provide the primary structure of the thesis. But within groups of chapters a narrative, or historical, or guide-book pattern is then followed. (In my experience a descriptive approach is rarely or never used in a matrix approach as the primary organizing dimension. People who like using externally given structures tend just to do a wholly descriptive thesis.)

A matrix approach offers many advantages for doctoral students. It almost always generates enough categories to slot your chapters into. Figure 3.6a shows a six-box pattern combining a primary argumentative dimension (a liberal view versus a Marxist interpretation in this case) and a secondary analytic dimension (compartmentalizing each approach into economic, political and cultural boxes in this case). Using this kind of graphical planning device is helpful because it will alert you to an alternative sequence shown in Figure 3.6b, where you go across rows first and move down the columns second. Here the

primary dimension is the analytic one, and the argumentative dimension is secondary. Exploiting the two-dimensional
space of a blank matrix like this means that you will often be
able to pull together more strands of your thinking than can be
accommodated in the more usual simple, linear approach.
Either way Figure 3.6 would generate enough boxes to arrange
the core chapters of a thesis in a strong and robust pattern.
Add a lead-in chapter at the beginning and a lead-out chapter
at the end to this core and you would have an effective eight-
chapter PhD.

(a)

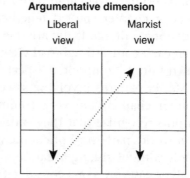

(b)

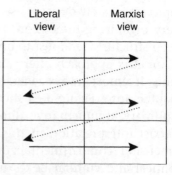

Figure 3.6   Examples of a matrix structure:
(a) the argumentative dimension is primary;
(b) the analytic dimension is primary

Conclusions

These three cuts on the macro-structure of your thesis each matter a great deal. Putting them together often entails making quite complex judgements, which can be hard to resolve. There is never just 'one best way' of organizing a long text. One consideration may pull you in a particular direction, and another in a divergent fashion. When you do settle on a pattern for your work, there will *always* be at least one other viable alternative structure that you could use, and some debate in your own mind about whether to switch over. Welcome then to the world of permanent authoring dilemmas, of which this is only the first. Some of the same issues recur at the micro-level of organizing individual chapters or papers, albeit in a more manageable way.

4

Organizing a Chapter or Paper: the Micro-Structure

> George said: 'You know we are on the wrong track altogether. We must not think of the things we could do with, but only of the things that we can't do without.'
> *A character in Jerome K. Jerome's* Three Men in a Boat   [1]

The building blocks of a completed thesis are chapters. Yet if these blocks are to hold together they must themselves be effectively structured internally, so that they can bear a load rather than crumbling away under pressure. A first step then is to divide the chapter into parts. In addition, two elements of designing internal structure are commonly mishandled: devising headings and subheadings to highlight your organizing pattern; and writing the starts and ends of the chapter and its main sections. I discuss these three issues in turn.

Dividing a chapter into sections

> The human mind is only capable of absorbing a few things at a time.
> *Stanislaw Lem*   [2]

> Nothing is particularly hard if you divide it into small parts.
> *Henry Ford*   [3]

A chapter of 10,000 words is impossible for you to hold in your head as an author unless it can be split into shorter component parts linked by a common theme. It is similarly difficult for readers to follow your argument without the cues provided by 'organizers', especially the sections of the chapter and their associated armoury of headings, which should convey in condensed form a sense of the argument being made. Fixing the sections to be used in any one chapter is normally straightforward, since chapters are much shorter and simpler than whole theses. But the scheme which you adopt has to work not just for this chapter but across all your chapters in a recognizably similar way, unless readers are to start anew in understanding a new scheme of organizers with each fresh chapter.

Whenever you are chunking up text, it is a basic principle to try and make sure that the sections you create are similarly sized. Dividing the text as evenly as possible generates consistent and hence more accurate expectations amongst readers about how long each section will be. Just as thesis chapters should be around 10,000 words (plus or minus 2000 words), so the sections inside chapters should all be approximately the same length and have the same importance for your argument. How many sections you need depends on the precise length of your chapter, but a rough rule of thumb is that you will need a major heading to break up the text every 2000 to 2500 words, or every seven to eight pages of A4 paper typed double-spaced. Both you as the author and readers will be able to hold this much information in the forefront of their attention at any one time, but will quickly lose track if sections get larger. And with only four or at most five main headings to keep track of in each chapter readers should have a clear idea of its internal structure. If you have more than (say) seven sections then readers will definitely find it harder to keep track of how the whole chapter is structured. And main sections shorter than around 2000 words will often seem bitty or insubstantial.

So in a standard-length chapter of 10,000 words you need four main sections. The titles for these sections are called 'first order' headings, because they are the top organizers, the ones including most text within each chapter. You can show their importance to readers graphically in three ways: by numbering them (for instance, 3.1, 3.2, and so on); by using a large font

size and format that makes them stand out clearly from the surrounding text; and by locating them prominently, for instance
on an otherwise blank line of their own and centred on the
page. For the smaller subsections inside each main part of the
chapter you will also need a set of 'second order' headings. You
can signal them as less important than first-order headings, but
more important than ordinary text, by: using an intermediate-
sized font; using a less prominent font format; locating them
less conspicuously (for instance on an otherwise blank line, but
placed at the left-hand margin); and by not numbering them.
In some cases you may also need some 'third order' subheadings, which are really only groupings of paragraphs. They are
signalled by using a less prominent font and emphasis than the
second-order headings; of course with no numbers; and located
so that they are less conspicuous (for instance, at the left-hand
margin, but with a main text paragraph starting adjacent to it
on the same line). Overall, the size, emphasis and location of
subheadings should be most prominent for first-order headings
(which are the only numbered ones), less for second-order subheads, and less again for third-order subheads (when they are
present). Of course, all headings should be more noticeable
than the ordinary text. In this way readers are given a clear
visual signal of where each section stands in the overall argument structure of the chapter.

It is worth trying to avoid regularly using four orders of subheading, which could be complex for readers to follow and hard
for you to manage. It is also best to let the headings express the
hierarchy of ideas, rather than to try frequently indenting text
from the left-hand margin, as some organizer programs on
word-processing packages will routinely do. Start each new paragraph which comes immediately after a subheading at the left-
hand margin, and thereafter use a tab to make paragraph starts
stand out. Short indented passages of text are used for lists of
points, with bullets or dashes in front of them. They can also
occasionally allow you to avoid introducing fourth-order subheadings, where it is convenient so to do. In this use, you can
flexibly group together sets of paragraphs in an *ad hoc* way into
indented passages, without burdening readers with any further
elaboration of your subheadings system. (The only other reason
for indenting passages of text should be for quotations longer

than 30 words. Run on smaller quotations in the text within single quotation marks, 'like this'.)

In addition to its component main sections each chapter will need a relatively brief, untitled section of lead-in text at the beginning, and a short section of lead-out text labelled 'Conclusions' at the end. Each of these smaller bits should be between 200 and around 1000 words only. Readers will universally expect that the text placed at the very beginning of each chapter is lead-in material, so you do not need to label it 'Introduction'. (Using this redundant subheading can often be a quick way to make your overall scheme of headings and sections start to malfunction badly: see below.) However, your lead-out materials will always need a heading to mark them out, preferably at second-order level so that readers will not expect to find here a longer section than they will actually get. Thus in outline my recommended complete schema of sections for a chapter (let's say Chapter 3) is:

Introductory text 200 to 1000 words		[no subhead]
3.1	**First main section** 2000 to 2500 words	[first-order heading]
3.2	**Second main section** 2000 to 2500 words	[first-order heading]
3.3	**Third main section** 2000 to 2500 words	[first-order heading]
3.4	**Fourth main section** 2000 to 2500 words	[first-order heading]
Conclusions 200 to 1000 words		[second-order subhead]

Since this pattern looks very straightforward, it may seem surprising that authors ever have difficulties with partitioning chapters. But in fact three mistakes are commonplace: underorganizing chapters; overorganizing them; and organizing different chapters in different ways.

(i) The simplest way of disorganizing a chapter is to *under-organize* it, perhaps including headings but only fake ones that do no useful work. This effect comes about because authors often create sections which are much longer or shorter than others, and then they assign the same order of headings to these dissimilar pieces of text, thereby mis-signalling readers and creating inappropriate expectations. Using first-order headings for the lead-in and lead-out materials virtually guarantees this outcome. It is very common to find a chapter (let's say, chapter 4) organized like this:

4.1	**Introduction**	[first-order heading]
	300 words	
4.2	**First main section**	[first-order heading]
	1500 words	
4.3	**Second main section**	[first-order heading]
	12,000 words	
4.4	**Conclusions**	[first-order heading]
	500 words	

Several things have gone wrong here. Titling the lead-in and lead-out materials as if they were main sections will generate expectations amongst readers that these are substantial bits of text when they are not. The middle two main sections are real ones, but they are completely unbalanced. Section 4.3 is eight times longer than section 4.2 (as well as being 40 times longer than section 4.1 and 24 times longer than section 4.4). So when readers encounter a first-order heading here they have no idea what to expect. It might be a section as short as 300 words or as long as 12,000 words. These headings will look well worked out on the thesis contents page, but in fact they do not effectively chunk up or organize the chapter at all. Virtually all the text (85 per cent) is actually in section 4.3, which at this length will be impossible for readers to follow or for the author to organize effectively.

(ii) It is also possible to *overorganize* a chapter by having *too many* levels of headings; making them too similar in their font size, appearance, and location; and then overnumbering them. For instance, if you split up a 10,000-word chapter into

12 sections, and have three or four second-order subheadings in each section, plus a scattering of third-order subheads as well, then readers will encounter 40 headings in total, effectively one every 250 words, or two per page. If the headings look alike (using similar fonts and occupying the same positions on the page) then confusion is guaranteed.

Text that has been overfragmented in this way often comes with a complicated numbering system that is supposed to provide guidance for readers. All modern word-processing packages have 'outliner' facilities which allow you to automatically create a numbered set of paragraphs in many different formats, often with varying levels of indentation as well. These features are mainly designed for use in short reports. The outlining facility can also be useful for making conventional notes when ploughing through a very hierarchic textbook or a similar source. After using this facility for these purposes in their earlier studies, quite a lot of doctoral students also adopt it for authoring large amounts of text. But applied over a very long text like a doctorate an outliner approach can often be counterproductive and seem like overkill.

In many technical or more mathematical disciplines the number sequence commonly adopted might look like this:

5.1	***First-order heading***
5.1.1	*Second-order heading*
5.1.2	*Another second-order heading*
	5.1.2.1 Third-order subheading
	5.1.2.2 Another third-order subheading

Alternatively in humanities subjects the same effect is often achieved by mixed-together different letter and number sequences such as this:

5.A	***First-order heading***
5.A.i	*Second-order heading*
5.A.ii	*Another second-order heading*
	5.A.ii.a Third-order subheading
	5.A.ii.a Another third-order subheading

In both these examples the number sequence is overdone and looks ugly and hard to follow. Extending it to fourth-order subheadings includes five or more numbers (such as 5.1.2.1.3, which occurs in some cases): this step sends a very clear signal to readers that you care little or nothing about the accessibility of your text. Readers will find it difficult to tell whereabouts they are in such an overcomplex hierarchy of headings, especially where the headings at different levels look very similar (as in my examples above). Adopting such a schema cannot give cohesion to an argument that has become much too fragmented. Nor can it impart genuine order and hierarchy when an author has not clarified her ideas sufficiently to organize her text in a more considerate manner.

It may also be that authors who adopt complex numbering schemas are actively encouraged by the availability of this device to chop their argument up into ever smaller pieces. Typically they may overdevelop an 'analytic' argument so as to create a 'fruit cocktail' effect, discussed above (on p. 70). They place so much reliance upon the chaining of numbers or symbols at the start of each subsection that their basic intellectual approach alters. They start making too many distinctions, in a kind of 'logic-chopping' manner. For this reason my personal practice has always been to recommend people to number only the main sections of chapters (such as 3.1 or 3.2); and to avoid using headings with more numbers in them (like 3.1.2 or still worse 3.1.2.1). Using numbered headings only for chapter main sections but not for smaller subsections seems to work best for the vast majority of humanities and social sciences PhD theses.

Take a flexible approach to this rule of thumb, however. In the humanities especially, you may want to try and do without *any* numbered sections, if other professional writings in your discipline have a very literary or understated feel. Here you would rely only on the differing font sizes, emphasis and location of various orders of headings to give a clear sense of their hierarchy to readers. At the other end of the spectrum, if your discipline has a strong 'technical writing' style, as some areas of the social sciences do, you may wish to use numbered second-order headings, for subsections within the main chapter sections (that is, numbers like 3.2.2). But it is wise to hold the line here and not to introduce four- or five-number headings (like 3.1.2.3 or 3.2.3.2.3) for smaller subsections, which will tend to encourage you to use overfragmented modes of exposition. It is also worth remembering that across most disciplines it will be much easier to get thesis material published as a journal paper (or even as a book), the less it seems like a report and the more accessible the text appears. Converting an overnumbered chapter into a paper is not a trivial task. If you have relied on the numbering scheme to give coherence, then you may have to redo all the links from one section to another, and much of the internal signposting in the chapter from scratch, if it is to work as a paper.

(iii) The final common problem with headings occurs when thesis authors do not use the same system of headings across all chapters, but employ different systems at various points. Most inconsistency problems occur because students write up their chapters one at a time, often beginning with a typical literature review which goes over length and becomes difficult to organize. As they write later chapters so they change their ideas about sections and headings, and start using different schemas, without going back to their earlier work and redoing the headings in the new format. Whatever scheme of headings you arrive at, it must be applied to give the same 'look and feel' throughout.

However, this requirement is quite consistent with the need for your scheme to be flexibly handled, in a way that responds to the nature of each different chapter and section, rather than being implemented in a mechanical or robotic-looking fashion. The system of headings stays the same throughout the main text, but some chapters may not need to use all the elements of the schema. For instance, you might use only first- and second-order headings in shorter chapters, with brief sections. But then you can introduce third-order headings in bigger chapters which have longer sections or which handle more complex material.

Just as a constantly updated rolling synopsis is a useful planning and revising tool, keeping you in touch with what the central argument of your research is really about, so it can be very helpful to maintain an 'extended contents page' showing the current sequence of materials in your thesis. This page may never be included in the final thesis, or used by anyone but you. Instead its role is to help your planning and your orientation thinking by displaying a synoptic view of how your thesis is organized down to your lowest order of headings and sections. Some authors find it helpful for their extended contents page to include headings and subheads and any numbering used, in the same font and layout as they are shown in the chapters, which may spread the material out over several A4 sheets. Others like to use a more condensed format for the extended contents page, showing differences of emphasis, but in more compressed ways. By keeping the extended contents page on at most a couple of sheets of paper this approach may give an easier overview of the structure of your material.

Devising headings and subheadings

> The best way to inform your reader is to tell them what they are likely to want to know – no more and no less.
> *Robert J. Sternberg* 4

Good headings should accurately characterize your text. In a very few words they should give readers a helpful advance idea of what is to come in each section or subsection, and wherever possible what your substantive argument will be. Devising effective headings is a difficult art that needs sustained attention from authors. You can tell that the task is complex because in the business world there are highly paid professionals who do nothing else, people like advertising copywriters, newspaper or magazine sub-editors, and Web-site designers. Intellectuals tend to make fun of many of these groups and to see their outputs as non-serious. But the job they do is not as easy as it looks.

Consider the following problem. It is 1989 and the Communist Party of Czechoslovakia has renounced its previous 'leading role in the organs of the state', bringing to an end over 40 years of one-party rule and state socialism, and opening the way for democratization and a transition to a capitalist economy. You are working as a sub-editor for a right-wing British tabloid newspaper, the *Sun*, whose daily audience of 4.3 million readers is mainly preoccupied with soap opera stars, footballers and the nude pin-up girls on page 3 of the paper. None the less, your editor has decided to lead on the historic Czechoslovakia story to please the right-wing proprietor. You are told to devise a front-page headline, to take up two-thirds of the page, but to use *no more than three words*, and four syllables (given *Sun* readers' limited attention span and linguistic competences). How are you going to get the essence of the story across within these limitations? This is a genuine question, and I would encourage you to get pen and paper now and try to come up with your own answer. In the notes for this chapter I have printed the brilliant solution that the *Sun* actually went with.[5]

The paper's achievement in this case was to give the essence of the whole story in its headline. Of course, tabloid newspapers have to try harder to grab readers' attention than most writers of doctorates. As a thesis author you can allow somewhat more words and many more syllables into your headings than the *Sun*. But the basic goal, of putting the message in the shop window, is just as appropriate for doctoral work. Taking it to the limit here, one approach much used in fairly short business and government reports is to use narrative headings and subheadings, which give a mini-précis of what each section or subsection covers. This style has a lot to commend it. Yet it is rarely used in PhD dissertations, mainly because it could get very wearing if repeated over a long text. Headings and subheadings in doctorates, and in journals and books, are normally much shorter, ranging from one or two words at minimum up to seven or eight words at maximum. Headings for main sections only might be a bit longer if they have two parts separated by a colon. However, subheadings should always stay quite snappy (on one line, without parts). None of these limitations is inconsistent with trying to get as much of the text's key message as possible into the heading or subheading.

There are four common general failings in how PhD and other academic authors title their chapters and sections:

(i) *Non-substantive headings* do little or nothing to cue readers about the line of argument you are making. People often choose headings which consist only of vacuous verbiage or are very formalistic. Some are process-orientated or refer only to the methodological operations you carried out, rather than to your findings. Some are completely vague. Others tell readers a little about what topic is being covered, but give no clue about what the author wants to say about the topic, what position is being argued, or what the 'bottom-line' or conclusion of the argument may be. This problem is far and away the leading defect with headings in academic theses and publications, especially when authors are using an analytic pattern of explanation. Poor headings often feed into mismanaging readers' expectations, because authors choose very grand or sweeping subheadings to caption small subsections, feeding a sense of disappointment amongst readers. To pick up cases in your own work, look through your extended contents page and test each of your headings for genuine content. Replace those which are formalistic or process-orientated with something more specific and substantive.

(ii) *Interrogative headings* consist solely of questions and end with a question-mark. Some very well-organized students quite late on in their studies have shown me PhD outlines which consist entirely of interrogative headings, sometimes as many as 15 per chapter, with an alleged 'plan' for the thesis as a whole defined by upwards of 150 questions. This approach often looks precise and informative at the planning stage, reflecting specialized knowledge on the author's part. But interrogative questions create only an illusion of professional expertise, for one critical reason. Questions are not answers. It is always much easier to formulate a set of interesting questions about a subject than it is to produce well-evidenced, coherent and plausibly argued answers to them. Most expert readers will be thoroughly familiar already with the kinds of questions one can ask around your thesis topic. They are primarily reading your work to find out what substantive solutions you have come up with. And here a series of interrogative headings obscures things as effectively as vacuous headings, and can be every bit as formalistic. Again check your extended contents page and if you use interrogative headings (ending in ?), replace all of them with 'answer' headings that convey instead your substantive argument.

(iii) *Inaccurate headings*, which actively miscue readers about the content of their accompanying section, occur all the time. They represent a fundamental failure of the key authorial role, to effectively manage readers' expectations. The heading says that a chapter or section will do A, but instead it does something different, perhaps something close to the author's intentions like C or D, or perhaps something much further away like M or N. This problem can arise in many ways. Authors often set out to do something with a detailed plan, but their text actually turns out to have an inner direction of its own and they then have difficulty in recognizing the fact. Perhaps authors promise readers to evaluate a decision but in the end they do something more modest instead, such as describing the process of reaching that decision. Perhaps they hope initially to make some form of intellectual breakthrough and end up with something more mundane. Often an author's initial headings link so poorly or loosely to what has actually been accomplished in a piece of text that she cannot see that the section is being radically misdescribed, that readers will expect one thing from the heading and get something different from the section text itself.

Combating most of these common problems in finished pieces of work is partly bound up with how far you edit, revise and replan your text, a topic discussed in detail in Chapter 6. But in the planning stages (before you have written out your ideas), it is also important to make sure that your headings describing sections and chapters are as accurate as possible. Look at your extended contents page and check that the fit between headings and what you plan for each section is a close one. Headings should capture the flavour of your substantive argument, but without overselling or overclaiming. The headings and the planned text should be commensurately scaled, and the heading should create only expectations that your text is actually going to meet.

(iv) *Repetitive headings* occur when anxious PhD students keep incanting words from the title of their doctorate in their chapter titles and section headings. Again this is a quick way to confuse and miscue readers, because different headings may tend to blur into each other and chapters and sections will lose a distinctive feel or identity. It is particularly inadvisable to reuse theoretical or thematic concepts taken from your whole thesis title in many different chapter or section headings. You do not achieve linkage by saying mantra words over and over, but by forging a closely connected working argument, whose development can be schematically traced in your headings.

Other instances of repetition may not confuse readers, but instead just make your headings longer and more boring than they need to be. For example, suppose the thesis title makes clear that the author is focusing on Korean post-war musical culture. It would be completely otiose to have later chapter or section headings repeat that the country reference is Korea or that the general time period is post-war. Similarly if a thesis focuses on a particular author or body of work it is unnecessary to have the chapter headings repeat that. Instead they should move on, taking the thesis frame of reference as given and providing more details of what that particular chapter or section is about. It is straightforward to check your extended contents page and make sure that chapter and section headings effectively partner with the thesis title itself, without repeating it.

Repetitive or overly similar headings often arise in the first place because students submit chapters to their supervisors or review committees as separate bits of work on widely spaced occasions. Hence they subconsciously may try to cram more of the thesis self-description into the opening chapter title than is needed. To avoid this problem, get into the habit of always putting your current overall thesis title and the latest version of your short contents page as the frontispiece for each chapter you submit. Your supervisors, advisers or departmental assessors will also be grateful to be given a clear view of where your current piece of work fits within the thesis as a whole. PhD students often blithely assume that their supervisors have a godlike ability to automatically retain a clear view of their overall thesis architecture from previous discussions, normally several weeks earlier. In fact supervisors inherently focus on your thesis a lot less than you do. They have other projects of their own to keep in view, and other PhD students to supervise. So they can only give concentrated attention to your work whenever you submit new chapters. Supervisors often find it very difficult to separate out the layers of different past discussions or to follow all the twists and turns of your thesis planning ideas and changes. Hence they will always appreciate being discreetly reminded of your overall title and current chapter plan.

Handling starts and finishes

> Creations realized at the price of a great deal of work
> must in spite of the truth appear easy and
> effortless ... The great rule is to take much trouble to
> produce things that seem to have cost none.
> *Michelangelo Buonarroti* ⁶

A central task for any author is to manage readers' expectations. But authors are often not fully aware of the number of different ways in which they create expectations. Once you have produced a piece of text, and you are familiar with its every nuance and wrinkle, you may assume that readers will be equally detailed in their approach. It is all too easy to picture readers as scanning your text carefully in the exact sequence that you wrote it, judiciously assigning weight to this factor or that argument, and carefully creating a balanced picture of what is said. But 'real life' readers, those who are not the fictional products of our authorial imaginations, do not operate like that. Instead they treat the text harshly, garnering first impressions quickly from obvious signs and stigmata, and then often coding up what they later read in detail to fit in with that initial frame of reference.

Although readers are famously diverse in their reactions, it is not hard to explain how their first impressions are mostly sourced, or to identify which elements of the text are most productive of expectations. Headings, subheadings and the sectioning of the text are very important, as the two previous sections make clear. Well-organized authors also signal to readers what a chapter or a section will do. They make promises: 'I will show that ...', 'The analysis demonstrates that ...'. These explicit hostages to fortune clearly need careful phrasing. But in addition you will often generate expectations more implicitly. Suppose you assign two-thirds of one chapter's text to aspect P, a fifth to aspect Q, and an eighth to aspect R. Readers will inevitably conclude that in your view P is more important or more interesting than Q, which in turn is more important or interesting than R. And if your literature review waxes lyrical on the defects of previous work, then readers expect that your analysis will do better, will transcend these earlier limitations.

And if you wheel an elaborate theoretical apparatus onstage at great length, or delineate a typology, or introduce your own neologisms – then readers will expect that these elements will justify themselves, will do useful work or create new insights or predictions that could not have materialized without them. How your text uses terminology, the concepts and vocabulary it deploys, and the style cues that you signal as author – all these will be used by readers to try and classify you and your text, to understand where you are coming from, where your scholarly tribal affiliations really lie. If these cues do not fit with your self-classification in the professional scene, or what you later say and do, then readers will receive incompatible messages – and code them as confused authorial purposes. Diagrams, charts and tables are also key attention points. Along with headings these are the items that readers will most quickly identify on a first scan through a piece of text. And like headings these attention points should ideally be independently understandable, because readers will commonly try to make sense of what they say on a first scan, without ploughing into accompanying text in detail (see Chapter 7 below).

It is unrealistic for authors to respond to these points by deploring the laziness or the lack of application or disorderliness of readers, their inability to unwrap your text in the same sequence that you have written it. And it would be naïve to imagine that examiners, however conscientious, will behave in a radically different manner. None of us read academic work like a good novel, ploughing through in one straight line from A to Z. Educated, professional audiences do not suspend disbelief. From the word go, from the first encounter with your arguments, academic readers will get on with criticizing and categorizing your text, trying to place you as an author, trying to find short-cuts to unravel your intent, determined to economize on the time they spend grappling with your thought. And they are right to do so, for this is a rational approach to allocating scarce resources of time and attention.

The most crucial parts of a chapter for generating readers' expectations, for setting up mental frameworks, for getting readers off on the right foot or the wrong foot, are the beginnings and ends of chapters and of sections. And, of course, these are also usually the most difficult passages to write. So here you can ease your difficulties a good deal by having a well-defined checklist or repertoire of things to include and strategies to try. I review: key elements for setting out on a chapter; beginning and finishing a section; and concluding the chapter as a whole.

Starting a chapter

Writing down the first few pages of a chapter can take far more time than completing much longer sections of the main body of the text. Partly this is the normal intimidating effect of a blank page or a blank screen, a problem built into the writing process at all times (see Chapter 6). But the problem gains extra intensity here because all authors know implicitly that beginnings are important in conditioning how readers view their work, as well as influencing how their writing will progress and the detailed directions it will take once they are launched into text production. Getting a satisfactory start to a chapter will often be a two-stage process. At the very beginning you need to write quickly a 'working' start, just a piece of lead-in text that gets you going, that helps you start the writing out of your ideas for the chapter. Later, when you have all or much of the text in being, you will probably need to go back and carefully reshape your start to frame what you have actually done.

At either of these stages, however, you must always include four elements in the following sequence:

◆ a chapter title;
◆ some form of 'high impact' start element, designed to particularly engage readers' attention;
◆ a piece of framing text which moves from the start element to some discursive comments on the chapter's main substantive themes, leading up to;
◆ a set of signposts to readers about the sequence and topic focus of the chapter's main sections (that is, those parts which have first-order headings).

Because of the special importance of starts in conditioning readers' expectations and the author's later progress, I analyse each of these requirements in detail.

A *chapter title* may seem obvious, but it is actually very common to find doctoral students submitting chapters to their supervisors without any title at all. This move makes it harder for supervisors to give useful feedback. It also means that the author has been writing the chapter all the way through without a clear focusing element to keep her on track. Chapter titles need to be carefully chosen, but this is not a reason to postpone choosing one until the chapter is complete. Choose a working title from the very beginning, which you can then re-evaluate when you have finished. Chapter titles can be somewhat longer than the headings used for sections inside chapters – for instance, it is acceptable to have a two-part heading with a colon in the middle, as I do in some chapters of this book. Remember that chapter titles operate inside the overall thesis title, and so they should not repeat elements of it directly.

A *high impact start* serves to attract readers' attention, to get them immediately engaged with the new chapter. It should set your new slab of text apart from what has gone before, and give it a distinctive 'feel' and character from the outset. In a 'big book' thesis it is very important that each chapter does a particular job which is clearly signalled to readers, and which is different from its neighbours. The chapters need to build up across the whole thesis in a cumulative way, adding new elements of the analysis. They must not seem to readers to repeat, or to go round in circles, or to wander without an obvious pattern across the possible landscape of your topic.

Start paragraphs must be conceived, written and normally rewritten with special care. The opening element (either a sentence, or a set of sentences, or a whole paragraph) should focus on some interesting general aspect or problem that the chapter particularly addresses. Later elements (again sentences or paragraphs) can come down to earth somewhat, feeding into the framing text (see below) which is specific in indicating what the chapter is about. However, the requirements to be interesting and to write with special care pull in different directions here. Most PhD students write their theses too defensively, and hence end up with *safe* but very low-impact starts. Three of the most popular false starts are:

I	'In the previous chapter, I argued that X and Y and Z. [Author may enlarge on this for several sentences, even a whole paragraph.] But there are also other issues of A or B which will be tackled here ...'
II	'In this chapter, I will discuss [repeat the chapter title at more length], in particular the issues of A and B.'
III	'The concept of A [a word mentioned in the chapter title] has been defined by Jones (1989) as "xxx" and by Smith (1998) as "yyy" ...'

In all these cases the capital letters in italics such as *A* or *X* stand for specific concepts or arguments in the thesis. False start I is deeply problematic because it makes readers focus not on the new chapter, but on its predecessor. This mis-signalling is almost bound to make them feel that the current chapter only repeats or extends in some small way what has gone before, a very demotivating beginning indeed. In a new chapter, always begin afresh. Never, ever, begin a chapter by looking back, by trying to make retrospective linkages between chapters. These links must instead always be made prospectively, at the very end of the conclusions of the previous chapter (see below). False start II does not actively mis-signal what the new chapter is about. But by only elaborating and repeating the chapter title it will look boring and low energy for readers. If key chapter title words are incanted exactly, often many times in the first few sentences, this start will also seem badly written. False start III is again very low energy, ploughing off immediately into definitions, normally quite boring for professional readers who will have seen this concept many times before. By linking these definitions to other authors, of course, this start also makes your work look derivative and unoriginal from the outset.

The key ways of getting to a better and genuinely high impact start vary a lot, depending on your discipline and type of thesis. Three common choices are: including quotations; introducing a strong example or other striking piece of empirical information; and setting out a paradox or intellectual puzzle.

Strong, memorable *quotations* can often be helpful in getting you over the hurdle of beginning from a blank sheet. In Johanne Goethe's words: 'It is just when ideas are lacking that a phrase is most welcome'.[7] You can integrate the quote into the opening sentence of your chapter. Or a whole-sentence quote can be printed as an epigraph, as at the beginning of chapters and sections in this book. (An epigraph is like a motto or subtitle, placed immediately after the title and above the main text.) If the quote is in the first line or first sentence of your main text then you will have to immediately discuss the theme or issue it raises. But if the quote is an epigraph then it implicitly characterizes the whole chapter (or section) and does not have to be discussed straightaway.

Do not select boring, mundane or anodyne quotes as epigraphs or opening sentence material, especially from contemporary authors working in the same field as you. Useful starting quotes really need to be something like epigrams (witty or striking thoughts cogently expressed in a short space), or particularly thought-provoking or fundamental reflections for your themes (if you pick a longer quotation). A beginning quote from a contemporary professional author working in exactly your field can make your work look derivative. So try not to cite such people. Instead pick much more general quotes. Classical or canonical or long-dead authors in your field (who may safely be quoted without looking derivative) are a good option. Contemporary non-professional authors (novelists, playwrights, journalists) make a good impression, and in some disciplines other modern sources (magazines, newspapers, music CDs or TV programmes like *The Simpsons*) are also appropriate. You can also use contemporary professional authors working in radically different fields from your own but making a relevant point for your work. Looking for more general quotes can run the danger of your falling for clichés or very tired, familiar aphorisms (such as those found in most dictionaries of quotations). Reasonably well-read readers may well see such quotes as routine: they can be no help to you. General purpose sources (Shakespeare, the Bible, major philosophers and so on) are helpful only if the quotes you use are apt and unusual. If you think that quotations may work for you, keep a sharp eye out for interesting observations as you read (both in general literature and professional sources), and record any possibles in a PC file as soon you encounter them. That way you can pick and choose from a large selection, and are more likely to find one that is really effective and appropriate in a given context.

A *striking example*, incident, event, conjunction, narrative or *other piece of empirical information* can also be an effective start, crystallizing and perhaps dramatizing a theme which the chapter will explain or develop at length. By presenting the chapter focus in a very concrete way, or an element that leads into it, such a start can achieve an impact which a dry recital of theories or ideas cannot. For instance, Michel Foucault's opening pages for his philosophical book *Discipline and Punish* starts with a detailed description of the gruesome logistics of a nineteenth-century public execution.[8] A similar effect can be created by using very key summary statistics or data as the 'attractor' element, especially where this information can be presented in a dramatic or novel way. The trick here is to handle a few key numbers in text (not in a table), concentrate on especially telling numbers, and lose all unnecessary detail in the data cited (see Chapter 7 for how to present numerical information in text). It helps if the point of the data is to show up a clear contrast or a not-widely-appreciated aspect of the chapter's theme.

The final way of achieving a high impact start is to focus on *a problem or paradox*, a puzzle which has no obvious explanation, usually achieved by bringing proposition A and proposition B into a conjunction, and exposing a tension between them. An effective chapter start in this mould will operate like the overall thesis question (discussed in Chapter 1 above), only this time defining a core focus of the chapter. Later main sections of the chapter must then deliver an effective answer to the problem or a solution of the paradox.

Framing text comes after the high impact start, and domesticates it, making the links and the transition from the arresting start material to the more prosaic or mainstream themes of the chapter. The object of the framing text is to 'warm up' readers to the chapter topic, perhaps indicating previous schools of thought about it, or the interpretation offered by earlier studies. The framing text may also handle any 'lead-in' material which it is necessary for readers to encounter before the main sections start, although this should be kept to a minimum length. General framing text must amount to at least one substantial paragraph, but it should not extend beyond three or perhaps four pages. If you have very substantial amounts of lead-in stuff to get across (for example, a lengthy historical or geographical background for a case study) then make that into the first main section of the chapter. All your framing material should set up and show off the rationale for the main sections of the chapter. You should not dive off unannounced into substantive exposition. The framing text should lead up to the signposts which end the (untitled) introduction.

The *signposts* provide a minimal indication of the sequence of main sections to come in the chapter. When you drive down a highway, the signposts say 'London' or 'New York' to show where you are going. But they do not provide any detailed pre-figuring of what you can find in these places. A signpost is not a guidebook. For the same reason, signposts in your text need to be kept fairly terse and under control. Readers must be given a very clear idea of how many sections there are in the chapter, and what sequence they come up in. You can include a phrase or two, perhaps a whole sentence, to very briefly characterize the subtopics considered in each section. But you must not blurt out what you will say in later sections or give a condensed summary of the chapter argument to come. If you do succumb to the temptation to write a mini-guidebook to future sections you will probably state your argument in too crude or vulgar a way now, and create an unwelcome sense of repetition for readers later on.

Signposts can be implemented in a more explicit or a more latent fashion. Explicit signposts should preferably use textual ways of conveying the sequence ('First, I consider ...', 'Second, I examine ...'). It is best to avoid referring to the section numbers directly ('Section 3.1 discusses ...') because this approach can make your signposting look too mechanical. It may then seem to readers as if you are just duplicating the headings themselves. More latent ways of signposting are briefer, simply signalling a sequence of subjects to come in the chapter, without linking them precisely to particular numbered sections.

Starting and finishing a section

The beginning of each of the main sections of the chapter also needs to be carefully written. Main sections generally should be numbered (2.1, 2.2, etc.) and have a short heading, probably around four to eight words. Section headings should be short and punchy. (The only exception concerns a 'narrative subheading' strategy where the headings are full-sentence descriptions that précis the section contents.) Do not use colons or partitions in subsection headings, which would make them too cumbersome. It is important not to repeat either the thesis title *or* the chapter title, both of which automatically frame what the section is about. Again, it is best to avoid interrogative headings. Instead try to get some of your storyline or substantive argument into each section heading.

Next you will need no more than one or two paragraphs of lead-in material. Ideally this should start in a somewhat higher impact way than normal text. Again a quotation can be used, or a very short empirical example or a smaller intellectual puzzle (one that will be wholly resolved within this section). But a section start must always be accomplished much more speedily and simply than that for a whole chapter. In longer or more complex sections you might need to end the lead-in paragraph with some low-key signposts setting out the rough sequence of topics that will be handled (within this section alone). Within-section signposts should always be briefer and less formal than those for the chapter as a whole. If they are not, there is a risk that readers may get confused, especially at the start of the chapter where they will encounter chapter signposts for the main sections at the end of the introduction, and then come across within-section signposts for the first section perhaps only one or two paragraphs later. It is important to ensure that readers do not run into different 'first, second, third' lists close to each other, which might be confusing.

Concluding a section is also difficult and worth doing carefully. You will need a last paragraph for each section that terminates it in a way that looks logical, well organized, and cumulative. It is best to avoid 'telling them what you've told them' in a mechanical fashion. Instead, the section wrap-up paragraph should let you step back a little bit and draw out a brief central message from the section as a whole. This could be an interim conclusion, or a summary of what the section has said but perhaps looked at from a different angle. It is important that the concluding paragraph for a section stick solely to what has been done in that section, and not discuss anything else. However, in the last sentence or so, the concluding paragraph can make forward linkages to the next section, so that it too can have a well-designed, higher impact kind of start.

Finishing a chapter

You should mark the end of the chapter by a Conclusions section which is at least two paragraphs long. It should have a heading displayed in a font which makes clear that it is not a first-order section. The first paragraph (or part) of the Conclusions should gather up the key points previously pulled out in each of the final paragraphs for each section, and re-present them so as to draw together the end points of each section. It is worth writing the opening sentence of the Conclusions carefully, preferably in a general way which clearly breaks away from the ending of the last section and instead encourages readers to look back across the chapter as a whole and to assess what they have learnt.

The second paragraph (or second part) of the Conclusions should 'open out' to briefly consider one or two broader issues raised. It should always end by establishing a forward link of some kind to the next chapter. With a descriptive sequence of chapters the link will normally be easy to make – for instance, in a historical or narrative sequence, what happened next? And in a 'guidebook' pattern, what links A to B? Where the chapters discuss a sequence of analytic or argumentative topics the link across will usually take the form of pointing to some open issues raised by this chapter, one of which the next chapter will address. Sometimes there are more tricky transitions, when a series of connected chapters ends and you have to link forward to a new grouping of chapters. In these circumstances you may want to leave a couple of blank lines to indicate that the conclusions for this chapter alone have finished, and that some more general comments follow. Then write a separate paragraph or two just of linking text, drawing the connected chapters together and possibly referring back to your opening chapter plan and the sequence outlined there.

Conclusions

In the UK's difficult and lengthy driving test there is a much-dreaded element called the 'emergency stop'. At the beginning of the test your examiner tells you that at a certain random point she will tap on the dashboard of the car with her folder, as a signal that you must bring the car to a halt as quickly as you can, under control and safely. Then the test starts and you drive off, usually quite quickly forgetting about this whole idea under the stresses and strains of negotiating traffic. Later on, as you are driving down some less populated section of road you suddenly notice your examiner apparently having a fit and lashing at the dashboard with her folder. As belated recognition dawns, you respond by bringing your car to a screeching stop amidst a copious cloud of burnt rubber from the tyres. For authors of doctoral theses (and indeed other professional works) it is a good idea to think of an analogous emergency stop test for your text.

Suppose that at some random, unannounced point I take the text away from someone who is reading your chapter. I ask her to explain (without looking at it again) whereabouts she is in the chapter, and what it is all about. If the text is adequately and appropriately organized then the reader should be able to respond:

> The chapter is about the four themes W, X, Y and Z and it has three sections. The first was about W (specifically subtopics w_1, w_2 and w_3). When the text was taken away I was in the middle of the second section covering X, having already absorbed subtopics x_1 and x_2. I believe that three more subtopics x_3, x_4 and x_5 would be handled later on in that section. I have a clear but general idea of the topics yet to come in the bit of the chapter I haven't yet read, namely that this third section will cover Y and Z together, and in a briefer way than the treatment of W and X.

If our mythical reader cannot respond as precisely as this, then the chapter is too weakly structured. The worst case result for an underorganized chapter would be if the reader responds to the emergency stop test by saying:

> I have no real clue what the chapter as a whole is about, because the title is very vague or formalistic. From what the author says at the start perhaps the focus is on some X and W themes in some way? The chapter just started out on a magical mystery tour, and has so many [or so few] headings that I cannot really say how it is subdivided. I can only tell you roughly where I have been up to the point where the text was taken away. And I have little idea of what was to come in the rest of the section where I was

stopped, and no idea at all what remains to be discussed in later sections. Every other page I turn throws up a new element or a new direction in an unpredictable manner.

While it is important always to adequately organize your text, how you chunk up your chapters must also depend a great deal on the material that you are handling. The advice in this chapter should not be read as a series of remedies to be mechanically applied to produce chapters which are all the same. Although chapters should generally average 10,000 words in length, with main sections every 2500 words, that does not mean that every chapter should have the same four main sections as every other. It is important to adjust your structures sensitively to the material you are handling, rather than to produce robotic-looking work. An excessively mechanical application of these (or any other) rules could mean that you subdivide and signpost text more than you need to, producing fake subsectioning and a text that is very boring for readers to plough through.

So you need to be flexible, tuning and adjusting the principles set out here so as to accommodate different lengths of chapters and sections, and different kinds of material across them. Chapters smaller than 10,000 words may need only two or three sections, while longer ones might need perhaps five sections or at most six sections (but not more than this). Main sections in long chapters may need to be well organized in subsections that are explicitly signposted, producing perhaps twelve or more first- and second-order subheads in all.

The text box below shows a flexibly applied structure for a middle-sized chapter (let's say, chapter 2), with each of the headings shown in its appropriate font, appearance and location. There are three main sections, plus a short (untitled) introduction and a brief conclusions bit. The box also notes where start and finish elements need to be more carefully written. In this plan section 2.1 has two subsections (each with second-order subheads), but section 2.3 is shorter and does not use any subsections. And although the larger piece of text in section 2.2 is subdivided, it is differently handled because of the nature of the material there, using three lighter-touch groupings of paragraphs denoted by only third-order subheads. Figure 4.1 on p. 102 shows the same structural information as the text box below, but in a more diagrammatic form. It illustrates the general point that having a clearly recognizable and standard set of headings across the thesis as a whole is perfectly compatible with having chapter structures which flexibly adapt to the demands of organizing different kinds of text.

CHAPTER 2: TITLE Opening paragraphs – from 1 to 5 Last paragraph signposts the section structure	
2.1: SECTION HEADING Opening 1 or 2 paragraphs signpost subsections *Subsection heading* Opening paragraph, main body, closing paragraph *Subsection heading* Opening paragraph, main body, closing paragraph	1st order 2nd order 2nd order

2.2: SECTION HEADING
Lead-in paragraphs signpost groupings of
  paragraphs
Grouped paragraphs heading leads into text, with
  wrap paragraph at the end
Grouped paragraphs heading leads into text, with
  wrap paragraph at the end
Grouped paragraphs heading leads into text, with
  wrap paragraph at the end
	1st order
	
	3rd order
	
	3rd order
	
	3rd order

2.3: SECTION HEADING Opening paragraph, main body of text, closing paragraph	1st order

CONCLUSIONS
First paragraph (or part) summarizes across
  sections
Closing paragraph (or part) points forward to the
  next chapter
	2nd order

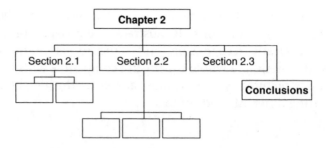

Figure 4.1 The tree structure of a chapter

Implementing effective chapter structures is closely bound up with writing and producing text more generally. But to have a clear idea of what you are doing and some rules of thumb of the kind set out here is a great advantage when starting out on the writing process. It should generate more initial ideas for you to try out. In the next chapter I carry the discussion down to an even more detailed level of writing, looking at two issues which often prove troublesome for doctoral students – writing in a good style, and including simple and efficient scholarly references.

5

Writing Clearly: Style and Referencing Issues

> Poorer writers have fewer readers.
> *Robert J. Sternberg*   [1]

An author with a well-organized piece of text must still pass two further hurdles before gaining credibility or approval in academic professional circles. The first is a test of style. Does the author communicate fluently, convincingly and appealingly in the professional manner appropriate for her discipline? Quite where success or failure should be determined here is difficult to specify in any general way. Evaluations of good or bad writing style are notoriously subjective. Much ink has been spilt on good style for novelists and creative writers (see *Further Reading* on p. 287 for some style manuals). But this literature offers little help to authors of doctoral theses or other large professional bits of text, like academic books. However, it is still possible to pull together some generally useful advice about conflicting style pressures, and some sensible ways of proceeding at a paragraph-by-paragraph, or sentence-by-sentence level, as I try to do in the first part of this chapter.

The second hurdle is a test of scholarship, more important perhaps in a PhD thesis than in any other piece of academic writing. Does the author acknowledge sources for her arguments or evidence? Does she chart her intellectual influences comprehensively and in an appropriate format? Obtrusive referencing is often one of the most obvious hallmarks of academic text, something that sets it apart from everything else. As a result PhD students often overdo referencing, and they can get trapped into embracing overelaborate systems or mystifying the issues involved. But in stark contrast to stylistic issues, good referencing practice can be clearly and objectively defined in terms of key principles. In the second part of the chapter I show how two simple core referencing systems meet these needs.

The elements of good research style

Below the zoom level of the chapter and the section, we enter the realm of new and smaller organizing entities, the paragraph and the sentence. Good style consists of stringing these tiny elements together in connected chains that strike the maximum number of other people, your achieved readers, as logical, meaningful, accessible and plausible. But it is wise to acknowledge from the outset that there is no single route to good style. Such judgements are particular, varying with the nature of the materials, the readership and the author's purposes. It would be easy to say also that 'good style' is a subjective issue, and to adopt a philosophy of 'each to their own taste'. But underneath this appearance of irreconcilable diversity I actually think there lie some more fundamental authoring dilemmas in professional writing. I begin by exploring these divergent style pressures in doctoral work. I move on to some checklists of style issues particularly relevant for writing dissertations, at the level of paragraphs, then sentences, and last vocabulary.

Conflicting style pressures

> Every difficult work presents us with a choice of
> whether to judge the author inept for not being
> clear, or ourselves stupid for not grasping what is
> going on ... Writing with simplicity requires
> courage, for there is a danger that one will be
> overlooked, dismissed as simpleminded by those
> with a tenacious belief that impassable prose
> is a hallmark of intelligence.
> *Alain de Botton* [2]

An approximate but still useful view of the basic tension in professional and academic writing is shown in Figure 5.1. Accessibility considerations (graphed on the horizontal axis) tend to make your writing clearer and easier to follow. Here they are shown pulling at right angles to 'value-added' considerations (shown on the vertical axis), which normally tend to make your text more packed with content. (This aspect of the diagram is a graphical oversimplification. Accessibility and value-added considerations certainly pull in different directions, but whether they pull in such sharply contrasted directions is a moot point.) Writing which is neither accessible nor contentful is simply ineffective, and this is often where doctoral students start off. Few PhD students move rightwards along the horizontal axis following the dotted arrow towards popular writing (highly accessible but low content). However, every year there are a certain number of fluent and competent writers who find themselves undershooting the doctoral standard for the content needed.

Instead most thesis authors follow the dashed arrows in Figure 5.1, increasing the content of their work as their research progresses, but often producing very complex, dense, and underorganized text by the time they reach the middle of their studies. Once they have coped with the value-added problem, they can then painfully achieve progress on making their text more accessible, and try to move closer to good professional text during their final draft stage. But this indirect progress is apt to be long-winded and fraught with difficulties. The advice

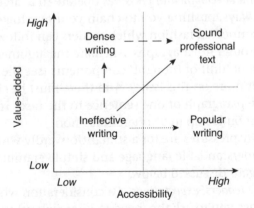

Figure 5.1   How PhD students' writing can develop

here aims to help you follow instead the solid diagonal arrow in Figure 5.1, moving more directly both to meet the content standards of the PhD and to produce text which is accessible for readers.

The message in Figure 5.1 can be made a bit more subtle by noting that PhD authors (like academics in general) are professional communicators operating in a specialized environment. There is no clear consensus on what constitutes good style, nor is it feasible to envisage one in the future, because there are *multiple* conflicting style pressures operating upon doctoral students. The exact mix of these influences varies a good deal from one discipline to another, sometimes from one time period to another, and from one university location to the next. But there is never any single resolution possible, no point where everyone will agree. There is no 'one best way' out there waiting to be discovered, only a balancing act to be achieved with one piece of text, then struck afresh with the next.

Four main pressures will unambiguously influence you towards producing text that can be easily appreciated; these are shown in the left-hand column of Table 5.1: the more they are emphasized the more accessible your text becomes:

◆ *Structural considerations*, such as those discussed in Chapters 3 and 4, push you towards producing writing with sufficient organizers, operating within a well-developed overall framework, for your own sake as an author as well as for readers.

◆ *Logical and developmental pressures* operate in a large number of other ways, pushing you to chain your text together in a closely connected fashion which readers can follow as they move through it. Paragraphs articulate the argument as a sequence of 'unit of thought' components (see the checklists below for more on this issue). And there must be clear links from one paragraph or one sentence to the next, so that the argument builds up in a coherent fashion.

◆ *Readability* pressures are for a straightforwardly written text using understandable language and simple grammatical forms, again discussed below.

◆ *Managing readers' expectations* is a consideration which encourages you to ask the 'need to know' question ('What

Table 5.1 How different pressures on authors improve or worsen the accessibility of their text

Factors generally increasing the accessibility of your text	Factors which initially improve your text, but may impede accessibility if taken too far	Factors generally worsening the accessibility of your text
◆ Structural considerations ◆ Logical and developmental pressures ◆ Readability ◆ Managing readers' expectations	◆ Push for parsimonious phrasing ◆ 'Say it once and say it right' ◆ Maximizing originality	◆ Professional authenticity ◆ Reproducing the feel of an original text ◆ Cramming in substantive content

do readers really need to know at this point?') all the way through your text; and then to deliver that, no more and no less. All these pressures make your style more accessible.

However, there are also three general pressures in academic work which will always push you towards reducing the accessibility of your text. As the right-hand column in Table 5.1 shows, the more these factors are emphasized the more difficult and the less accessible your text will seem:

◆ *Professional authenticity* is often seen (especially by younger scholars) in terms of mastering a specialized argot, learning and using an 'alchemical' terminology confined to insiders and hence incomprehensible to outsiders. Like all specialized vocabularies there is often a case for using professional jargon where it is more precise, fine-tuned, and helps avoid the multiple meanings and normative or value connotations often inherent in equivalent ordinary language terms. But students often lose sight of this rationale behind a prolific use of complex vocabularies and grammatical constructions, designed only to demonstrate the writer's qualifications as a member of the 'initiated'.

◆ *Reproducing the feel of an original text* [or a case study or a field experience or a data set] has a somewhat similar effect. Here an analyst's style of writing is pulled towards the subject she is covering. For example, an expositor of a philosopher may end up imitating the sage's portentous style. Or a commentator on a literary text may come to mimic its mannerisms in her own approach, perhaps unconsciously. Similarly a researcher analysing a particular bureaucracy or organization can often unconsciously copy officials in overusing organizational acronyms and employing the bureaucracy's ponderous and passive phrasings as her own.

◆ *An effort to cram in substantive content* is the last of this set of influences. Academic authors often try to convey a great deal of detail about their argument methods and research techniques, resulting in a text which looks close-packed with material and dense to read. All these imitative influences tend to make your text more esoteric, more polysyllabic, more specialized. There are some widely used measures of readability, like the 'fog index' which increases with average sentence lengths and the number of multi-syllable words per sentence. Many theses will top the outer limit at the top of the fog index scores.

A third set of style pressures has a different type of impact. As the centre column of Figure 5.2 shows, emphasizing these factors will make for better style and a more readable and accessible text up to a certain point. But carrying on beyond this point, overemphasizing these factors beyond an optimum level, will thereafter begin to make your text more and more difficult to read.

◆ *A push for parsimonious phrasing*, a style eliminating all redundant text, follows through on a 'less is more' policy. This stance can be a force for good or ill depending on circumstances. In a loosely knit text, full of 'waffle', making cuts down to the bare bones of the argument will generate important improvements in style and readability. It will often cut out pointless, minimally reshaded extensions of a core argument, and help sharpen up the profile of the author's thought for readers.

> An unnecessary word does no work. It doesn't further an argument, state an important qualification, or add a compelling detail. (See?)
> *Howard Becker*   3

But with an already pared down and well-organized text the same stance can have different effects. Cut out all unnecessary words, leave only what is strictly essential (no asides, no 'for examples', no flavouring), and you may end up with a piece of writing too dense or too formal for many readers to make inroads. Journal editors and referees often stress this kind of paring away of closely written text. But it can produce excessively hard-boiled, remote, underexplained and unnecessarily difficult pieces of text. As de Botton notes in the epigraph to this section, making life hard for readers will trigger two reactions, neither of them encouraging for the reception of your text. If readers blame you as author for being obscure there is a direct threat to your passing the final examination without having to make revisions. If readers blame themselves for not being able to measure up to your text, this may rebound in unsympathetic views of your work. Triggering realizations we would all prefer to avoid is not a way to get widely read.

- The *'say it once and say it right'* approach urges you not to blur the argumentative impact of a single connected set of points about X by dissipating them in dribs and drabs, a little bit here and then again there and somewhere else a third time. Instead you should pull together all the related little 'x's into one, big bloc X argument. In weakly organized text this idea can again be a great force for good. Nothing is so corrosive of readers' confidence in an author than the feeling that they are simply re-encountering material already described in a disorganized text, or are revisiting in only a marginally varied form points made already, perhaps for the third, fourth or fifth time. But some degree of linkaging back and forth across a text is inevitable and necessary. For instance, cross-referencing and short 'reminder' passages can often be justified on the 'need to know' criterion. Radically overdoing a 'say it once and say it right' logic may sometimes push an already well-structured text into inaccessibility, denying readers the 'warm-up' links that they need to grasp a wider pattern of argument.
- *A concern to maximize the originality* of your text is a positive impulse so long as it is well-grounded and your efforts focus on clarifying and framing the value-added elements of your

work. Making these components more apparent and ensuring that their significance is recognized by you as author and then communicated to readers will improve accessibility. You can start to overdo this concern, however, if your originality ceases to be well grounded in your research, and instead you try to inject value-added 'artificially', as it were. It is not being genuinely original to coin new concepts or terminology that are not really needed or do little effective work, or to write overly dense or elliptical text that is difficult even for other professional readers to follow. Sometimes in the social sciences people can overdo things in an analogous way, by adopting a very formalized or algebraic way of expressing arguments where this is not strictly necessary or insightful. Stating things in equations rather than words will always cut your readership numbers – perhaps dramatically if you give no alternative, informal account of your argument. So take the step to formalization only when it shows clear intellectual or analytic dividends. And even then try to provide in parallel the best possible intuitive explanation of the operations carried out in the formal analysis, and what they show.

Recognizing that there are multiple pressures acting on your style, and that they pull in different directions, may help you to appreciate how much any piece of professional writing entails striking a balance. All of the ten influences reviewed above are perfectly valid and legitimate ones to take into account in fixing on an appropriate writing style. None of them can simply be ignored. All of them will need to be pursued in a constrained way, going as far as you can in one dimension without damaging how your text appears in another dimension. And if your text reads wrong in some way, the solution you need will almost always entail tweaking your writing a bit to re-emphasize a consideration that has become neglected. It will not usually entail scrapping completely the way that you do writing, or trying to start all over again in some completely inauthentic voice. 'If your face is not clean, wash it,' said George Bernard Shaw, 'don't cut your head off.'[4] Solutions for style problems are usually about rebalancing more than revolutionizing your writing.

Constructing paragraphs

> The paragraph is a great art form. I'm very inter-
> ested in paragraphs and I write paragraphs very,
> very carefully.
> *Iris Murdoch* [5]

> One thought alone occupies us: we cannot think
> of two things at the same time.
> *Blaise Pascal* [6]

A paragraph is a unit of thought. In English writing, much more than in many other languages, the pattern of paragraphs is a very critical element in making an argument look coherent and well organized. In general a paragraph should make one point, or one component part of a single broader point. Where a paragraph handles instead miscellaneous unconnected points, as is sometimes necessary to round out an argument, this role should be explicitly signalled to readers – because they will not expect it. Normally readers will expect a paragraph to have a single focus and one role. Overlong paragraphs, with too many sentences in them, have numerous drawbacks. Your text becomes underorganized and difficult to follow. And the internal focus of the paragraph becomes blurred, with too many different elements stuffed into a single bulging bag.

But paragraphs must not become too short either. A paragraph is not a sentence. It is a grouping of sentences, a way of carving them up into connected sets so as to reduce the diversity of your thought to manageable proportions. If paragraphs reduce to just one or two sentences, then they cease to have this organizing rationale and become heteronomous cogs, turning as your argument progresses but not doing any useful work. For English-speaking readers, short paragraphs in academic work will also make your work look bitty, fragmented and uncertain. You will appear to be casting around for what to say, starting to make points but then not properly developing them.

The optimal length for paragraphs varies a great deal from one kind of writing to another. In journalism paragraphs will be short, often around 50 words and never more than 100 words, because newspapers and magazines are set in narrow columns.

Read any book-form reprint of a journalist's collected writings and you will notice that these short paragraph lengths do not work at all with larger pages. Instead the journalist's text comes across as far too chopped-up, with up to six or seven paragraphs on each book page, and twelve or so on each double-page spread. Professional academic work is always configured for printing as books or journal articles. Here the printed page typically holds around 500 words. The ideal length for paragraphs is one that divides each page several times, but not too frenetically. A good aim point is hence around 150 words (half an A4 page printed double-spaced). But paragraph lengths of between 100 and 200 words (a third to two-thirds of an A4 page) are perfectly acceptable.

A good way to keep track of paragraph lengths is to make sure that you can see each paragraph in its entirety on the screen of your PC (using 1.5 or double spacing to make your text easily readable). Where a paragraph goes appreciably longer than a single screenful, consider whether it should be split up. Where a paragraph occupies only a small part of your screen, ask yourself whether it should be merged with the paragraph before or after it. Never leave very short (one- or two-sentence) paragraphs hanging around, because they are disruptive of the overall flow of the text. Always integrate them into one or other of their neighbours.

The sequence of material within paragraphs should generally follow the Topic, Body, Wrap formula. The first 'topic' sentence makes clear what the paragraph addresses, what its focus is on. The main 'body' of the paragraph comes next, giving reasoning, justification, elaboration, analysis or evidence. The final 'wrap' sentence makes clear the bottom-line message of the paragraph, the conclusion you have reached. Readers will always pay special attention to the opening, topic sentence of a paragraph, to glean as economically as they can what it is about. And they will also focus more on the last, wrap sentence, trying to garner the guts of your argument without reading the whole paragraph in detail. Many readers may only 'eyeball' the 'body' text, or will skim it in advance of detailed reading, in effect deciding whether to read it and how intensively. Such people may fasten on little else but the topic and wrap sentences, which hence need to be written with especial care.

Some PhD students bridle at this advice, arguing that it would be wrong for them to adjust their writing pattern to accommodate 'lazy' or non-serious readers of this kind. But it is always an author's job to maximize her readership and to convey information accessibly. It is wise to bear in mind that readers have very diverse needs, which they know best and which authors cannot anticipate fully. Skim reading, for instance, is an entirely rational strategy for all readers to adopt at some stage, however serious-minded or committed to your topic they may be. An author's task is precisely to attract and retain skim readers or 'eyeballers', and to convert them into intensive readers by providing text which is as accessible and as interesting as possible. So as with chapters and with sections, the beginning and end parts of paragraphs are crucial.

It is especially important that each topic sentence should accurately characterize a paragraph and give readers a sense of progression as they move on to that paragraph from its predecessor. A very common problem occurs when authors instead misplace the wrap sentence, so that it misleadingly appears as the topic sentence of the next paragraph. Here the author uses the first sentence of paragraph Y to sum up the previous paragraph X or to link back to it, instead of to launch Y out on a distinctive point of its own. The effect is very off-putting and misleading for readers, because it suggests that paragraph Y focuses on exactly the same theme as X, rather than moving the argument on.

Another very common bad paragraph beginning is to put some other author's name as the very first word, leading off thus: 'Smith (1997, p. 56) argues ... '. Sometimes even accomplished authors will construct a whole sequence of paragraphs on 'random author list' lines, where every topic sentence starts in this obvious and boring fashion. The implied message that readers always get is not that you have read the literature but that the paragraphs concerned are completely derivative, lacking in all originality or value-added content, merely précising someone else's work. You should eliminate derivative-looking paragraph starts wherever they occur in your text. Replace them with topic sentences focusing on the substantive point of the paragraph. Your text will also look more organized if instead of reporting the views of individual authors you categorize them (accurately) into an appropriate school of thought. The paragraph can then set out what that school of thought or intellectual position stands for, and only cite the relevant authors in support of this characterization. Where references are needed try always to place them at the very end of sentences, preferably in the Harvard format or by using endnotes (see next section). You may sometimes need to introduce the names of schools or authors into your main text outside references, but do so sparingly.

The wrap sentences at the end of paragraphs are often easier to write than the start, because you now have the paragraph text to go on. But wrap sentences should not just reiterate what has already been said. Readers are not goldfish. They will perfectly remember what you have written, especially when your paragraphs are not too ponderous or too long. Instead the wrap sentence should close the paragraph as a unit of thought, and clinch or reinforce its main point. It should have at least a little added value of its own. A last sentence is a good place to give a more clear-cut evaluative judgement, or to assess the significance of what has been established in the paragraph. It is a chance for a wise author to draw together the phenomena covered in the paragraph as a whole (stand back and spot the shape of the wood around here), rather than just itemizing details (inspecting trees in close-up, one after another).

Writing sentences

> Words differently arranged have a different meaning, and meanings differently arranged have different effects.
> *Blaise Pascal* [7]

In English sentences the inner core is a subject linked to a verb linked to an object: Subject–Verb–Object. Different languages have different conventions. But if you want to write straightforward and accessible English sentences, these three components should be closely bonded together. This means that a real subject, main verb, and real object should always be clearly identifiable. There must be no equivocation about who or what is the subject of the sentence. Fake or implicit subjects can arise in several ways. Some thesis authors pick up the passive verb forms and anonymized subjects favoured by government bureaucracies or lawyers: 'It was felt that...', 'It was decided that ...'. Others create implied subjects by verbal means, such as using 'this' without an accompanying noun as the subject: 'This entailed...'. All such usages need to be carefully excised. There must be no ambiguity either about which is the main verb. It should be highlighted in the sentence structure, and it should be clearly superior in importance to any other second-ary verb forms included in the sentence. Not all sentences have objects, but most do and it is worth following through the same discipline for them also. Do not interpose any other element between subject, verb and object. Nothing should impair their double-bonding or break up the sentence core. This rule means that qualifying or subordinate clauses are always best placed at the beginning or ends of sentences, never in the middle, which should be reserved for the core. And other terms or phrases in sentences, such as adjectives and qualifier or descriptor words, should generally be placed before or after the subject/verb/object also.

In order to keep the subject/verb/object core clearly visible, sentences should not get too long and they should have the simplest feasible grammatical construction. Many PhD students seem to feel that writing professional-looking text requires them to construct great, rambling sentences. The tone of their writing differs markedly from their conversational approach. It becomes replete with subordinate or qualifying clauses, so that their sentences require complex grammatical construc-tions to hold them together. All the main word-processing packages have facilities which will identify for you the average number of words per sentence in any piece of text, and usually the maximum sentence length also. (Look under 'Tools' for the 'Word Count' facility in Microsoft's Word, and under 'Document Information' in Wordperfect.) My suggested rule of thumb here is that you should never write a sentence longer than 40 words, and that you should aim for an ideal sentence length of around 20 words. Wherever a sentence is more than 40 words long, you should always chunk it up into two or three sentences. Where it is between 20 and 40 words, you should assess if it would be better split into two. Problems with long

sentences usually reflect either the author writing inauthentically in a pompous style, or trying to do too many things
within a single sentence, typically by loading in qualifying
clauses beginning with 'although', 'however' and so on. A
sentence should express a single thought or proposition, not
multiple ones.

Each sentence is also important as a fundamental building
block of your thesis as a whole. You should routinely run a
checklist over new sentences in turn to ensure that you maintain quality control. The basic ethos here is that sentences can
only do one of three things for you – build, blur or corrode.
They can build the thesis, forming part of the coral-reef accre-
tions of your core argument. Or they can blur the thesis,
creating patches of text (like repetitions) which perhaps are not
actively damaging but which fail to advance the argument.
Or they can corrode your argument, mis-stating propositions
and actively weakening your chances of getting a doctorate.
Unless a sentence builds your thesis, you are best cutting it out.
You must ruthlessly eliminate all corrosive sentences, which are
liabilities if left alone. You may need to retain a few blurring
sentences with little new content, to help give continuity or to
make rhetorical linkages at certain points.

> Every author has a meaning in which all the
> contradictory passages agree, or he [or she] has no
> meaning at all.
> *Blaise Pascal* [8]

Three other questions are helpful to bear in mind when checking:

♦ Is the sentence *correct*? Is it argumentatively substantive and
  logically put? Is it factually right? Do all parts of the
  sentence work together to meet these tests?
♦ Is it *appropriate* for PhD level work? Some propositions may
  be factually true or argumentatively sound, but just not
  what we would expect to see people saying or discussing at
  the doctoral level. For instance, we would not expect a car
  engine designer to tell us that: 'Internal combustion engines
  go brmm, brmm you know' – even though that is
  completely correct.

◆ Does the sentence *say exactly what you want*? Read it aloud. If anything niggles at the back of your mind, if you have some undefined uncertainty about the sentence, always rewrite it.

Choosing vocabulary

> We only think through the medium of words.
> *Abbé Etienne de Condillac* [9]

How you pick words makes a difference to how sentences work. Doctoral authors are renowned for overusing jargon and producing pompous prose, perhaps wrongly but certainly not without some cause. In the humanities and social sciences many people routinely substitute longer noun forms of words where they could use short verb forms, saying 'configuration' instead of 'configuring' just to get an extra syllable. Or they choose complex forms of words which sound more abstruse, for very little reason. For instance, 'methodology' means the science or study of methods, but many social scientists use it just to replace 'method' itself, because it seems to give a more 'professional' feel to do so.

You cannot avoid necessary jargon in your discipline, nor should you try to do so. Academic jargon often does specialist things, has more precise meanings and allows expositions or conversations to quickly reach targetted subjects which would be hard to reach or cumbersome to define in other ways. But you should maintain a constant check that you fully appreciate the meanings of words you use. Do not pointlessly substitute portentous vocabulary for ordinary language words where there is no extra value in doing so. In general, try to write as you would speak if you were sitting across the table from someone in your discipline and giving a carefully grammatical oral explanation of your work. Trying for a professional 'voice' more strained or more pompous than you would use in such a considered conversation will not make your work seem more doctoral. It will make it seem inauthentic, and perhaps ungrounded, since you will be more likely to make mistakes in meaning.

> No wise man [or woman] will wish to bring more
> long words into the world.
> *G. K. Chesterton* [10]

Managing verb forms and tenses well can have important consequences for your text. Using active verb forms with real subjects will make your text much more lively, and fits closely with the subject/verb/object focus above. You should strictly avoid passive verb forms because they tend to create avoidable ambiguities. If you are using Microsoft Word the spellchecker facility will automatically highlight all the passive sentences in your text, and offer a more active way of saying the same thing: make sure that you do not just click 'Ignore' at these points. If your doctorate is in history or any of the social sciences, you can save yourself a lot of time by writing chiefly in the past tense. If you write any passages in the present tense about real-world events or situations, then developments after you write are likely to render what you say anachronistic or inaccurate within the span of your research period. During the time that your thesis sits on library shelves in unpublished or published forms this danger obviously grows. If you write: 'In autumn 2001 American public opinion supported military intervention in Afghanistan', your proposition will not go out of date. Whereas if you write: 'The British public supports limited military intervention in Iraq' (which was true in early 2002), the statement is falsified when a majority of people no longer endorse this strategy. Never use the pluperfect tense, and avoid the future conditional form beloved of biographers: 'In a small cottage a new baby cried, who would in less than two decades become a force in world history.' In other humanities disciplines, such as literature or cultural studies, these rules may not apply universally. But it may still pay to be cautious about writing in the present tense.

Intellectuals are prone to some particular style lapses, which can sometimes spill over into quite serious flaws in reasoning. People who use greater than normal levels of theorization and abstraction can sometimes commit two classic errors. 'Reification' means that you convert an abstraction into a 'thing', to which you then ascribe agency, the power to act, as in: 'Society can exact a price for non-conformity.' It is a short step from there to 'anthropomorphism', where you ascribe human capacities or attributes to non-human entities, as in: 'A learning organization always wants to look after itself.' Combining the two, you can first convert an abstraction into a thing, and then endow this artificial agent with humanlike qualities, as in: 'The hurt done to society causes it to seek retribution.' Each of these conceptual slips creates a broad pathway to writing absurd propositions.

A closely related problem concerns the handling of collectivities. Academics should know better than to use generalizing stereotypes. But in fact when discussing the behaviour of groups of people they often write in a style using the 'archetypal singular'. Here a statement is made about the behaviour of a mythical archetype who somehow stands for all the people occupying a certain role or having certain characteristics. For instance: 'The bureaucrat is interested primarily in achieving a quiet life and a comfortable sinecure, whereas the politician seeks only to be re-elected.' Or: 'The writer's lot is not a happy one.' The problem here is that any statement using an archetypal singular is only true if *everyone* in that role or with that characteristic behaves in the way cited, a claim that is almost always bound to be wrong and is additionally never provable. Some bureaucrats are no doubt interested in slacking, but we could never establish that *all* are, just as some writers will be happy and others miserable. Any author who uses the archetypal singular, in virtually any context, will immediately degrade her intellectual grip on whatever she is discussing, debasing her reasoning to a sub-professional level and affecting adversely the accuracy of her text. When discussing collective entities use plural forms of phrasing, such as: 'Politicians are interested only in re-election.' The great virtue of the plural form is that as soon as you read this sentence, a question will occur to you: Do I mean *all* politicians, *most* politicians, *some* politicians, or *normal* politicians? And then you might further ask: What evidence or other argumentative token can I offer to corroborate my claim? In this way you might end up with worthwhile empirical propositions that positively build your doctorate – whereas any sentence including an archetypal singular can only be a corrosive liability.

A miscellany of other minor but common errors in theses are discussed in the style guide books listed in *Further Reading* on p. 289. Be careful in using other well-known style guides that are now quite old: they tend to be more tolerant of complex grammatical forms and overlong sentences than current professional standards. And they often mix up advice for creative fiction writers with that for non-fiction authors. The sources I recommend are worth consulting, but do also bear in mind the caveats I make about each book and the general need not to overdo a search for style improvements. Let me close by briefly pulling out just one instance of this detailed advice here, concerning capitalizing words and acronyms. It is best to minimize the use of capitals in your text for two reasons. Capitals tend to make the text less readable, especially when used in headings for sections or for tables, charts and diagrams. Try to keep all these elements in lower case after the first letter, except for proper nouns that are normally capitalized. In addition, most journals and book publishers pursue a minimum capitalization policy, so that you will reduce later editing changes by following this pattern in your text from the outset. Be careful also about the use of acronyms in your thesis. A page with lots of acronyms, that is, with many organizations or concepts reduced to initials, will be less readable than normal text. Only use acronyms for specialized concepts that recur a lot (at least three or four times) and choose the simplest form of the acronym possible (for instance, Nato or NATO, but not N.A.T.O.). Each acronym should be carefully explained on first use, and if you start reusing it after a period when it has not been present. Consider sometimes using substitute words or descriptors instead of an acronym on pages where it appears a lot: it will make your text easier for readers. You must also post a comprehensive glossary of acronyms and abbreviations at the start of your thesis, placed just after the contents page and the lists of tables or figures, so that bemused readers can remind themselves what you are referring to.

Effective referencing

> When a thing has been said, and said well,
> have no scruple. Take it and copy it.
> *Anatole France* [11]

Fairly or not, doctorates are notorious for being over-referenced. This aspect of authoring often absorbs a disproportionate amount of time and attention amongst PhD students, especially in the humanities and social sciences. There is no reason that it should. I examine the principles on which your referencing needs to be built; how to choose an appropriate system; and two standard systems that do the job simply, Harvard referencing and endnotes.

Principles for referencing

The 'need to know' criterion provides the basic rationale for what should be sourced, and in how much detail. Two, three or four readers, the examiners, have particular responsibilities to guard the portals of the PhD against incorrect or stolen work. Meeting their needs does impose a much higher standard of referencing than is common in academic books or even most journal articles. For instance, in these sources authors extensively use 'whole book' citations, where they designate a book as a source without specifying where to look within it, as (Foucault, 1995). Doctoral authors should strictly avoid this approach, because in theory the examiners should be able to check every source referenced. Obviously it would take them a long time if they had to read the whole of Foucault's book to find the one point which you say is in there. So thesis references must always be fully precise, ideally sourcing citations to particular pages, as (Foucault, 1995, pp. 56–9), or at worst indicating a specific chapter, as (Foucault, 1995, Ch. 4). In practice the examiners will very rarely follow up references, unless they have reason to think either that you have misquoted another researcher or perhaps that there is 'unacknowledged quotation' (plagiarism) in your text, which is a quick way to instantly fail your doctorate. Yet they will rightly become a bit suspicious about your scholarly qualities if they see that you are providing less than full and precise details for every citation and quotation.

Your referencing system also needs to reflect a more general principle of good authoring, namely that it should prove a *one-stop look-up* facility. Readers should have to go only to one place to follow through the sourcing of all quotations and citations. They must never be asked to look in two or more places in order to find out which source is being referred to.

For instance, it is still very common to find books where an author uses footnotes or endnotes in the main text, but when you turn to the note there is a Harvard referencing system in use, showing only Smith (2001). This means that you have to look further on again in the bibliography at the end to find out which source this is. Another example of two-stage look-up occurs often in humanities disciplines (like history) where many authors still use pointless and anachronistic Latin abbreviations. Here you may find in an endnote or footnote a reference such as 'White, *op. cit.*' or 'White, *loc. cit.*', where the Latin bits mean 'the same work as when White was last cited'. You then have to embark on a complete magical mystery tour of looking back through dozens of previous notes, trying to find the last time White was cited. The most careless and discourteous authors will pursue this *op. cit.* logic across several chapters, asking you to ransack possibly hundreds of notes to find the last time White was referenced. This approach would be a very rash one to adopt with PhD examiners or assessors. Both these examples illustrate the dangers to you as an author of not using a one-stop look-up system. If readers have to dig around in several different places to track down where you got a point from, they will form a worse view of your text and of your competence as an author compared with if you make their task straightforward.

Within the two principles of meeting the examiners' need to know precise sources for *everything* quoted or cited, and providing a one-stop look-up, try to guard against a tendency towards over-referencing. A classic 'thesis paranoia' symptom is inserting supporting literature for every point, even ones that no one in their right mind would dispute or need to do further reading about, such as: 'The United Kingdom is a country with a long and chequered history (Davies, 1999; Trevelyan, 1966; Chesterton, 1923).' If you find this problem in your text, check whether you are overciting more generally. Later on an excessively overcautious referencing approach also signals 'PhD thesis' immediately to journal editors and reviewers, and to book publishers. So it may make it harder than it otherwise would be to get your work published. Referencing details are also generally unattractive, so if overdone they can detract quite a lot from the 'look and feel' of your text.

Choosing a referencing system

You will not get to choose a referencing system if the PhD regulations in your university specify a format which your thesis simply has to follow. However, the most common situation is that the doctoral thesis rules are vaguer, only requiring full referencing to be provided in a particular recognized and consistent format or in one of several commonly used formats. Here you still get a choice of system. There is an extensive literature of reference books dedicated to informing you in great detail about the very many different referencing formats that exist, all of which come in subtly complicated varieties. In addition many influential professional associations produce style guides for their areas, some of which are helpful, such as the Modern Languages Association guide.[12] If your university regulations do not specify a particular system then check whether the professional association for your discipline and your country has a recommended format.

Even if you are studying outside the USA, you should none the less carefully consider whether the equivalent American association has a preferred format – because this will commonly be used also by many journals in your field. American referencing has certain basic features which people from smaller countries may need to take into account. Virtually all American references include the first names of authors and the initial of a second forename, as well as the family name (surname), as: Alvin B. Stiegler. In a country of over 260 million people much more specificity in citation is required than in smaller countries, where reference lists often only include one forename initial. The advent of the World Wide Web means that citation searches are now frequently global in scope, and with only a surname and initial they will generate thousands of 'confuser' references. So the American convention is the only feasible one now, and it should be universally adopted. You can always abbreviate to one or two initials later on if that is what a particular journal demands. But finding author first names to fill out dozens of references where you only have initials is a good example of a referencing 'time bomb' which can blow up in your face later on. In addition, most US journals will require details of both volume and issue numbers for journals, whereas in Europe volume alone is usually given. Again the only safe rule is to collect the fullest possible details from the outset.

Making a commitment to a particular referencing system used to be a difficult decision. If you got it 'wrong' you could find that you had a lot of extra work to do every time you wanted to publish something, shifting the referencing over to the format required by the particular journal you are targeting. There was always a pretty dismal chance of picking an optimal format here, since academic journals have remained quite stubbornly differentiated in the way that they handle references, across countries and across disciplines. Somewhere along the publishing line you are bound to have to redo your referencing for one purpose or another.

However, much cheaper and easy-to-use PC software for storing notes and referencing on computer has now transformed this problem. As early in your PhD studies as possible you should consider adopting a well-known citations-handling package like *Endnote* as the basis for all your references.[13] Ideally your university will provide one of these packages as part of its central IT facilities, giving you free access when you work on campus. But most doctoral students also work extensively from a home PC now, so you will also need a copy of the same software for home or personal use, which your university IT services should be able to supply at a strongly discounted price. So long as you can meet the cost, this initial investment will normally pay off many times over in several ways. The package will store all your citations in a single database. You enter the full details only once but the packages can then deliver citations in many different alternative formats, enough to satisfy even journals with the most esoteric requirements. You thereby save enormously on retyping or copying across references between other documents. With a central database, finding the references you need for any chapter, conference paper or article can also be accomplished at the touch of a button. In many universities you can also now download book or article details from the main library catalogue or Web-based bibliographic systems straight into your referencing database, without any retyping or editing on your part. Apart from their extra cost, the only drawbacks of the packages are the learning costs of mastering a new separate package and of making it work with less commonplace word processors (such as Linux or Apple ones). But the integration difficulties have now been solved for the major PC word processors. Your university library or IT services should provide free training courses in using their preferred referencing package, which are well worth attending.

Alternatively you may choose not to employ a specialized package, but to try and get along with creating a large central references file in your existing word processor (such as Word or Wordperfect). There are several ways to do this, of which the worst is just to create a straight text file. Instead try to find out how you can construct a searchable table or database in the package that will meet your needs. Word and Wordperfect also have very sophisticated facilities that can help here. For example, both include a powerful facility to automatically switch footnotes over into endnotes, or to convert endnotes into footnotes. You can also use a database that comes as part of your standard office package (like Access in Microsoft Office), from which material can be easily moved across to your word processor. These options are well worth exploring, especially because most of us use only a fraction of the facilities in our extremely powerful word-processing software. If you have not used the relevant menus or buttons before, try searching the on-line 'Help' pages for tutorials, look in the company's package manual (if you have one), or consult one of the many helpful guides to packages written by external authors and stocked in bookshops. Best of all, ask around amongst your colleagues for someone who is using these facilities and get them to show you how they work. Whatever you do about handling references, make sure that you start very early on in your PhD work; that you do it on a PC (bin that card index if you still have one!); that your approach is a systematic one which creates a centralized reference storage facility; and that you always regularly update this central file (and back it up several times) as you go along.

Harvard referencing

This approach is one of two widely used referencing systems which I review in detail here because they meet the principles of full referencing and one-stop look-up. (The other alternative is endnotes, discussed below.) Harvard referencing is perhaps the most widely used approach in academic life. There has been a long-term trend for more journals and book publishers to switch over to it, mainly because it saves space and tends to deliver a cleaner and simpler text than do notes of any kind. The system requires only two elements, an in-text reference, and a single, integrated bibliography at the end of the thesis, book or article.

◆ The *in-text reference* includes only the author surname (family name), the year date of publication, and page number details, all enclosed in brackets. For example: (Jones, 1999, p. 14; Jones and Crank, 1997, pp. 86–7).

   An alternative way of citing page numbers leaves out the p. or pp. and just puts in a colon after the year date, followed by the pagination, as (Jones, 1999: 14–17). Chapters can be indicated by Ch. or Chs. Whole-book references can be given with just the author surname and date. Where the same author has several publications with the same year date included in the bibliography, add single letters to the date to differentiate, as: 1999a.

◆ The *bibliography* lists every source cited in the work, arranged in alphabetical order of the first author's surname, and then date order, for example:

Jones, Terence B. (1999) 'Academic time-wasting in universities', *American Journal of Scholasticism*, vol. 12, no. 4, pp. 12–71.

Jones, Terence B. and Crank, Arthur (1997) *One Book Academics: What Goes Wrong?* (London: Futuristic Press). Second edition.

Jones, Terence B. and Winge, Steven A. (2001) 'Deconstructing post-modern writers' angst', *Times Literary Supplement*, 26 September, pp. 70–1.

Notice that authors' single-author works come before those written with others, and thereafter dual-authored works come before triple-author works, and so on. If a first author has several co-written works with the same number of people involved, use the alphabetical order of the second co-author's surnames to set the sequence (thus Jones and Crank comes before Jones and Winge in the box above).

◆ For journal articles the bibliography reference must include in sequence: author surname, full forename, second forename initial, year date, article title, journal title, volume number, issue number, and pagination. I have included vol. and no. here because some journals and publishers require it. Others will ask for the volume number and issue number without these labels, separated by a colon, as 4: iii. But deleting or replacing elements that are already in your references is much easier using 'find and replace' facilities on your word processor than it is inserting them from scratch.

◆ For magazine or newspaper articles use the same sequence as for journal articles, but replace the volume and issue numbers with the day and month date of publication.

◆ For books the bibliography reference must include in sequence: author surname, full forename, second forename initial, year date, book title (and subtitle if there is one), place of publication, and publisher. Add any essential information on the edition or translation that readers might need to know. For a republished later edition of a work give the first publication date at the end of the reference, as: 'Originally published in 1847'.

One great advantage of the Harvard system is that it provides a clean-looking text which includes immediate information for an expert reader (who will often know what source is being cited from the in-text reference alone). Yet it also gives easy access to more detailed information. The second great advantage is that every thesis has to have a comprehensive bibliography organized on exactly these lines anyway. Thus with any notes system you have to provide referencing for each source at least twice, once in a bibliography format, and then again in notes format, as well as repeating note citations of the same source. The Harvard system eliminates all this duplication and along with it the difficult 'version control' problems which often arise whenever you have two different citations of the same source. If you find that you have a source wrong there is only one place to change the reference under Harvard (although you will need to update the in-text referencing if the author name or year date is altered). You also do not have notes taking up some of the valuable space within the doctorate's word limit.

Finally Harvard referencing has big advantages because it tends to discourage authors from proliferating and expanding 'subtexts' in footnotes or endnotes. In any notes system the temptation for authors to create learned subtexts is normally irresistible. Critical asides and authorial digressions multiply, along with methods comments, lower level data, debates with opponents, and similar materials. Where authors rely on notes, it often looks as if the main text is surrounded by a forest of subsidiary commentaries, especially in academic books or articles with long footnotes at the bottom of the page, which sometimes squeeze the main text into less than half a page. Harvard referencing should prevent this completely, and yet it is still possible to put in special endnotes to include some bulky but indispensable subsidiary information (see below). Harvard referencing is attractive for publishers and journals precisely because it discourages subtexts, forcing you to make up your mind about what is key in your sources and what is not. Being constrained to pursue a single line of argument through your text can improve the clarity of your writing and your thought.

Many students who are used to notes systems anticipate that if they try Harvard referencing they will have four main difficulties. In fact these commonly cited 'problems' are all familiar ones, to which easy solutions exist:

♦ If you have to reference a large amount of literature at one point in your text, more than three or four works, then (but only then) it is permissible to add an endnote to accommodate the references. This exception violates the one-stop look-up rule, but it is preferable to having an unsightly wodge of referencing disrupting your main text. If you find that this is a common problem in your work, you may want to check whether you are over-referencing.

♦ Primary texts and older works may require unconventional referencing different from that shown above. For instance, you may want to refer to books, chapters and verses in sources like the Bible or the work of pre-modern philosophers, or to the acts, scenes and lines in plays. This problem arises because the page numbers for a classic work or other specialized text inevitably vary from one edition to another. Yet you want to make references in such a way that other people can find the passage you cite whatever edition of the work they are using. Legal case referencing also has its own forms. And citations of documents in historical archives should also follow referencing and numbering conventions, often ones particular to that archive. In all such cases you should preferably use a convention that is already well established in your discipline for the Harvard in-text reference, explaining what you are doing on first use for that source. The idea here is to maximize the ability of other professionals to retrieve and check the documents or other material that you cite. If no convention exists for your source then establish your own rule clearly on first use, giving readers a brief reminder about it later on when needed. Primary sources that are constantly referred to can also be abbreviated, so long as you explain the shortened form used to readers on first use and include it in the glossary of acronyms. For example, a reference to John Locke's *Treatise on Civil Government*, Book 4, Chapter 3, section 6, might appear as (Locke, *TCG*, IV.3.vi). This kind of abbreviated reference is perfectly neat to use many times over in your text, but is also accessible enough once you have explained the convention being used. Where your thesis revolves centrally around the use of a set of primary sources, then it is often useful to discuss them in a Research Methods Appendix, and this is a good place also to explain the referencing conventions you have followed.

◆ Unpublished and un-indexed sources, such as documents located in a depository that is not a well-organized historical or other archive with retrieval numbers, can be handled in a similar way in the Harvard in-text reference. Establish and explain your own referencing or naming convention as for primary sources above. Include a set of convenient abbreviations, ideally acronyms that will be intuitively understandable (as with the Locke reference above).

◆ In-text references for interview material are also sometimes cited as a problem for Harvard referencing, but are in fact straightforward to handle. 'On-the-record' interviews should be cited in a similar way to primary sources, by establishing a convention including the interviewee's surname, the fact that it was an interview and the interview date, as: (Smithers, interview, 26 October 2000). Your Research Methods Appendix should then include full details on who interviewees were; where and when you talked to them; how interviews were conducted (for instance, face-to-face, by phone, using a questionnaire or a dialogue mode, etc.); and how you recorded the material (for instance, taped or noted). If you want to cite evidence from 'non-attributable' interviews then referencing issues do not arise, because you cannot link particular points to any definite respondent. Instead you need to find a way of introducing phrases into your main text which give as much useful contextual information about your informant or source as possible, while yet fully preserving their anonymity. Material from 'off-the-record' interviews cannot be cited or referred to at all without breaching normal academic research ethics. (Make sure that you carefully discuss with your advisor any possible issues in referencing different kinds of interview material at the examination stage.) In all these last three respects there is no significant difference between the difficulty or ease of citing sources under Harvard referencing and using alternative systems like endnotes or footnotes.

A final issue worth noting about bibliographies concerns segmentation. A single unified bibliography arranged in a strict and predictable alphabetic ordering is best for all textual materials. In some older works, and in the PhD regulations for a few more old-fashioned universities, it is still possible to find bibliographies broken up into primary sources (such as unpublished documents) and secondary or published sources, or even separate listings for books and articles. All such devices breach the one-stop look-up principle, because from the in-text reference alone readers normally cannot tell what kind of source they are being directed to. With any kind of segmented bibliography they may have to look in several places to find the reference they need.

Endnotes

The main viable alternative system for referencing consistent with full citation and one-stop look-up are endnotes.

♦ The *in-text reference* is reduced to a minimal superscript number, as.[8] The numbers should restart at 1 with each new chapter. The number is automatically entered in your text

by the word-processing package when you create an endnote. Note numbers should always be located at the end of
sentences, not in the middle. You should also avoid having
multiple note numbers at different points inside or at the
end of the same sentence.

♦ The *note itself* must give full details on first citation of
a source, covering the same items as required for Harvard
bibliographies (see above), but with the component items in
a different sequence, as:

---

8. Terence B. Jones and Arthur Crank, *One Book Academics: What Goes Wrong?* (London: Futuristic Press, 1997), second edition. Terence B. Jones and Steven A. Winge, 'Deconstructing post-modern writers' angst', *Times Literary Supplement*, 26 September 2000, pp. 70–1.
9. Terence B. Jones, 'Academic time-wasting in universities', *American Journal of Scholasticism* (1999) vol. 12, no. 4, pp. 12–71.

The main changes here from the bibliography format are:
the author's first name and second initial now come before
(instead of after) their surname; and the year date of
publication moves from early on in the reference to a
position just ahead of the volume number for journal
articles, and just behind the publisher name for books.
In any form of notes system you are duplicating the
bibliography to a large extent. However, on second or
subsequent citation of the same source in endnotes it is
possible to reduce the level of detail in referencing, so long
as the source remains unambiguously identifiable. You can
here retain author surnames only, plus a shortened form of
the book or article title, as:

---

10. Jones and Crank, *One Book Academics*, p. 87.
11. Jones, 'Academic time-wasting in universities', pp. 15–16.

Using a chapter endnotes system involves some inconven-
ience for readers. They have to flip from a note number to the
note itself, which is located either at the end of that chapter or
at the end of the thesis as a whole. 'Big book' theses in typescript and bound as one volume are bulky. So readers might
find it easier to use endnotes located on the last pages of each
chapter, rather than at the end of the whole thesis. But if your

thesis gets published as a book readers will face no extra difficulty in using notes placed all together at the back. The great
plus point of endnotes, even more than the Harvard system, is
that it creates a clean-looking main text, with only relatively
unobtrusive in-text note numbers, ideally not too numerous or
overdone.

Footnotes follow the same format for full details and subsequent references as in the two endnotes boxes above. But these
citation details are given at the bottom of the same page as the
note number. Footnotes maximize one-stop look-up. Endnotes
are clearly less convenient for readers than footnotes. None the
less footnotes are still a slightly worse system to use for authoring
a thesis, even with the rapid advances made by modern word
processors in handling them. They are somewhat harder for you
to control and keep up to date when you cut and paste text, as you
will have to do extensively. Usually there will be some enhanced
difficulties in maintaining version control between footnotes and
a bibliography compared with endnotes, where all your references
for a chapter are at least gathered together and printed in one
place. And repagination problems tend to increase with footnotes.
Footnotes also maximize the clutter of referencing that readers
see. Especially in PhD dissertations, they often give a ragged and
uneven appearance to your final printed pages, with notes apparently 'squeezing' the main text. Because of these and other problems journals and almost all book publishers have moved away
from footnotes. For instance, if readers are accessing journals on-
line (as more and more are doing), then it is often hard for them
to keep two different-sized fonts on the same page readable. Either
the main text is in focus but the footnotes are too small; or the
footnotes are visible but the main text is then too big.

You will often need to rearrange both footnotes and endnotes for publication. This task is a very easy one for your word
processor if it entails swapping endnotes to footnotes, or vice
versa. But swapping between notes systems and Harvard referencing is only easy if you are using a citations-handling package like *Endnote*. The most difficult rewriting occurs if you are
redoing notes for a journal or a book using Harvard referencing
and have to eliminate subtexts. Using footnotes has its most
likely adverse impact on authors' intellectual habits here,
encouraging you to create subtexts and then carry on vigorous

side-shows there. Endnotes have less impact on authors here, because endnotes are in a much less visible location.

Finally, for completeness, let me mention a newer citations-handling approach which is even less obtrusive than endnotes. 'Popular science' writers follow this style, partly in hopes of broadening their appeal to readers, especially those outside the academic community. They provide a full slate of references at the end of the book, but there are no note numbers or Harvard references in the text to trigger them. Instead the reference list gives a page number, perhaps also a line or paragraph number, and the first few words of a quote or other phrase on that page. This leads into a full relevant citation in endnote form. This approach may become more popular in future with academic books in 'soft' disciplines, where authors strive for a better literary feel. But at present it would still be an unconventional referencing procedure to use for completing a PhD.

Conclusions

Constructing your text crisply and handling your references competently are small but quite important parts of achieving a convincing approach to professional writing. There is no reason to worry overmuch about either aspect. Do not try to achieve a perfect style by endlessly polishing or tinkering with your text. And do not get hung up or obsessed about referencing issues. Once you have achieved a certain level, your substantive arguments and the quality of your research will be decisive in shaping readers' reactions. So these fundamentals should always get most of your attention. Getting style and referencing aspects of your writing right simply helps readers focus on the substance of your argument and the qualities of your research, instead of being distracted, confused or annoyed by presentational defects. Producing cleanly written, well-referenced text will also help maintain your morale as an author. If your text reads well you will be better motivated to write more and will have a clearer picture of where you are going. It should give you the confidence to tackle and surmount some inevitable major difficulties of the writing and revising process, to which I turn in the next chapter.

6

Developing Your Text and Managing the Writing Process

> Never ignore, never refuse to see, what may be
> thought against your thought.
> *Friedrich Nietzsche*   [1]

For creative non-fiction the heart of the authoring process is a person sitting at a desk, surrounded by information, notes, scribbles and sources, or otherwise jammed with ideas, and struggling to organize their thoughts on a blank screen or sheet of paper. This particular image is so dominant in our thinking about authoring because it is so awe-full, so hard to manage your way through at the time, so difficult to capture what you were doing afterwards, and so psychologically stressful or unnerving to contemplate at almost any time. In another field, writing novels, its practitioners' collective obsession with the angst of an author imagining something out of nothing has gone even further, as John Fowles noted ironically:

> Serious modern fiction has only one subject, the difficulty of writing serious modern fiction .... The natural consequence of this is that writing about fiction has become a far more important matter than writing fiction itself. It's one of the best ways you can tell a true novelist nowadays. He's not going to waste his time over the messy garage-mechanic drudge of assembling stories and characters on paper ... Yes, all right. Obviously he has at some point to write something, just to show how irrelevant and unnecessary the actual writing part of it is. But that's all.[2]

Of course, Fowles is pointing out that this degree of navel-gazing is deeply unhealthy, even disabling for his field. Thankfully, creative non-fiction is a more prosaic area than novel writing, an area where well-primed authors generally find it easier (more routine) to do writing. But most of us encounter some similar problems in handling the self-exposure involved in authoring, facing up to our own limited ideas and contribution, and coping with the inevitable separation between our planned piece of work and the one that actually materializes on screen or paper.

Three key strategies can help ease the myths and difficulties surrounding the writing process. One step is to rethink the writing process not as a single creative act but instead as a multi-stage process, where each stage is as important for your progress as any other. Authoring does not just involve producing a first draft. It is just as much about how you reflect on what you have done, try out the arguments on other people, replan your text in the light of comments, and implement revisions. Second, where a piece of writing is not working in its current form, it is useful to have in reserve a specific and reliable method for radically remodelling problematic text. A third strategy is to plan your writing sessions carefully and to review some detailed suggestions which may help you maintain progress and avoid running into potential road blocks.

Drafting, upgrading and going public

> Everything is proceeding as I have foreseen.
> *The Emperor, in* The Return of the Jedi   [3]

Writing up a chapter plan into the very first joined-up version of your text will produce literally dozens of changes in what you expected to do. All of them will be disappointing. What seemed feasible, concise, coherent or original on your plan will turn out weaker, lengthier, less accessible or more familiar in practice. Howard Becker notes that many PhD students adhere to the illusion that there is some 'one best way' of authoring any given piece, sitting out there in a landscape of potentialities, just waiting to be discovered.[4] The writer's task then is to hunt high and low for this optimal path. Taking this view, you may easily get the feeling part-way through writing that you have been thoroughly mistaken about where this best way lies, and now have lost track of it entirely. Countering these setback feelings entails taking a longer view of, first, the whole set of stages involved in developing a professional text; and second, the process of exposing it to consideration and debate by others.

Stages in the writing process

> Don't get it right, get it written.
> *James Thurber* [5]

> Outlines can help, but not if you begin with them.
> If you begin, instead, by writing down everything,
> by spewing out your ideas as fast as you can type,
> you will discover ... the fragments you have to
> work with.
> *Howard Becker* [6]

The major myth of the authoring process is the critical character of breaking fresh ground, filling a blank screen or a blank page *de novo*. An essential antidote is to recognize that this is only a first stage in authoring, and not necessarily the key one for the development of your argument. Authoring is a multi-stage process and, as the quote from James Thurber above makes clear, there are divergent rationales to go with these different stages. The logic of a first draft is to make text where there was none, to get something written, to get the elements you have in play more or less defined, even if only in a preliminary way and often in the wrong order. As your text grows you will also necessarily lose some control over it. By the time a chapter is 30 or 40 pages long you cannot possibly hold its entire argument in your head at one time. Nor can you even fully understand what you have written or why the argument turned out as it did. Rebuilding this mastery is a key element in the second stage of the writing process, where you can follow through a logic of organizing text in a coherent fashion. Building an extended text will necessarily change your thinking. It will make clear aspects of your own views that you could not have known in advance, and allow you to weigh, test and sift the varying levels of commitment you have to different propositions. Someone quoted the maxim, 'Never begin a sentence until you know how to end it' to the novelist E. M. Forster. He replied: 'How can I know what I think till I see what I say?'[7]

A second essential philosophical change of view with this approach is to recognize that there is no 'one best way' of saying something. There is no Platonic perfect form sitting out there waiting to be searchlit by a peculiarly perceptive advance plan, or, once identified, capable of being written up intact by a more self-consistent or more talented author. Instead all that you can say is constructed, created, not found or discovered ready-made. Difficulties arise because very often we confront authoring dilemmas, choice points in the creative process where two or more options lead further on but you can only maximize one of your valued goals or purposes at the expense of another. There may be no 'right' choice in such dilemma situations. There often is no common currency in which to measure the different kinds of costs attaching to each of the options leading forward. So you can only make conditional choices to follow one route rather than another and to see what happens. But later on it will be helpful to recall those prior decision points in re-evaluating what you have done. Perhaps an alternative choice might be better after all.

Going from a poor version of your ideas to a radically improved and viable text takes time, distance, alternative perspectives and a concerted effort at remodelling. Writing is an act of commitment. So no one can constructively renounce text that they have just produced – that is, see what is wrong with it or what might be changed to remedy defects. With a newborn text you can only renew and reiterate your commitment (perhaps tinkering around with perfectionist embellishments) or reject it non-constructively ('It's all rubbish – I'm wasting my time!'). You need at least some days to pass, other things and other thoughts to intervene, and other people to read what you have written in order to begin to see things differently. And when you start to revise and replan it can be helpful to have built that stage into your thinking and your timetable in advance, and to have some appropriate expectations about it.

You will almost always need to carry out five operations on any piece of text: print, edit, revise, upgrade and remodel:

♦ *Print* your material to achieve a shift of perspective from writing on your PC. If you only edit text on-screen your changes will be too confined to small corrections and changes at a verbal level. Working on paper will help you see how more thorough-going alterations are feasible, such as moving large chunks of text around over several pages.

♦ *Edit* means a word-level edit of your raw text to remove mis-spellings, grammar mistakes, tiresome repetitions of the same word or phrase, and other infelicities. Do not leave your text untouched with these problems still around. So long as they remain uncorrected, their presence will tend to obscure other defects from you. Getting to a clean text lets you see beyond the clutter, to any deeper intellectual problems.

♦ *Revise* covers a paragraph-level reconsideration of how one idea chains to the next. It focuses on improving things by small-scale switches around in the order of sentences or paragraph chunks. It can also cover more substantive changes, especially in the beginnings and ends of paragraphs (remembering the Topic, Body, Wrap sequence).

♦ *Upgrade* involves going back from your piece of text to your original materials and considering whether you can strengthen the arguments in any way. Can you cite more scholarly support for points you have made? Or bring in additional empirical evidence? Or reanalyse your data to knock out possible competing interpretations? Can you extend your key arguments, or develop them in a more formal or systematic way? You need to be clear when your approach needs more sustenance and underpinning. But avoid slipping into 'thesis paranoia' by overarguing or overciting on non-controversial points.

♦ *Remodel* refers to a much more radical restructuring of a chapter or article, which usually requires a very specific method, described in the next subsection. Text that is already in a satisfactory condition may not need full-scale remodelling. But you will normally have to make radical changes in at least one or two chapters out of eight, unless you are a very disciplined and consistent writer.

Producing a piece of text finished in 'first draft' form involves both your private efforts to generate raw text and improve on it, and seeking outside commentary and advice. The overall process can be pictured as having four phases, moving from most personal and private to most public. Going public with your commitment, a text that crystallizes your thought and for the moment fixes it in one configuration, is a particularly sensitive stage that needs to be handled carefully.

In Phase 1 you write out a semblance of the argument to an approximate length of the chapter you are embarked on. This stage produces raw text, words on screen or handwriting on a page, arguments played out or attempted, facts marshalled, connections made, positions expounded – but maybe not yet in any satisfactory joined-up form.

In Phase 2 you stockpile and reassess your text for a while, looking for ways to upgrade it and tighten it up. After leaving a short gap (because some time and distance are needed here), you can review what you have, looking for omissions or inconsistencies, trying to trace the development of the argument and to see places where moving things around can improve things. During this shape-up stage it can also be useful to show bits of text to friendly readers, that is people close to you, such as fellow PhD students, friends, relatives, significant others or lovers. Even people without a background in your topic can be helpful foils, sympathetic readers who can look at your text dispassionately and tell you how accessible or well written it seems. A trusted, intelligent but inexpert listener can also help you test your key arguments by letting you say them aloud and more accessibly. If you are very lucky and get on really well with one or more of your supervisors, perhaps you may get them involved in this shaping-up stage. Phase 2 may involve you in making multiple small revisions as you go along. But it normally ends with you making a first systematic run through of your work, inserting additional materials, tying down loose referencing, moving and reknitting text in an improved pattern, and consolidating lots of small upgrade changes into a revised form.

In Phase 3 you begin to go public with your text, accumulate comments, and incorporate them in a more fundamental revision or remodelling. In professional contexts you can only go forward a certain distance on your own, after which you need to get some radically different views of what you are saying in order to make progress. Your supervisors or advisers are the first port of call. One of their primary roles is to look at and comment on your formal written text. You need to make sure that they give you effective feedback on your work. Normally advisers are reassured and even grateful when they get chapters to look at. It is not easy for them to operate solely at an oral level in someone else's research topic. They need your help in the form of a regular sequence of chapters in order to offer useful advice and commentary. But supervisors are also very variable in what they say, for various reasons. Some are famously diffident or difficult people, like the Oxford philosopher whose three-word written comment on a student's painfully produced 12,000-word chapter was: 'I suppose so'. Different supervisors also follow different strategies. Some will comment in vigorous detail on early drafts, where others deliberately stand back for fear of being too critical of your nascent ideas. Some very well organized supervisors put their effort in very early on in your text production process, demanding that you get a near-perfect chapter draft to stockpile before you can move on to another chapter. In this perspective, once you have reached the right 'doctoral' level in one chapter, it will become easier for you to deliver subsequent chapters to the same standard. Other advisers (like me) feel that it is only important for you to get a broadly acceptable chapter draft before moving on, lest you drag out early writing with perfectionist anxieties and erode your later research and authoring time. In this perspective, going from a first full draft of the thesis to a final version of the text will normally produce so many changes that overwriting early chapters, before the neighbouring chapters are written, will too frequently be wasted or redundant effort. The detailed stylistic and argumentative choices you make in your first two years' work are likely to be extensively overturned by more mature insights and by the alterations inherent in crafting the thesis into an integrated whole.

Beginning to go public should take other forms than just showing material to your supervisor, however. Presenting a chapter in a 'friendly' public forum such as a departmental graduate seminar can be very helpful, even if the audience does not include many people who know a great deal about your topic. The point of these exercises is for you to think through how your text can be presented and explained to people knowledgeable in your discipline but not in your specific topic. The changes that you make in order to mount an effective presentation and the comments that you get back can often be very helpful foretastes of how people in your discipline generally will view your work. Some PhD students resent being asked by their departments to do regular presentations once or twice a year to such groups, feeling that so inexpert an audience has little to say to them about their own specialist research. But at the end of the PhD other 'generalist' audiences in your discipline will make crucial decisions about your future as an academic, such as deciding whether or not to appoint you to a university job or to allocate you a post-doctoral grant. It is far better to have to appreciate early on how the profession as a whole may see your work – so that you can make adjustments in the orientation or presentation of your text in time to improve these later perceptions.

> Talking is a basic human art. By it each
> communicates to others what he [or she] knows
> and, at the same time, provokes the contradictions
> which direct his attention to what he has
> overlooked.
> *Bernard Lonergan*   [8]

> Conference makes a ready man [or woman].
> *Francis Bacon*   [9]

After your supervisors or advisers have commented on your draft, and perhaps you have also accumulated some 'outside' commentary, then you should quickly make any changes that seem necessary, while these criticisms and reactions are still fresh in your mind. This second round of revisions is the final element in producing a settled first draft of the chapter. Your first draft will normally be a long way from your original raw text. It is a version of the chapter that you can safely bank, leaving it as it is, not to be reassessed until you have written a complete draft of the whole thesis and are moving to a final version of the entire text (see Chapter 8). It is important for your later morale that before you 'bank' the chapter you make some effective modifications to meet suggestions or comments from your advisers and criticisms in seminars.

This does not mean scrapping and starting again. Nor does it mean throwing up your hands and filing your existing version of the chapter with a lot of disabling commentaries attached, your own and other people's. Instead keep faith with your chapter, and with the work that it embodies, but try to find a way of adjusting what you say and how you say it that meets or skates around the points made against your argument. It may not be a good idea to painstakingly try to remodel the chapter into a completely different form now, because later changes when you move from first draft to a final text could supersede any major restructuring which you do now. But when you 'bank' your chapter in first draft and move on to the next, it is important that it is in a reasonable working format, one that counters criticisms and incorporates important suggestions. In that way you will think of the banked chapter as viable, up to date, genuinely a first draft – rather than seeing it as imperfect, conditional or in need of a major overhaul before reaching proper first-draft status.

Phase 4 of developing text is a desirable but more optional one, of going public in wider professional settings by giving seminars at other universities and papers at conferences. Do not attempt this stage until your chapter or paper is well worked-up, so that you are reasonably confident about taking outside criticism of your ideas. If you meet this test then presenting to an outside seminar at another university can be a very useful first step. Alternatively there may be small-scale specialist group meetings which occur regularly within academic professional associations. These occasions can offer more focused criticisms and evaluations from people working in exactly your field. Any outside audience (especially at conferences) will tend to be more heterogeneous, less committed to the theoretical ideas or methods of research that hold sway in your home department or university. They will be franker about possible problems and more radical in challenging your ideas with alternative approaches. Going beyond this level involves presenting a paper to a larger professional conference, at national level.

Later on in your doctorate, when you have a developed version of a chapter in a tightly written and short conference paper format, then you may also find it valuable to apply for international conferences. As you go up this ladder of increasing scale the potential audience for your paper widens. But the time you get to present it falls, from 30 to 40 minutes in a university seminar, to maybe only 15 or 20 minutes at large conferences.

Remodelling text

> One changes one's ideas the way an animal sheds its coat, in patches: it's never a wholesale change from one day to the next.
> *Umberto Eco* [10]

All of the advice above assumes that your text already works tolerably well, sufficient for you to be able to absorb comments and to upgrade it incrementally. But sometimes, perhaps rather frequently in the early stages of developing your thesis or with more argumentative or theoretical chapters, you may find that the overall feel of a chapter is not right. Here more fundamental changes may be needed. Text remodelling is a particularly powerful technique for this kind of situation. It is psychologically difficult to use, because none of us likes to admit to ourselves that some writing we have produced really does not work. The idea of starting over can seem very threatening and non-constructive if you have no clear alternative idea of how to proceed.

Remodelling is designed to cope with the fact that at the normal full-chapter length of 30 to 40 pages any piece of text becomes very difficult for us to hold in our heads as a whole. We tend to cope by selectively forgetting parts of the text as we move through it. Authors use many different linking words, phrases and sentences to convince readers that one paragraph leads on seamlessly to the next. These devices can all effectively disguise the structure of a chapter from the author as well. Even if you have gone over a finished chapter several times making incremental changes and revisions, the chances are still very high that you will not fundamentally understand what you have done.

Three steps provide the foundations for remodelling:

– Write out the chapter heading in full, and then all the
  subheadings in full as they come up, in the same font as
  used in the chapter. It is best to do remodelling with pen
  and paper, and not on a PC. (There are a couple of specialist
  PC packages which might assist authors doing extensive
  remodelling, especially people whose research already uses
  a lot of interviews or case study materials.[11])
– For each paragraph in the chapter, write a one-line summary
  of what it says. Try to express the argumentative *core* of what
  the paragraph says. Be cold-bloodedly realistic, or perhaps
  downright cynical or sceptical. For instance if a paragraph
  only says a bit more on a point already made, express that
  judgement in your summary line. It is very important not to
  let these summaries lengthen out beyond a single line.
– Number all the paragraph summaries in sequence from the
  beginning to the end of the chapter.

You should now have a drastically summarized version of what
your chapter says, one that records all the key points being made
within one or two pages. This view should be much more accessible and comprehensible than your previous impression of the
chapter.

With the couple of pages showing this chapter skeleton on
the desk in front of you, begin a series of basic checks:

◆ Is the chapter structure simple (good) or complex (bad)?
◆ Is the argument pattern clear and logical (good) or
  unclear (bad)?
◆ Do the current sections and subsections divide up the
  chapter text evenly (good) or unevenly (bad)? Even division
  shows up because each section or subsection has much
  the same number of component paragraphs as the
  others at the same level.
◆ Does the chapter's argument have a developmental or
  cumulative feel about it (good) or does it by contrast seem
  recursive and repetitive (bad)? You need to follow a 'say it
  once, say it right' philosophy, gathering together closely
  related points which can be handled at one place in a
  full-force way, not dissipated across different bits of the text.

◆ Does the chapter use an analytic or argumentative mode of exposition (generally better in terms of organizing and personalizing your argument) or does it rely on a descriptive approach (generally worse for organizing and personalizing your argument).

These checks will only take you five minutes to do for a normal chapter, but the answers you get may sometimes surprise you. You may find that what you have written is a considerable distance away from what you planned to do in advance, but also from what you thought you were doing in producing the raw text and making any edits since. Sometimes the text may seem to have a life or tendencies of its own, and this can be an important datum for you to consider. If you find a mismatch between the initial chapter plan and its implementation, do not immediately conclude that your text must be flogged back into line with the master plan. If in the end this is how you wrote it, that may be because this is how that text *had* to be written by you. And if your initial structure was different, perhaps it is that which should be changed? Sometimes your sectioning, headings, subheadings, signposts and promises reflect your original plan while the body of the text you have written in fact does something different. Bringing the two back into sync by dropping an unrealistic plan can sometimes sort out problems very straightforwardly.

> Books do not always obey the author's orders and this book … quickly became obstreperous.
> *Claire Tomalin* [12]

> A show has a mind of its own, and it's wrong to push it in a direction it doesn't want to go.
> *Neil Simon* [13]

The next stage of remodelling can be as psychologically uncomfortable as realistically summarizing each paragraph. If the text does not read well, you must try to generate *one alternative schema* for the chapter, a new structure that differs substantially from the existing one. On a new sheet of paper, set out some alternative section and subsection headings for the chapter, spacing them out evenly from top to bottom of the new sheet.

The idea here is to surface a different way of organizing things, a different sequence of ideas. Once you have specified the section heads and subheadings you can then indicate the kind of body-text to go inside each section by simply inserting paragraph numbers from your existing text-skeleton onto the new plan, in the rough order needed – which may be very different from their current sequence.

To really assess this alternative schema you now have to flesh it out a bit, which means moving back from pen and paper to working on your PC. Save your existing text twice as different files, once under its customary name and again under a new name (perhaps adding 'revised' or 'Rv' to the front of the old name). Now at the top of the revised file insert the new section headings and subheadings you have created. Then cut and paste your numbered paragraphs from one location and sequence to the alternative one. This stage of the operation is called 'chop and stick', because you are only cutting out paragraphs and putting them back together in a different sequence. You are not yet rewriting the beginnings or ends of paragraphs to make them fit together, merely regrouping them. The next stage is to print out the reconfigured file with a couple of blank lines at each point where the new sequence differs. Then read through the text in the new sequence, marking it up as you go along. Think about how you could rebuild the whole chain of links in the new sequence, from one paragraph to another, and from one subsection to another. Pencil in ideas for doing this on your print-out.

Next comes a key evaluation decision. Which works best – the new sequence (roughly hewn though it still is) or the old one? The point of looking at a whole alternative approach is to compare like with like. Left to ourselves most of us are quite conservative and risk averse. Faced with a choice between some finished-looking text and a still unspecified alternative version, we will tend to cling tenaciously to what we have. But sketch in a new structure, and show yourself how the text would look if quickly remodelled, and you may be able to overcome this inertial attachment. With a rough-hewn alternative physically in front of you, you have a chance to make a much better informed decision. In my experience, people who have got this far with text remodelling techniques almost always proceed with the reshaped version – even when they previously felt dissatisfied with their text but pessimistic about finding any better way of organizing it.

From here on you need do only a limited amount of work to finish off the remodelled version of the text. The principal task is to refocus the beginnings and ends of sections and subsections, the signposts and promises made to readers. You will also have to remake some linkage points between paragraphs at all the points where the sequence has changed under the new structure. But you should have a clear plan of what to do by now, and almost all of the text used in the new version is already written. With these elements on the desk in front of you, producing a fully polished and connected new text should be much easier than it was to generate the original version.

There are then only a few remaining checks that you need to make on the remodelled chapter:

◆ Look at each subheading in turn and ask: is it the right level of heading, and in the right place? How many paragraphs follow each subheading (easily checked from your new plan)? Your subheadings should neither be too spaced out, nor come too frequently. It is especially important to avoid having two headings next to each other, with no intervening text. (Also look out for cases where there is only a single lower-order subheading inside a section: creating subsections is redundant unless there are at least two of them.) Do the subheads divide the text evenly so far as possible? Are the subheadings effective and informative? Do the headings give readers good clues about what the storyline or the 'bottom line' is in each? It can be very useful to crosscheck the subheadings with your one-line paragraph summaries for that subsection and see how far they match up.
◆ Check each of the linkages between paragraphs in the new plan. Is there a good reason why this paragraph follows that? Does the first and last sentence of each new paragraph signpost the contents well, and make good verbal links from one paragraph to the next?
◆ Practice the 'emergency stop' test on the new text. Suppose that I suddenly clap my hand over the bottom of the page

at a randomly chosen point in the chapter and ask readers to explain what the structure of the argument is and how far they have come in it. Will they be able to give a reasonably easy and assured answer? If the answer is no, strengthen the signposting in the text, review the headings and subheadings again, and try to tighten up the structure and make it as simple and straightforward for readers to access as possible.

Organizing the writing process

> Biting my truant pen, beating myself for spite,
> 'Fool,' said my Muse to me, 'look in thy heart, and
> write.'
> *Sir Philip Sidney*   [14]

> I write when I'm inspired, and I see to it that I'm
> inspired at nine o'clock every morning.
> *Peter de Vries*   [15]

Your experience of the writing process can become unnecessarily off-putting if you do not approach it in the right way. Writing is difficult to do, and most of us tend to put off doing hard things for as long as possible. I often think of multiple tasks that I must complete before I can even try to bang out words on screen or put pen to paper. Perhaps I start what was meant to be a writing session but then find some displacement activity, like following up scholarly references, or doing a word-level edit of last week's writing, which allows me to wriggle away from starting new writing. After a few less productive sessions like this, I can end up writing hard against a deadline – which is far more stressful than starting in good time and trying to consistently rack up some words. Repeat this experience a dozen times and it can quickly become habit-forming. Nothing useful gets written except when a deadline really looms. So the new writing process becomes inextricably associated in your mind with high-pressure working. In turn this link reinforces the tendency to postpone getting started on it, like putting off going to the dentist. There is no magic cure for these common problems.

But it can be helpful to review some fairly commonsense issues around the writing process, and to do what you can to make creating new text easier and more straightforward for you.

A first step worth thinking through is how you programme your writing slots.[16] Nothing is more demoralizing than to plan on doing a certain amount of writing in a given week or month, only to find that the time has elapsed and you have made too little progress on your planned levels. Start by being realistic about all the competing demands you face, from family, friends and social life, from employment or other means of paying your way, travel time, teaching, studying courses, lectures and seminars, and so on. You need to take out appropriate amounts of time from any given week and be realistic about what is left. When estimating how much you can write in a session, build in some slack time also for editing and catch-up activities. Sometimes in doing these sums it will become clear that you just need to prioritize your writing more, to set aside much longer or more frequent periods for it than you have been doing.

The time slots you earmark also have to be useful ones. A writing session cannot normally be squeezed into small bits of time, a half-hour here and there, a short train journey, or a small interval between coursework sessions. These lesser chunks of time can be used very productively for other things related to writing, like jotting down ideas, reviewing previous jottings, or word-editing raw text. But writing raw text from scratch, or substantially remodelling stuff you already have, generally both require a substantial commitment of time, perhaps around three or four hours minimum for most people. This has got to be completely free time – not eroded by phone interruptions, not a time when you do e-mailing or surf the Web, and most especially not a time when family members or friends will interpose quite different demands on your concentration.

You need a half-hour space at the start of each writing session in order to get warmed up on pre-writing activities, reviewing your notes and organizing ideas for the piece from your last writing session. You may need to build up your confidence, morale and sense of clear direction in order to reach the point of committing words to screen or paper. It can help to type notes and organizing ideas into the document you are working on below the existing joined-up text, in the rough sequence you want the unwritten sections to follow. Then as you write up new bits of joined-up text, you can delete the appropriate notes or organizing ideas, so as to give you a sense of progress and to keep focused on what is yet to be completed.

You also need around half an hour at the end of today's writing to leave off in a proper fashion. It is important to finish in a controlled and chosen way, rather than just depleting your stock of ideas, evidence and argument to nothing and going away hoping that 'something will turn up' in time for your next session. Try to finish a writing session by gathering together all the materials you may need for the next day's piece of writing, like quotations, references, data or other attention points, bits of argumentation or especially juicy or telling phrases that have occurred to you. Type sufficient notes into your PC file or a possible skeleton of the next passage of text to get you quickly restarted again whenever your next session is scheduled. Some people find it helpful to print out and pin up these elements on a big noticeboard next to their writing desk, where they can be seen as a whole, and also physically moved around and reorganized if need be. The longer the gaps between writing sessions the more care you will need to take over this prefiguring exercise. It is also very helpful to sustain your sense of making progress by printing today's new pages and putting them in a file or pinning them on the noticeboard for editing outside the writing session itself, in some smaller or less useful slice of time.

For the main body of each writing session you need enough time (perhaps two or three hours) to rack up several hundred words at least, such that you will see a distinct accretion of new text by the end of the session. Once you get stuck in to writing it is a good idea to keep plugging away at it for as long as possible, resisting the seductive idea of having a break and a cup of coffee, because you will only need to warm up all over again. But it is not a good idea to make writing sessions too long, because as with all other kinds of work there will be diminishing returns to effort after a while. You need to check how good your endurance is, and also what times of day or night are most productive for you. Keeping a log may help you to find this out more clearly.

However long your writing sessions are, it is critically important to remember to energetically flex your arms and hands regularly when typing (at least every 15 minutes). Repetitive strain injury (RSI) is now something of an occupational disease for PhD students and academics. In very serious cases its onset can create a high level of disability, making it impossible for you to touch a keyboard, to write with a pen, to drive a car, or even to turn a key in a lock. In acute cases RSI can mean months without being able to do academic work at all. And once significant RSI symptoms have appeared they never completely go away. It is therefore incredibly foolish for any would-be academic or researcher to run risks like typing for hours on end uninterruptedly, especially when working close to fixed deadlines. As well as flexing regularly, you can also help ward off RSI by always using an 'ergonomic' keyboard plugged into your computer. This step should be mandatory if you are using a notebook or portable PC, all of which have very cramped keyboards which are particularly prone to triggering RSI symptoms. More generally, make sure that you get up and walk around every half hour of your writing session, perhaps doing a few stretches. Again, using a noticeboard to organize elements for your text, or using an impromptu standing-up desk (like the top of a four-drawer filing cabinet) to do drafting, may help keep you more mobile.

> My foot is a writer too.
> *Friedrich Nietzsche*   [17]

How many writing sessions do you need to accomplish the physical task of banging out 80,000 words in a coherent whole? Different perspectives suggest very diverse answers. An encouraging way of looking at things sees a thesis as 'a mountain with steps', capable of being surmounted a bit at a time. Zerubavel points out that if you can write even 500 words in each writing session, you will need only 160 sessions to complete 80,000 words.[18] Even if every word has to be redrafted twice from scratch, you will still only require 320 sessions. Seen in this salami-slicing light the wonder is that it commonly takes three or four years of full-time work to find the space for these few hundred necessary writing sessions, when there are 200 working days per year. If you can manage 1000 words per day, which is perfectly feasible for all but the most painstaking or complex bits of text, then writing the whole thesis twice over should only take 160 days. And at 2000 words a day the time involved shrinks to just 80 days.

But look at how much time you have in a day and the perspective is not so benign. Allow 7.5 hours for sleep every night, the current average for people in the USA, about an hour short of what is medically best for us. That leaves a total of 1440 waking minutes per day, according to James Gleick.[19] Say we take as a rule of thumb the idea that even the simplest of daily tasks takes somewhat under five minutes (having a shower, brushing your teeth, making a cup of coffee). Then in a normal day we can each of us only do 300 things, across every life activity we have. In a four-hour writing session you can do maybe 50 things – like switching on your PC and waiting for it to lumber into life, checking a reference, writing a couple of sentences, editing a paragraph, making a note or two (that is 10 per cent of your time gone already). Yet it is by combining a myriad such protean activities that an integrated professional text has to be constructed.

How much you manage to do in any writing session will be shaped by many different influences. The traditional mind/body way of looking at scholarly pursuits pictures a struggle between your intellectual push to complete authoring tasks and the physical artificiality of spending long hours in front of a PC or sitting writing at a desk (see the quote from Aquinas below). There is something in this perspective, since writing on your own is normally a more sedentary activity than (say) working in an office, especially if family distractions pen you up in your study in order to get any writing done at all. You can counteract these tendencies, however, by ensuring that even on heavy writing days you insert time outside your writing sessions for walks, fresh air, getting out and about, going to the gym or the swimming pool, or whatever works best in helping you focus. It is important to remember that authoring is not a leisure activity, but work. You need to be fit and well to do authoring properly, just as much as for more physically demanding jobs.

> The soul has an urge to know, and the body an inclination to shirk the effort involved.
> *St Thomas Aquinas* [20]

> The whole calamity of man comes from one
> single thing, that he [or she] cannot keep quiet
> in a room.
> *Blaise Pascal* [21]

> Our thinking subject is not corporeal.
> *Immanuel Kant* [22]

The mind/body way of picturing difficulties in writing is far too crude, though. Normally problems in concentrating and focusing, getting up steam and then keeping going, are the results not of physical resistances to being chained to the keyboard or the desk but of mental cross-pressures. Your progress will depend most upon your intellectual morale (itself closely reflecting how the work is going) and the level to which other worries and business impede upon you. These are the influences which tend to generate displacement behaviour instead of writing (such as overperfecting earlier bits of text, refiling your notes and papers, or breaking off for a cup of coffee and some light-relief daytime TV). Making an effort to persist with writing for your full session length is usually a worthwhile response to such pressures. Taking some small steps can also strengthen your morale by giving you more perceptible indicators of progress and better incentives to continue. For instance, find the starting number of words in your chapter (using the 'Tools/Word Count' buttons in Word or the 'document information' button in Wordperfect), and then type it into the beginning or end of your document file. Then update the word count at the end of each session, and perhaps keep a record of the words racked up. Comparing these figures with your target level also guards against overwriting, otherwise an important source of potential extra delay for hard-working people.

Keeping up your intellectual morale can be very difficult while working up a chapter on your own. Planning the structure of a new piece of text tends to be an optimistic stage, because you are still shielded from difficulties of implementation. But writing up raw text for the first time tends to be inherently dispiriting, especially if you subscribe to the 'writing equals one-off creation' myth and hence do not take account of the multi-stage nature of the authoring process. In looking at

last session's raw text try to bear in mind the extent to which
you will normally be able to edit, revise, upgrade and remodel
your work. You can always make big changes by taking out
infelicities, adding in strengthening evidence, developing and
extending arguments, formalizing or systematizing frameworks
for analysis, uncovering new relationships in your data, boost-
ing scholarly referencing, and so on.

> Work makes the companion.
> *Johanne Wolfgang von Goethe*   [23]

> In order that people may be happy in their work,
> these three things are needed:
> > they must be fit for it;
> > they must not do too much of it; and
> > they must have a sense of success in it
> – not a doubtful sense, such as needs some
> testimony of others for its confirmation, but a sure
> sense, or rather knowledge, that so much work has
> been done well, and fruitfully done, whatever the
> world may say or think about it.
> *W. H. Auden*   [24]

As you are writing up new text you are likely to be strongly
influenced, consciously or subconsciously, by ideas about how
your readership or audience might respond to what you are
saying. Normally these are constructive influences, for instance,
if you think seriously about how to represent ideas to readers,
or use the 'need to know' criterion to set an appropriate level of
detail for your argument. Anticipating how professional readers
will interpret your text is also a vital element in composing raw
prose and then editing it into a more acceptable form. But it is
also possible for this thinking ahead to become overdone and
disabling, creating a 'writer's block' syndrome where authors
are so constrained by their readership's anticipated reactions
that they have difficulty getting any text up on screen at all, or
showing what text they have got to other people. The good
news is that this problem is strongly linked to previous success
or anxiety about your reputation. So perhaps it more commonly afflicts established authors in middle age trying to repeat
earlier successes than it does young people just starting out.

But the off-putting and obsessional character of the doctorate in general, especially when a 'big book' thesis is involved, probably more than makes up for this age-protection effect.

> Trouble has no necessary connection with discouragement – discouragement has a germ of its own, as different from trouble as arthritis is from a stiff joint.
> *F. Scott Fitzgerald* [25]

> Some people misinterpret what writer's block is. They assume you can't think of a single thing. Not true. You can think of hundreds of things. You just don't like any of them.
> *Neil Simon* [26]

Part of the positive help that comes from exposing your text to a fairly wide range of commentators, from family or partners to supervisors, fellow students and wider seminar audiences, is that it can help counteract the development of disabling private standards of criticism. Going out into the professional world at conferences is also generally encouraging for PhD students, since it tends to show you that standards there cover quite a broad range. Doctoral researchers normally cannot match the sweep of large-scale confirmatory research projects or the thematic ambition of major authors. But in terms of doing well-based and consistently-pursued research many PhD students can match or outclass most academics doing conference papers. The important thing is to have a realistic image of your likely professional audience, one that encourages you to 'see what may be thought against your thought' in Nietzsche's terms (from the epigraph to this chapter) without paralysing you from composing, developing and upgrading your text.

Conclusions

> To learn from experience is to make backward and forward connections between what we do to things and what we enjoy or suffer from things in

> consequence. Under such conditions, doing
> becomes a trying, an experiment with the world to
> find out what it is like; the undergoing becomes
> instructions – discovery of the connections of
> things.
> John Dewey   [27]

At whatever level you choose to look, producing effective text is a very iterative experience. Once you formulate an overall architecture for the thesis, it is important to keep it updated as your planned research activities work out in practice. At the micro-level you need to consider alternative ways of structuring or sequencing materials, comparing your status quo arrangement with a viable and well-specified alternative. At the detailed sentence level, you need space and distance in order to be able to spot what can be improved in your writing. Running through all these aspects is the common thread of considering how your text will be read. How will it be deconstructed? What intended or inadvertent messages will you communicate? In its current form does this sentence/this paragraph/this chapter positively build the thesis? It can help your confidence to keep in mind that producing an integrated professional text is a multi-stage process, and that a lot will change as you progress raw text towards an effective finished form. And remember too that completing the thesis as a whole is a further key stage for making improvements in your final text, a phase which I discuss in detail in Chapter 8. Before then, however, I focus in the next chapter on some important non-text elements of many theses – charts, tables and diagrams.

7

Handling Attention Points: Data, Charts and Graphics

> Standards of what counts as good presentation in
> reports are not static. They increase over time,
> reflecting changing information technology
> capabilities and practices in other large
> organizations. ... Effective graphics and
> presentation of data require close attention to
> detail and zero tolerance of defects.
> *UK National Audit Office*   [1]

When readers first scan your text they will pay disproportionate attention to any organizers and summaries they
encounter, but also to visually distinctive 'attention points'
which stand out from the main text – especially tables, charts,
diagrams, maps, photographs and text boxes. At this 'eye-balling'
stage readers will often try to make sense of each attention point
on its own, without reading closely the accompanying text, since
they are trying to decide whether to focus down for serious study,
and where. If data presentation is important to your thesis, or
other elements play a key role in the exposition (for instance, diagrams in a theoretical argument or photographs in project
work), then how you handle attention points will strongly
influence readers' views of the professionalism of your approach.
Even if attention points are few and far between in your text,
PhD examiners and subsequent readers (such as journal editors
and reviewers) will expect them to be competently delivered.
Later, too, you will go to conferences, and have only 15 or
20 minutes to give an oral presentation, or possibly secure only

a poster session in a crowded conference venue. On these occasions people focus a lot of attention on your presentation slides or other exhibits. Usually these slides will either be versions of your existing attention points or designed on similar principles.

Yet the prevailing academic standards for handling attention points (especially numeric data and tables) are normally poor, and can often be appalling, creating unnecessary aggravation for readers and audiences. The rock group Radiohead famously called on the 'Karma police' to arrest someone who 'speaks in maths' and hence 'buzzes like a fridge ... like a de-tuned radio'.[2] And it is a cliché of the conference circuit that business speakers will always illustrate their talks with well-designed, legible and visually attractive computer presentation slides. However, university speakers will instead routinely put up undesigned, text-heavy overhead projector slides crowded with impenetrable text or littered with dozens of complex numbers (like regression coefficients to three decimal places), printed in a small, almost invisible font. Sometimes an academic presenting data says deprecatingly: 'I don't know if everyone at the back can read this, but what this number shows ...', pointing to a smudge of microscopic typescript in the midst of column after column and row after row of visually identical and completely unreadable smudges. Similarly in the social sciences, academic journals are often stuffed with tables full of jumbled, overdetailed and mostly irrelevant data, which their authors have barely analysed. These pathologically poor communication behaviours are amusing at one level, of a piece with the academic novels that mercilessly dissect contemporary university life. But endlessly repeated they are just about as destructive for the external reputation of academia, cementing ever more firmly an image of a professional group which does not even have the basic courtesy to communicate its ideas intelligently and accessibly.

Since poor presentation is so endemic, developing a more consistent approach to handling attention points involves convincing people that there are sound intellectual reasons for making more of an effort. I begin with a little 'back to basics' excursus, looking at the first principles of authoring and how they apply in this area. After that, I examine in turn some key issues in handling tables, and then figures or charts, and finally other forms of attention points like diagrams.

At this point two groups of readers may be wondering about skipping ahead to the next chapter, but they should perhaps reconsider. The first are people who are confident that their thesis will not include any attention points at all, because it has no data in it. They plan to write their whole dissertation in straight-text mode, that is, page after page of word after word. If you are in this category you should certainly skip the second and third sections below (covering tables and charts). But it could be worthwhile your looking through the first and last sections of this chapter, because when you do presentations to conferences or seminars you will normally have to distil a lot of text into a small compass. Perhaps you plan to read out the entire text of your paper, a practice still traditional or even expected in university seminars amongst philosophers and a few other groups. But in most of the humanities and all the social sciences disciplines it will be seen as professionally unacceptable behaviour. And at most academic conferences the time allowances for speakers are much too short to let you read a whole paper. So how are you going to achieve a compressed form of your message? And what visual guidelines will you provide the audience with to keep them in touch with your thought?

The second group of readers who may feel that they can skip ahead are those who routinely work with large amounts of data and believe that they have nothing more to learn about how to analyse or present numbers, charts etc. In fact this chapter is entirely relevant for your needs. It will not tell you anything new about generating data. Instead the focus is on *reducing* data and communicating it more effectively, rather than throwing an unprocessed mass of information at readers. The techniques discussed here are simple and straightforward to implement. They are not esoteric in any way. But they are very commonly ignored by data-junkie PhD students and their supervisors.

Principles for presenting data well

The essential principle vital for selecting and presenting all forms of detailed evidence effectively is the 'need to know' criterion. Ask first: 'What will my readers need to see or need to know in order to accept the conclusions of my analysis?' Then set out to provide information that meets exactly these needs, no more and no less. If different types of readers have strongly divergent needs then you need to segment them, handling one group's demands in one place and another group's needs elsewhere. For instance, most non-specialist people aiming for a straight-through read of your text may need to see only strategically important information provided in the main text. At the same time, readers particularly interested in professionally checking or evaluating your analysis (like your PhD examiners) may want to see detailed appendices giving chapter and verse to back up the main text exhibits. Finally an even smaller group of readers may want to replicate your analysis in detail, or use some of your basic evidence in different analyses of their own. For this small group it may be appropriate to provide full documentation of all your evidence and source information.

In theses with a lot of data and numerical information, segmenting your readers in this way means providing in the main text fairly accessible charts and tables, and only summaries of your detailed analysis results. Then your Research Methods Appendix can explain in detail the methods and techniques used in your analyses, and a data annex could include full print-outs of the results. Finally you could provide all your data sources in full on a CD bound into the back cover, for anyone keen to replicate your analyses. In theses without numerical data but with a great deal of documentation analysis or interview material lying behind the main text then a similar approach could prevail. The main chapters might include either multiple short quotations run on as normal text, or longer extracts handled as indented quotes or in text boxes. (Boxes are an increasing trend given the enhanced capabilities of modern word processors.) These selective citations can be backed up by full extracts from documents or transcripts of interviews included in appendices or on an accompanying CD. The 'need to know' criterion sets out what should be included in the main text, what should be placed in annexes or appendices, and what need go only on the back-up CD for reference. It is important for your thesis that incongruous elements are not introduced into the main text, like huge tables printed 'for the record' or overly long interview quotations which disrupt the flow and development of your argument.

The 'need to know' criterion should also play a key role in helping you decide what level of reportage is appropriate, the right degree of detail. Suppose that I want to quote a UK labour market number at one point, and official sources give the number of unemployed people as 1,215,689. The usual academic procedure would be to just quote this number in full, unmodified in any way. But a number of issues arise. Do readers really need to know this exact number? Do they care whether the number is exact to the nearest one person, or the nearest ten, or the nearest hundred or thousand? In the context of your argument would they lose any significant information if the number was expressed as 1.21 million unemployed, or even 1.2 million?

Some university people will immediately bristle here at the idea that as authors they should fillet out or reduce the level of detail conveyed by their text. Their view might be that it is not their job to 'pander' to lazy readers, or to make things easy for people. In the social sciences, some critics suggest that there are many academics who suffer from 'physics envy', a desire to ape practices in the physical sciences in pursuit of enhanced academic prestige. Whatever the truth of such claims, there are certainly many people who seem to regard the citation of complex numbers and multiple decimal points as essential talismans of systematic scientific endeavour. Not for them the production of 'easy' text, but instead an emphasis on precise accuracy in reportage at all times. But consider for a moment the 'scientific' implications of reporting 1,215,689 unemployed people. Including such a precise number in your text suggests that you believe the accuracy of government counting systems is plus or minus 1. Quoting this number in full also means that you are confident the real figure is not 1,215,685 or 1,215,691 people, but exactly 1,215,689. In fact it is highly unlikely that the official statistics are that accurate. A genuinely scientific approach would be to report information only correct to the number of digits where we can have reasonable confidence in the data.

Worse examples of completely bogus 'scientism' in the handling of many numbers occur in many PhD theses. It is common to see students making elementary mistakes like the following. Suppose that in a national survey of 1021 respondents, 579 people report that they have tried surfing the

Internet. A very naïve analyst will compute (579 ∗ 100)/1021 and report that 56.71 per cent of respondents have tried Web surfing. But in a national sample survey of this minimal size the standard error in sampling the population will often be + or −3 per cent. So reporting the surfing number as 57 per cent of respondents would be reasonable, but would mean only that there was a 95 per cent probability that the actual rate of surfing in the whole population sampled was between 54 and 60 per cent. Someone writing 56.71 per cent into their text is not being any more scientific. Instead they simply reveal that they have not the least idea of the accuracy level of the basic data which they are handling.

The 'need to know' criterion can also help in determining what *kinds* of attention points are needed or are most appropriate at different points. A simple and unobtrusive way to drastically cut the complexity of numerical data for readers is to picture them in charts and graphs instead of providing them in tables. In an appropriately scaled chart showing how the number of unemployed people has moved over time, an original data figure of 1,215,689 may effectively show up for readers as 'somewhat more than a million'. If that is an appropriate level of information for readers to have then you can deliver a lot more data much more accessibly by using a chart. A picture here can certainly be worth more than 1000 numbers in the cells of a table.

Somewhat less obviously, the 'need to know' criterion can also help you choose between giving a text-only explanation of a theoretical argument or condensing some of the conceptual relationships involved into a diagram. Using a diagram lets you exploit the two-dimensional space of the page to locate multiple concepts against each other. And employing a recognized set of diagrammatic conventions (such as the square boxes, circles and arrows in flow charts) can let you capture different relationships very synoptically. If you are describing a complex pattern of causation or interaction then offering readers a diagrammatic view will help make things clearer and more accessible for most people. However, remember that some readers may tend to skip diagrams, so always provide an intuitive text explanation as well. Where the concepts involved are fewer and the relationships between them are simpler, diagrams may have little value-added, and if they are included readers may find them disappointing.

The 'need to know' criterion also implies that all tables, charts, graphs and diagrams should be independently intelligible so far as is possible, in order to help skim readers make intelligent evaluations, and to aid readers who are referred back to the exhibit from elsewhere. In addition:

◆ All exhibits will need a unique number derived from a consistent system including the chapter number first and then sequence numbers. The normal approach is that tables, charts and photographs are numbered in separate sequences (for instance, Table 4.1 and Figure 4.2), as I have done here. Some authors prefer to label both tables and charts in a single sequence of figures. Diagrams need to be included with charts in the figures tally. And if photographs are integral to your thesis exposition they should also be incorporated. A few text boxes may not need to be numbered in their own sequence. But if they are extensive, cross-referred to a lot from different locations, or play a large part in the exposition, they may be numbered in their own sequence. In the social sciences separate numbering is common where a chapter uses a lot of case studies or case examples.

◆ Alongside their number, all attention points should have a clear overall heading or caption which accurately describes exactly what is being shown.

◆ Full subsidiary labels are also needed inside the exhibit – for instance, labels for horizontal and vertical axes in charts and graphs, and clear labels for rows, columns and cell contents in tables. Labels must spell out precisely what is being shown, for instance, making clear what units of measurement are being employed without any ambiguities or vagueness. It is best to avoid abbreviations if possible.

◆ All charts should have keys showing what their different types of lines, shadings or colours mean. These keys are called 'legends' in spreadsheet programmes. Legend labels should also include full details of the measurement units used where appropriate, or any other aspect that readers need to know.

- Very brief details of the sources for data are normally useful. They are given in a special source note immediately under tables and charts, along with any very short methods notes that would assist readers' interpretation of the attention point as a whole – for instance, brief essential information about how composite variables are defined or on how indices have been computed. By contrast, purely referencing material, small details or extensive methods descriptions should all be handled in endnotes to the chapter in the normal way wherever possible, to avoid cluttering up the bottoms of tables or figures with long messy-looking addenda.
- Many business reports include a short explanatory comment at the top of tables or charts. It can be placed just underneath the heading (often in a contrast colour and smaller font) and should sum up in one or two lines the exhibit's key message. This practice is still rare in academic circles but it is one well worth copying, because it can greatly assist readers' interpretation of what is shown.

A subsidiary principle for effective attention points is total quality control. There are often good reasons for *not* loading graphics especially, but also tables held on spreadsheets, into your main text files. Although modern word processors can easily accommodate these elements, including them tends to create very large files that are harder to save on diskettes and to send via e-mail. So especially at draft stages most authors still hold these elements in separate files. But then 'version control' problems can arise when the text is remodelled and revised, while the attention points held in separate files are not similarly updated. It is important to ensure that your main text and accompanying attention points are always reviewed and revised together, so that they stay in sync even in small ways. For instance, how a graph is labelled must agree completely with the description of the graph in the accompanying main text.

Total quality control should also reflect the changing expectations that examiners and other readers now have about how tables, charts and diagrams should be done. As in other areas, advances in information technology have had ambiguous effects. On the one hand, it is now easier to make sure that exhibits are always properly handled with an appropriate soft-ware package – either a sophisticated word processor, or a spreadsheet or a presentations package. And it is now much quicker to produce a given output of satisfactory appearance. On the other hand, because examiners and readers are aware of the reduced effort-level involved, their standards of what counts as a professionally presented exhibit have also upgraded over time.

Handling tables

> Statistics is the plural of anecdote.
> *Daniel P. Moynihan* [2]

Tables communicate precise numerical information to readers. They have traditionally been heavily used in any PhD with an extensive numerical data component. Designing effective tables is not rocket science. But it is frequently mishandled for the most trivial and banal of reasons, through a series of small-scale inattentions by authors to the needs of readers. Authors with data-heavy dissertations live and breathe their numbers, and come to know them closely. So they often tolerate a level of detail or confusion in their data presentation which readers cannot and will not bear. Consider Tables 7.1 and 7.2, which show the same table presented in different formats. I hope that it is obvious to you that Table 7.2 is a much better presented table. But why it is so much more readable may not be so clear. Here are the main differences.

Titles and labelling. Table 7.1 has an overly short heading which says only what kinds of organizations are being com-pared, but does not give the country location, the time period, or what is being measured. The title is in the present tense, which will go out of date. The first column is not labelled at all, and the second column label uses pointless abbreviation (to fit text into a spreadsheet column space) and omits any denomi-nator for the population. Readers would have to look in the main text to be sure what the table showed. None of the head-ings and labels use a distinctive font from the rest of the table. Some of the row labels are printed on two lines, despite lots of

Table 7.1   How health boards compare

	Trtmnt rates/pop
Argyll & Clyde	33212.42
Ayrshire & Arran	33200.32
Border	72331.01[1]
Dumfries & Galloway	31699.21
Fife	22876.55
Forth Valley	29748.33
Grampian	27681.49
Greater Glasgow	31827.22[2]
Highland	33855.18
Lanarkshire	23909.83
Lothian	31768.41
Orkney	21727.37
Shetland	28233.25
Tayside	50259.21
Western Isles	30840.19

[1] Includes Berwick in 1997–98 only.

[2] Estimates only due to data problems.

space (perhaps because they were transferred in that form from a spreadsheet), which gives the row numbers an uneven appearance. By contrast, Table 7.2 has full and complete labels, in clear fonts, which give all the missing information, and avoid unnecessary abbreviation. Even the row labels are tidied up, eliminating the ugly ampersand signs (&), which are not needed, and printing each label within a single row.

Decimal points, index numbers and details in the data numbers. Table 7.1 does not tell readers exactly what measurement units are being used: in fact they are the numbers of eye cataract operations per 1000 population. This gives large numbers, stretching from 21,727 at the low end to 72,331 at the high end. They are made less readable by not putting in commas to separate the thousands, and also by citing the numbers correct to two decimal points. Given the data range in Table 7.1, including any decimal points at all is a ludicrous level of detail: no reader would conceivably need to know this, so the decimal points are just clutter, obfuscating whatever the table's message is supposed to be. By contrast, Table 7.2 eliminates all decimal points and goes further by rebasing the index number to cataract operations per 100,000 people. Most readers will find it

Table 7.2   How Scotland's health boards compared in treating cataracts, 1998–9 financial year

Health boards	Treatment rates per 100,000 people	
Border	723	*Upper outlier*
Tayside	503	*Upper outlier*
Highland	339	
Ayrshire and Arran	332	*Upper quartile*
Argyll and Clyde	332	
Lothian	318	
Greater Glasgow	318	
Dumfries and Galloway	317	*Median*
Western Isles	308	
Forth Valley	297	
Shetland	282	
Grampian	277	*Lower quartile*
Lanarkshire	239	
Fife	229	
Orkney	217	
Mean treatment rate	335	

Notes: The range is 506; midspread (dQ) is 55. Two upper outliers, no lower outliers.

Source: National Audit Office, 1999.[4]

more difficult to handle very large numbers (above 1000), and very small numbers (such as smaller fractions of 1, like 0.0032 or 0.00156). Wherever possible it is best to try and rebase index numbers to run from 0 to 100, the number range that all readers are most comfortable operating with. In this case, however, such an effort would mean rebasing to cataract treatments per 1,000,000 people and would have two drawbacks. First, decimal points would be needed to differentiate some observations from each other. And second, this measurement unit could be rather misleading, suggesting to readers that the Scottish health boards being covered actually *have* populations in the millions, whereas none of them do. So here rebasing on cataract treatments per 100,000 population delivers tractable numbers running from 217 up to 723. It also makes visible the differences between observations, but without any clutter of decimal points.

The principles here can easily be extended to any kind of data numbers. Express very large figures in units of hundreds of millions, or millions or thousands as appropriate. And multiply very small ratio numbers to get rid of fractions of 1 and the need for several decimal points. You can also go a long way by rounding numbers up or down (so that 10.51 becomes 11 for instance, while 10.49 becomes 10). Or you can just cut numbers by eliminating all decimal points (which would mean that both 10.51 and 10.49 are expressed as 10). Some people find it helpful to design tables using as a rule of thumb that there should never be more than three 'effective' digits in any cell, and hence no more than 3 numbers vary from one cell to another. On this rule you might enter 1,215,689 in a table either as 1.22 million, or as 1,220,000 (that is, rounding to the nearest 10,000). If you went to four effective digits the same number would be 1,216,000 (rounding to the nearest 1000). In any table showing such large numbers rounding to the nearest 100 is almost always sensible in cutting away pointless detail, and often to the nearest 1000. This is especially appropriate where numbers are being analysed in main text tables, but the same data are also included in a reference annex or a data CD. Here there is no need to overburden the main text tables simply in order to read a precise number into the record.

Numerical progression. The sequence of rows in Table 7.1 is set alphabetically, so that the data in the second column are completely jumbled, with one number succeeding another in a completely unpredictable way. Readers will find the table very hard to follow, and must fend for themselves in trying to work out the central level of the data or which health board is doing well or badly. By contrast Table 7.2 reorders the rows to give a clear downward numerical progression. Health boards' performances here are visible at a glance, with strongly performing boards at the top of the table and weakly performing ones at the bottom.

Never keep data arranged in alphabetical ordering of rows or some other customary order if this obscures the numerical progression in the table. Some authors argue against this advice because they want to present data for cases or other units in the same standard sequence from one table to another. Most of the

time, though, this strategy helps the author, who is very familiar with the data's complexities, but actually only confuses
readers by creating badly jumbled numbers in the tables.
Always apply the 'need to know' criterion rigorously before
accepting any deviation from numerical progression. A numerical progression is desirable in *all* tables, with only two clear
exceptions: those showing over-time data, and those covering
categorical data which have to be kept in fixed order to be
meaningful (for example, survey response options on a scale
like 'agree strongly/somewhat agree/somewhat disagree/
strongly disagree'). Other departures from numerical progression are only very occasionally justified. There might be one or
two cases where readers need to make comparisons across a
small set of easy-to-read tables, and where they would be helped
slightly more by having a standard row sequence across tables,
rather than being given a clear pattern in each table's data.

In the case of larger tables with multiple columns, achieving
numerical progression is a little trickier. You need to determine
which is the most important column and rearrange the rows so
as to get a numerical progression on that column. Make sure
that the progression column is visible by placing it first (closest
to the row labels) or last (where it will stand out as the salient
column). If you can, try to achieve a numerical progression not
just down the rows but also *across columns* in the table, either
ascending (smallest data numbers in the first column and
largest in the last) or descending (largest data numbers in the
first column and smallest in the last). Here you reorder both the
sequence of rows and the sequence of columns to maximize
a table's readability.[5]

Statistics for central level and spread. Table 7.1 provides no
help for readers at all here, but Table 7.2 gives two different
'averages', the arithmetic mean, and the median, the observation coming in the middle or half-way through the data set as
a whole. It also shows the upper and lower quartiles, where the
top quarter and the bottom quarter of the data begin. Readers
can hence see the position of the middle mass, the middle
50 per cent of observations lying on or within the two quartiles.
The data shown here clearly straggle upwards at the top, which
explains why the mean is so much higher than the median,

because it is distorted by the top two scores. The table's notes give the range (the variation between the highest and lowest scores) and the midspread (the variation between the quartiles). They also confirm that the top two observations are upper outliers (that is, they lie more than 1.5 times the midspread above the upper quartile), and hence are highly unusual.

Layout. Table 7.1 is made hard to read by being overly spaced out across the page. Many students (and some journal and book publishers) still seem to believe that every table should use the full width of the page, no matter how few columns it has. The effect is always that the row numbers are put further away from their labels than is necessary, an impact intensified here by not using boxing or shading inside the table and by having the row numbers in column 2 spaced unevenly because some of the row labels use two lines. In addition the table uses a smaller font than surrounding text even though there is plenty of space on the page. It includes small superscript note numbers inside the table cells, which cloud the second column. And a succession of note numbers also clutters up the bottom of the table with unnecessary details. There is no clear finish to the table at the bottom and no source is given. By contrast Table 7.2 uses minimum-width columns without overspacing, bringing row numbers and labels into closer proximity. Within the available space, always use the largest possible font size for tables, up to a maximum set by the main text font, as here. With large tables use a whole page in landscape layout to keep table fonts readable. And as here, you should box the rows and columns (which usually helps readers). The median and quartiles are highlighted in Table 7.2 with light background grayscale shading (you could also use yellow or very pale shades of other colours with a colour printer). The design is uncluttered by note numbers within the table or other distractions. If some form of reference detailing needs to be given that is not essential to understanding the table, it is best handled by using an endnote in the main text accompanying the table. Table 7.2 uses a line under the notes and sources to achieve a clear finish to the table.

All these differences in Table 7.2 from Table 7.1 are generally applicable to every table you have to design. Just to recap, the most important principles are:

◆ Always have completely informative headings and labelling, including full details of units or measurement and what the cell contents show.
◆ Use the 'need to know' criterion to pick an appropriate level of detail for numbers. Choose the minimum number of decimal points needed. If you make use of index numbers or ratios, choose levels which give the most easily understandable numbers for readers. Consider how many 'effective digits' are needed, and use rounding or number simplification appropriately.
◆ Design all tables to show a numerical progression (*except* for tables showing over-time trends or categorical variables with a fixed order).

The final issue to consider about tables is whether you really need them at all. Would it be better to use a chart or graph instead of a table? In most cases charts will be better because they are clearer and more visual. Tables should principally be retained for the following circumstances:

– There are only a small amount of data to present, so that a simplifying chart is unnecessary.
– Readers need to know numerical values more precisely than would be shown in a chart, for instance if there are fairly small variations in results.
– The data to be displayed have very strong variation between the lowest and highest numbers so that it would be difficult to display the range of the data effectively in a chart. For instance, isolated high numbers for one or a few years in an over-time chart might necessitate a scale which would mean that readers could not detect any visible differences in other years' figures, whereas in a table they could still be seen.
– You want to compare data scaled in very different kinds of units or indices, and they could not easily be accommodated on one chart. Alternatively you might have the numbers in different columns which are of the same kind, but of such different sizes that they would be hard to scale together on a graph. Here tables can save space, since otherwise you

would have to provide a series of different charts for each column of numbers being covered.

- You want to both present some primary data numbers, and then show calculations of how index numbers or ratios or compound statistics are derived from them.
- Tables are being used to put reference material onto the record, for instance in Annexes or Appendices.

Designing charts and graphs

We live in a graphical age. In general if it is possible to display data in chart form rather than in tables it is desirable to do so, subject only to the exceptions enumerated just above. Charts and graphs automatically screen out too much data being thrown at readers. They are easier for you to analyse correctly as an author, and for readers to interpret. Charts are especially important in showing the relative importance of different components or phenomena; giving trends over time and rates of growth; and illustrating more complex patterns in data than just linear relationships, such as 'curvey' relationships. There are now many different types of chart for displaying simple data available on spreadsheet packages (like Excel or Lotus) and widely used data-analysis programmes (like *SPSS* or *Stata*). Both PhD students and established academics often make mistakes about choosing the right kind of graphic to go with their data. Figure 7.1 shows eight of the most commonly used charts and for each of them points out a few uses for which they are well or poorly adapted.

As with tables it can be useful to briefly compare a poorly designed and a well-designed chart version of the same data tables discussed in the previous section. Figure 7.2 (on p. 182) is a vertical bar chart version of the table in Table 7.1; and Figure 7.3 (on p. 183) is a horizontal bar chart version of the table in Table 7.2. The differences in the accessibility of the two bar charts are every bit as noticeable as in the readability of the two tables, and again it is worth briefly itemizing why.

Labelling.   Figure 7.2 has a very poor heading and axis labels compared with Figure 7.3. The choice of a vertical bar design for Figure 7.2 means that there is no space for the health board

Figure 7.1   Eight main types of chart (and when to use them)

(a)   *Vertical bar chart*

A (hypothetical) index of US potato production, 1997–2003

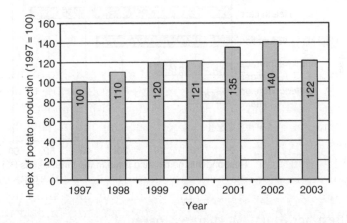

Use a vertical bar chart when:
– you have simple over-time data that are not really
  continuous, but cover discrete time-periods;
– you have other appropriate comparative data where
  the labels for each bar are short enough to fit
  underneath it.

Don't use vertical bar charts if:
– the bars in the chart have long data labels, especially
  not where you would need to use numbers or a key for
  labels to fit anything in the column labels.

Points to watch:
– put numbers inside columns, not on top of them;
– if data is not chronological or in categories with a
  fixed order, aim to achieve a numerical progression.

(b) *Horizontal bar chart*

British voters' views of the most important political issues, September 2001 (hypothetical)

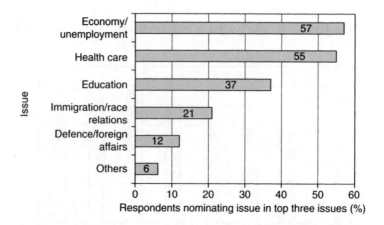

Respondents nominating issue in top three issues (%)

Use a horizontal bar chart whenever:
– you have comparative data where the labels for each bar are too long to fit underneath columns easily.

Don't use horizontal bar charts if:
– readers will expect to see columns (e.g. for over-time data).

Points to watch:
– put numbers inside columns, not outside their right-end;
– aim to achieve a numerical progression in almost all cases (unless data is in categories with a fixed order or is chronological).

(c) *Pie chart*

The main sources of finance for major consumer purchases in Europe, 2001 (hypothetical)

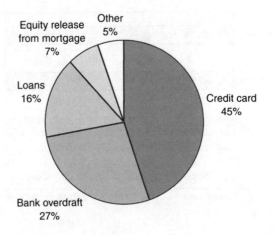

Use a pie chart whenever:
– you want to show the shares of something or percentages.

Don't use a pie chart if:
– data is over-time or more complex.

Points to watch:
– put the pie slices into a descending numerical progression (unless data is in categories with a fixed order or is chronological);
– start with the largest pie slice at the top, and arrange slices in declining order going clockwise;
– label each slice and show the percentage share as a number inside or outside it.

(d) *Percentage component chart*

How consumers in three countries financed major consumer purchases, 2001 (hypothetical)

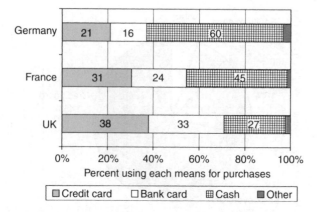

Use a percentage component chart whenever:
– you want to show how the shares of something or percentages vary across a number of different cases or areas.

Don't use percentage component charts if:
– the data is over-time or more complex;
– you have only one case (use a pie chart).

Points to watch:
– put the bars into an order that gives the clearest numerical progression you can achieve (unless the data is in categories with a fixed order or is chronological);
– avoid sequences which give a jumbled appearance – unless a pattern is visible don't use this type of chart;
– show the percentage shares as a number inside the bar components (at least for large components);
– use clearly distinct shadings and labels for components.

(e) *Grouped bar chart*

**Changing patterns of electronics appliances
purchases, UK 1994 to 2002 (hypothetical)**

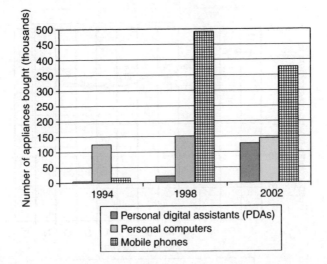

Use a grouped bar chart whenever:
– you want to show how the levels of several indices
   vary across a number of different cases or areas or time
   periods.

Don't use grouped bar charts if:
– the data are really shares of something (normally
   better to use a percentage component chart).

Points to watch:
– put the bars for each unit into an order that gives the
   clearest pattern across the cases (ideally a numerical
   progression within each case);
– use clearly distinct shadings and provide labels for
   each bar.

(f) *Line graph*

Proportion of the UK survey respondents seeing their governments as doing a good job in 2001 (hypothetical)

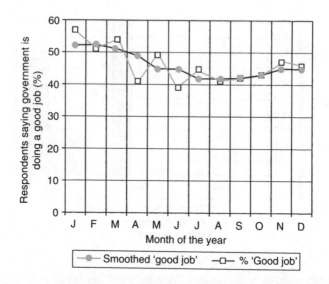

Use a line graph chart whenever:
– you have continuous over-time data.

Don't use line graph charts if:
– the data are over-time but are not really continuous;
– you have very few observations: in both these cases use a vertical bar chart.

Points to watch:
– if you have more than one line, make sure that they are each visible.

(g) *Layer chart*

Proportion of UK survey respondents rating the performance of the railways as 'very good' or 'fairly good', 2001 (hypothetical)

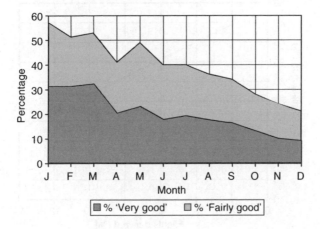

Use a layer chart whenever:
– you want to show how the relative size of two positively associated variables varies across time.

Don't use a layer chart if:
– your two variables are not really linked.

Points to watch:
– put the layers in an order that gives the clearest visible pattern, e.g. a numerical progression with the largest layer at the bottom and smaller layers towards the top;
– if the variables have to be kept in a fixed sequence but this gives a jumbled appearance to the layers, then use another type of chart.

(h)   *Scatterplot or 'X and Y' graph*

The relationship between flight delays and customer satisfaction levels, airports in USA 2000 (hypothetical)

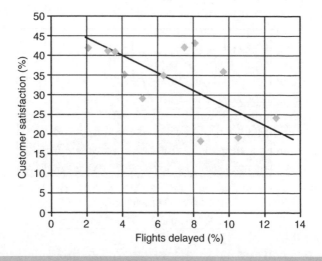

Use an 'X and Y' chart or scatterplot whenever:
– you want to show how the level of a dependent variable (shown on the vertical Y axis) varies depending on the level of an independent variable (shown on the horizontal X axis).

Don't use an 'X and Y' chart if:
– the two variables are not meaningfully associated or you are not positing a causal link from the X variable to the Y variable.

Points to watch:
– make sure that the variables are the right way round: the dependent (= influenced) variable must always be on the Y axis, and the causing or influencing variable on the X axis, or otherwise readers will be deeply confused;
– adding a regression line (or line of 'best fit') will help readers see the nature of the association more clearly. This line is the one which minimizes the *vertical* distances from the line of the data points above and below the line.

names on the horizontal axis, and so a separate key is needed to show which number denotes which board. Where bar labels are lengthy, always choose a horizontal bar design, like that shown in Figure 7.3 where the health board names are easily accommodated. Aim to use a fully informative label wherever possible, with minimum abbreviation. This approach follows the one-stop look-up principle discussed earlier in connection with referencing systems.

Numerical progression. In Figure 7.2 the bar chart format cuts out the mass of details in Table 7.1. But even so without any pattern across the bars, the chart in Figure 7.2 is a jumble of data. By contrast Figure 7.3 reorders the bars in a descending sequence, showing completely clear results. The median and the two quartile bars are also indicated, which would not be feasible without a numerical progression. In all charts (except those showing over-time patterns or categories where the sequence of values is fixed) achieving a numerical progression is just as vital as for tables.

Showing specific numbers. In Figure 7.2 the choice of a narrow vertical bar layout and the use of an index of cataract operations per 1000 population with very large data numbers makes it impossible to show any numbers for the bars. By using a horizontal bar layout, and an index showing cataract operations per 100,000 people, which generates simpler numbers, Figure 7.3 can give precise numbers for all observations. Note that these numbers are included *within* the bar space. Avoid adding numbers above the bar area with vertical bar charts, or to the right of the bars in horizontal bar charts, because in both these cases the number will detract from the proper visual scale of the bars. Although Figure 7.3 has an appropriate number of gridlines and tick points for readers to be able to scale the bars, including the numbers removes any difficulty in readers having to estimate what the individual scores are.

Scaling and grid lines decisions are often messed up. The two figures here are both scaled fairly well, but the vertical scale in Figure 7.2 could have been greater to allow more variation amongst the small scores to be seen. With more extreme ranges in the variation of data it is common to see charts where the vertical scale for the bars has been set automatically by the spreadsheet. This may highlight unusually high or low observations, but at the price of making almost invisible patterns in the

Figure 7.2   How health boards compare

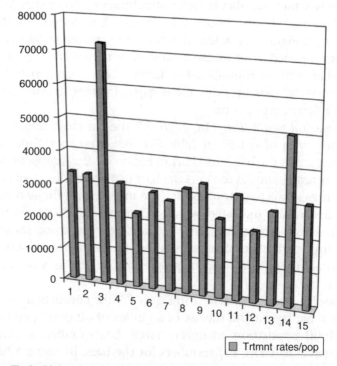

Key: The health boards are as follows: 1 Argyll & Clyde; 2 Ayrshire & Arran; 3 Border;
4 Dumfries & Galloway; 5 Fife; 6 Forth Valley; 7 Grampian; 8 Greater Glasgow; 9 Highland;
10 Lanarkshire; 11 Lothian; 12 Orkney; 13 Shetland; 14 Tayside; 15 Western Isles.

variations of most of the other scores. Try to use zero wherever
feasible as the scale starting-point for a graph. Where you must
choose a starting-point different from zero (called 'suppressing
the zero'), always indicate that you have done so, usually by
inserting a zigzag bit at the lower end of the relevant scale line,
or including a note to remind readers. It is also common to see
far too many gridlines and tick points being used on the vertical
or horizontal scales, which can make charts look cluttered.

  Two- or three-dimensional charts.   Figure 7.2 is made more
complex to read by the choice of a three-dimensional format,
with a 'depth' axis added by the spreadsheet. Many PhD students choose 3D charts, thinking that they will look more
sophisticated but not focusing clearly on what extra value-
added the extra dimension gives (which is very little with only
one data series, as here). Where several data series are shown
together, adding the third dimension is potentially more useful,

Figure 7.3 How Scotland's health boards compared in treating cataracts, 1998–9 financial year

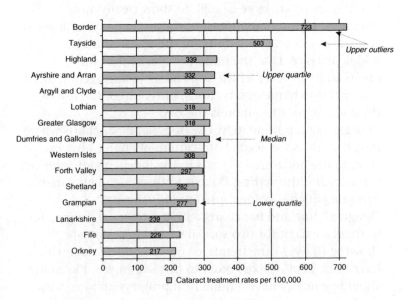

Cataract treatment rates per 100,000

but it will sometimes obscure blocs of data where several indices are shown together, unless they are very well designed. New users of 3D charts also may not realize that it is often tricky to achieve a consistent angle, orientation and appearance across a succession of 3D charts, making them harder for readers to interpret. This is also a key reason why journals and book publishers are less keen on them. By contrast Figure 7.3 uses a simpler two-dimensional (flat) format, which is much easier and quicker to design and implement in a consistent fashion. It is preferred by most journals and academic publishers, and is straightforward for readers to interpret.

All these differences between Figures 7.2 and 7.3 are generally applicable to every chart you have to design. The most important principles are:

◆ Always have completely informative headings and labelling, including details of units of measurement. Appropriate labels and scales must be shown for both horizontal and vertical axes, and legend labels are needed wherever the chart includes multiple data series (shown in several lines, bars or shadings).

◆ Use the 'need to know' criterion to pick an appropriate level for numbers, so that the chart can be easily scaled. Make sure that the charts are large enough to show clearly any important features mentioned in the accompanying analysis.

◆ Scale charts so that variations are still apparent in the middle mass of data (the middle 50 per cent of the observations). Never let the scale be set just to accommodate one or two extreme observations, untypical of the rest of the data. Try not to suppress the zero.

◆ Allocate axes appropriately. Use horizontal bar charts where long bar labels are needed. In scatterplot charts, always allocate the horizontal (X) axis to the independent (causing) variable, and the vertical (Y) axis to the dependent variable (the one which is being caused or influenced).

◆ Design all line and bar charts with a numerical progression in them – except for two special cases where you are showing (i) over-time trends, or (ii) categorical data which have to be kept in fixed order to be meaningful. Pie charts should generally have a numerical progression also, with the largest pie starting at the upper vertical and the wedge going right and downwards, followed by the second largest wedge, then the third largest, and so on, all going clockwise. The only exception here is a pie chart showing fixed-order categorical data. (Of course, you should never use pie charts to show over-time data.)

Overall, the most important test for charts and graphs is to try and ensure that each of them is independently intelligible to readers who have not lived with the data for months or years, as you will have done by the time that the thesis is printed and bound. Again make sure that your charts are revised and updated with your main text as it changes. Far more often than tables, charts tend to be held on spreadsheet and presentation packages, separate from your word-processed main text. There are good reasons for this, notably avoiding creating very long document files which cannot then be backed up on diskettes. But it does mean that stronger version control problems can arise unless you are careful to keep charts and their accompanying main text passages in close agreement. All charts should clearly show what the main text says that they show.

Other techniques for data reduction

> The only way to grasp a mathematical concept is
> to see it in a multitude of different contexts, think
> through dozens of specific examples, and find at
> least two or three metaphors to power intuitive
> speculations.
> *Greg Evans*   [6]

To present data well you have to really understand them. And
to do that, you have to look hard at them for a long time, and
ask an array of well-thought-out questions about what they
show. Yet modern PCs and software give all of us the ability to
crunch far more numbers than perhaps we have fully analysed,
and then to inflict them on our readers in an undigested way.
Data reduction means simplifying the numbers we are working
with. The field of exploratory data analysis offers many powerful techniques for doing this, and has an interesting literature
which I will only briefly touch on here.[7] Properly exploring and
reducing data is an essential principle for making progress in
understanding any set of numbers that you have to analyse, let
alone conveying that information accurately to readers. The
key principles of data reduction are:

♦ Look hard at your primary data. Do not rely on analysis
  packages to give you an intuitive picture of what you are
  dealing with or to tell you what questions to ask. Analysis
  packages can only work well for you if you already know
  what shape of data you have. This is easy enough in
  coursework where you are replicating someone else's prior
  analysis, but often very difficult for brand-new information
  that you have just generated by research.
♦ Always put your data in a numerical progression (easily
  done in any spreadsheet). Chart them wherever possible,
  and then look hard at the results. Never engage in more
  complex forms of multivariable analysis, such as
  correlations or regression analysis, without understanding
  the visual shape of the primary data you are handling.
♦ When trying to see patterns in your data remove as much of
  the 'clutter' as possible. For instance, try looking at a version

that cuts out confusing and unnecessary decimal points or where numbers are rounded. And transform your data using index numbers or ratios so as to put the data in number ranges that are most easily understandable, ideally between 0 and 100. Operating with unsimplified numbers (especially very large or very small ones) will make it more difficult for you to find patterns in them.

To get more of a fix on exploratory data-analysis techniques, I briefly consider three useful approaches: stem-and-leaf analysis (including measures of central level and spread); box-and-whisker plots; and data-smoothing for over-time graphs.

Stem-and-leaf analysis is a simple technique for looking hard at a set of data. Suppose that some data collection you have done generates the following 27 numbers for a particular variable (in the random order of their occurrence in your data set):

25	46	52	29	15
23	22	18	12	33
19	22	34	19	22
34	18	31	17	3
19	22	21	32	20
32	33			

One way to analyse these data would be as a bar chart or frequency count. Here we could set up some category boxes and count the number of cases in each, yielding a result like this:

Category	No. of cases
50+	1
40–9	1
30–9	7
20–9	9
10–19	8
0–9	1

This pattern looks like a conventional single-peaked one (the misleadingly termed 'normal' distribution, popularised as 'the bell curve'). But we have lost a lot of information here about the precise numbers in the original data, and may be missing a trick as a result.

Stem-and-leaf analysis goes a little bit further because it retains more of the information given in the original numbers. Each number is divided into two parts, the larger 'stem' part and the smaller 'leaf' or unit part. We choose what to set as the stem in relation to the range of the data being analysed (the variation from top to bottom score). Here we could set the stem as equal to 10s, just as in the frequency table above. But since we want to look a little deeper we could set the stem as fives instead, with (for instance) one stem running from 20 to 24, and another stem running from 25 to 29. On this basis the first number in the set is 25, which would separate into an upper 20s stem and a leaf of 5. The next number 46 would separate into an upper 40s stem and a leaf of 6. The next number 52 would separate into a lower 50s stem and a leaf of 2, and so on. Working through the whole set of numbers above would give a stem-and leaf analysis as follows:

Stem (5s)	Leaf (1s)	
5	2	Upper outlier
4	6	Upper outlier
4		
3		
3	1 2 2 3 3 4 4	Upper quartile = 33
2	5 9	
2	0 0 1 2 2 2 2 3	Median = 22
1	5 7 8 8 9 9 9	Lower quartile = 19
1	2	
0		
0	3	

It is clear here that there is not just a single-peaked curve (one bell curve). Instead there is a main bulge of observations scoring from 15 to 23 (including 13 data points), and then another smaller bulge from 29 to 34 (including 7 data points). Since there are 27 observations we can find the median by counting up or down until we reach the fourteenth observation (shown in bold in the listing above). And we can find the quartiles in the same way by partitioning in half the observations above and below the median (the quartiles are the averages of the seventh and eighth observations going from the top or from the bottom). From the stem-and-leaf we can quickly generate a table giving summary indices of central level and spread as follows:

Median = 22
Top point = 52   Bottom point = 3
Range = 49
Upper quartile = 33   Lower quartile = 19
Midspread = 14

With small amounts of data stem-and-leaf techniques are easily applied using pen and paper. There is also a great deal to be said for using them in this way because it keeps you in close touch with your data (which might well be outputs from other statistical packages, like frequency counts or charts). Where you get a large number of data points (more than about 30) you can use a PC package to do all the exploratory data-analysis techniques set out here: for instance, *SPSS* has stem-and-leaf facilities.

Box-and-whisker plots are a way of displaying the statistical results of a number of stem-and-leaf analyses. They are like a vertical bar chart, with a vertical axis showing the scale. The difference is that you draw in a box only from the upper to the lower quartile points, and add a thick line to show the position of the median, as shown in the right-hand bar of Figure 7.4. To display the remaining data points, stretching away above and below the middle mass, insert a single vertical line (the whisker). The further away from the middle mass an observation lies, the more unusual it is. There may be a greater chance that it is a fluke or a piece of bad data, or alternatively that it is a significant extreme case, requiring detailed explanation. Outlying observations (those lying a long way from the middle box, specifically more than 1.5 times the midspread above the upper quartile or below the lower quartile) are shown by blobs on the whiskers (see the middle bar in Figure 7.4). Outliers are often worth labelling individually with their name, to remind you exactly which observations are highly unusual.

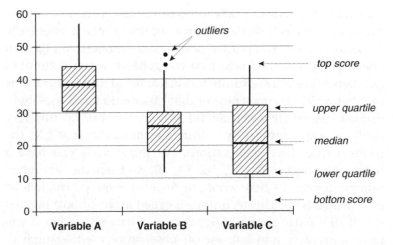

Figure 7.4   An example of a box-and-whisker chart comparing across variables

It can be useful to look at a single box-and-whisker plot of the statistics from one stem-and-leaf. But these plots' real value is in allowing you to compare the variation across different sets of data points, as shown in Figure 7.4. Here one can see at a glance:

◆ variations in the central level of the three different sets of observation, as shown by comparing the vertical position of the medians and of the middle boxes; and

◆ variations in the spread of their data, shown by the vertical size of the shaded middle boxes, the vertical size of the boxes plus whiskers, and the presence or absence of outliers.

This is a sophisticated, multi-indicator comparison, yet accomplished in a very intuitive and accessible way. It can greatly assist your understanding of the data, and it can also convey a lot of information effectively to readers.

Smoothing data is another very useful data-reduction technique for any kind of information that is analysed using line graphs, especially over-time movements of any kind of index. There are many cases where we acquire a large number of observations in a volatile data series, one that zigzags up and down a lot, such as the movements of stock markets, or commodity markets, or public opinion polls showing the popularity of a government. The key difficulty here is to try and separate out the meaningless or temporary fluctuations from the underlying, long-run changes or transitions that can occur in the central level of the data series. Smoothing data is a way of doing this. It essentially works as follows. You put the actual data numbers you have in one column, and then next to it you generate a new column of numbers. Here you substitute for each actual data number a new number which is an average of that observation and the observations immediately before and after it. You can do this very easily on a spreadsheet by writing a formula that will take the mean of the three observations. For instance, if you have a series of numbers like 52, 56, 74, 60, 58 then the smoothed number for the 74 here would be $56 + 74 + 60 = 210$, divided by 3, which is 63. This technique is called mean-smoothing and it will eliminate 'normal' fluctuations in data series. But if you have some very unusual one-off observations (either high or low) then they may still push the mean-smoothed figure up or down a lot. For instance, if we revise the series of numbers above by changing the 74 to a very unusual 124 we get the series: 52, 56, 124, 60, 58. Here the mean-smoothed figure for the 124 will be 80, which still sticks out well above the level of the surrounding numbers, despite being a solitary unusual observation.

Median-smoothing works in the same way but this time you replace an observation with the *median* of that observation, the one before and the one after. Take the series above, 52, 56, 74, 60, 58. The median-smoothed number for the 74 is the middle one of 56, 60 and 74, which is 60. This technique is much more powerful than mean-smoothing in screening out one-off, unusual observations. For instance, if we again replace the 74 by 124 to get the series 52, 56, 124, 60, 58 then the mean-smoothed figure for the 124 will still be 60, meaning that the unusual observation has been completely discarded and has no impact on the median-smoothed numbers. You will need to repeat the median-smoothing operation a second time, by median-smoothing your first-smoothed numbers again into a third column. This is necessary to get to a fully stable smoothed series, and one that places real enduring changes in the trend line of your data at the right place. (Median-smoothing a data series only once may misplace such real changes up or down by one period, for instance suggesting that a real change which took place in May of a given year actually occurred in June.

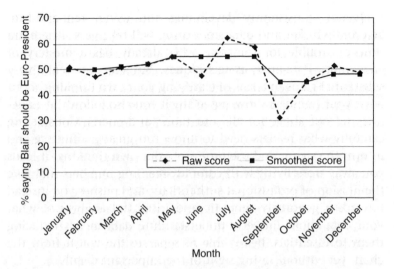

Figure 7.5 An example of median-smoothing – the percentage of British voters saying Tony Blair should become President of Europe during 2001 (hypothetical)

Median smoothing twice will get the change back to taking place at its real time in May.)

To see how median- and mean-smoothing work look at Figure 7.5. The chart shows some opinion poll figures I have made up, purporting to show the proportion of UK citizens who believed that Tony Blair should become President of Europe in 2001, with median-smoothing applied. The smoothed series is shown as the solid line here, with the actual data observations as a thinner dashed line, a technique which allows readers to focus most on the smoothed trend but still retain the ability to see how the actual scores moved over time. Observations for very unusual months show up very prominently as big divergences between the two lines, inviting you to give a special explanation of them. (One small digression point on methods here. You will need to have data for a few observations before and after the period you want to look at, in order to be able to get smoothed data covering the whole period you are interested in. There are techniques for finding starting and finishing values for smoothed series where you do not have this extra data.[8])

Overall, consistently developing and using stem-and-leaf, box-and-whisker and data smoothing will take very little extra time or trouble for someone who already has a mastery of elementary data-analysis techniques. But you can make very substantial gains in terms of clarifying your own thinking about what your numbers show, especially if you also follow the guidelines set out above for all your tables and charts. Considering carefully what readers need to know can greatly influence and inform the rigour and usefulness of your own thinking. It leads you away from living with complex-seeming numbers that give the illusion of professional authenticity, and pushes you instead towards a genuinely synoptic and insightful analysis of what your data show. Properly understanding data means reducing them to essentials, being able to separate the wheat from the chaff, yet without losing sight of the important details.

Using diagrams and images

> Thinking is not just the application of pure concepts arising from a previous verbalization, it is also the entertaining of diagrammatic representation.
> *Umberto Eco* [9]

Some attention points are not in the least numerical, but simply visual. They work by using the two-dimensional space of a blank page to permit more complex orderings and re-presentations of relationships than can be easily accomplished by text descriptions. Text is essentially linear. It arranges things in one dominant sequence, but a purely literary explanation is liable to get vaguer and harder for readers to follow as the patterns being described get more complex or convoluted. Here a good diagram can provide an invaluable spine for readers' understanding, allowing them to form a core mental image of how concepts, events, causes or institutions interact, which can then be fine-tuned and elaborated by your textual account. Readers pay special attention to diagrams of this kind, and they expect them to do a useful job of work. If they do not, if they seem redundant or dispensable elements in your explanation, then readers will be disappointed. If they put effort into understanding a diagram that turns out to shed no extra illumination, or perhaps is more confusing and less clear than the text which accompanies it, then readers may feel resentful. Such an attention point only detracts from the overall impact of your argument.

So diagrams need to be very carefully designed and implemented. As author you need to ask all the time what readers need to know, what value-added the diagram (or a set of diagrams) gives, and how comprehensible and accessible it will be for them. In short you need to manage readers' expectations in a very active way. Some key rules include the following:

◆ Always design diagrams using proper packages appropriate for this task, of which the best known are Microsoft's *Powerpoint* or Lotus's *Freelance Graphics*. Simpler illustrations may also be feasible to do in Word or Wordperfect. Hand-drawn or pencil-and-paper diagrams are no longer acceptable in PhD theses. Nor is it a good idea to use non-specialist software (like programming languages or general PC drawing packages) to try and produce professional-looking finished designs. If you will need a large number of diagrams, or you will be giving conference or seminar presentations, it is worthwhile going on a proper training course to learn your chosen presentations package thoroughly. It can sometimes be far more time-consuming in the end to try and take a shortcut by hacking-and-seeing or relying on the packages' on-line tutorials rather than attending a few classes.

◆ When designing diagrams always follow well-known conventions for constructing organization charts, algorithms, or flow diagrams. Conventions speed up your communication with readers, because they can recognize more quickly what is being shown and what you are trying to do, without their having to rely on the accompanying main text. They also impose a discipline on you, preventing you from lurching off into graphical idiosyncrasies which will be impenetrable to readers. For instance, flow charts outline a sequence of operations or provide a picture of how a set of cases breaks down into several subsets. In the social sciences most authors use a simplified format which focuses

on processes shown in square boxes connected
by horizontal or vertical arrows. There is also a more
'engineering' style of flow chart, which uses square boxes to
indicate processes, diamond boxes to indicate decision
points, and rounded shapes to indicate both the start points
of a set of operations and outcomes.

◆ Diagrams should be consistently designed across your thesis,
and not vary widely in their appearance. They should look
as simple and uncluttered as possible. If you are using boxes
try and give them a standard shape so far as possible. Do not
adjust box sizes erratically simply to accommodate different-
length labels. Try and align boxes on the page using simple
row and column (or grid) patterns, rather than spacing them
about erratically. Avoid using more types of shapes than are
strictly necessary. Different shapes (for instance, rectangles
or square versus circles or ovals) should always signal to
readers different types of things being diagrammed.

◆ Connect boxes up in diagrams using the minimum number
of straight vertical and horizontal lines or arrows. Try to
keep 'kinked' or cross-over lines or arrows to an absolute
minimum. Always avoid diagonal lines or arrows wherever
possible, because their slopes usually have different angles.
Diagrams can easily look a bit messy and unprofessional
when diagonals run at different angles. Make clear the status
of any lines or arrows used to link boxes with a proper key
and completely clear labels. Readers should never be left in
any doubt at all about what is being shown by connecting
lines or arrows. A line without arrows is generally more
difficult for readers to interpret, because it has no
directionality in it. Use this device only to indicate cases
where two-way flows or linkages of exactly the same kind
occur. Non-directional lines are also feasible in those types
of diagrams where normal conventions give the line a
reasonably clear meaning, as in organization charts
(or 'organograms' as they are also called). Arrowed lines are
generally more helpful and informative for readers so long
as they know very clearly what an arrow linking A to B
stands for. Does it mean that A *causes* B? Or that A
communicates to B, for example passing B information or
sending them an invoice or a product, or what? Or perhaps

A *controls or oversees* B? Try and avoid using double-headed arrows, which are very confusing for readers, and usually indicate that you do not know what is going on. If you have a situation where A gives B orders, and then B passes information back to A, you should show this by using two different kinds of one-directional arrows, a command and control arrow from A to B, and an information flow arrow from B to A in a different colour or format.

These recommendations may seem fairly obvious and basic. But a large minority of PhD students infringe many of these suggestions in their attention points, as indeed do too many senior academics in published articles and books. Most professional readers now are quite sceptical about diagrams and other images which do not follow proper conventions and guidelines. They will interpret poorly designed or badly labelled diagrams as signs either of careless authoring or of intellectual soft-headedness on your part. The ultimate useless diagram is one with a large number of boxes, each of which connects using double-headed arrows to all the other boxes in the figure. If that is what you have got to, you need to recognize what its subliminal message is for readers: 'Everything influences everything else. But don't ask me how, because I haven't got a clue.'

Conclusions

Good attention points can greatly strengthen your text, but their importance does not stop there. The further you go on in your academic and professional career, the more likely it will be that you will need to summarize or dramatize long screeds of text for an impatient audience. You will begin with seminar presentations, then go on to conference papers, then perhaps journal articles, and if you go into university teaching then lectures to wider public audiences. Learning the skills of designing effective attention points early on will always pay dividends. In the social sciences especially it is becoming harder and harder to publish text-only articles in many fields, and here papers with data components and good charts and tables are generally much more attractive for editors and reviewers. Some of the humanities subjects (like history) show not dissimilar trends. And the days when university teaching consisted of academics rereading from their previous works have long since gone. There is a strong emphasis instead upon designing and presenting even primarily textual materials in an accessible and imaginative way. If you progress from your PhD into other walks of professional life, like business or most professions, the premium on graphical communication and on simple, readable tables and charts is far greater than within universities. So handling attention points well is a key life skill, not just a thesis skill. In its own way it can be almost as important as the ability to get things finished (and published), to which I now turn.

8

The End-game: Finishing
Your Doctorate

> The tension between making it better and getting
> it done appears wherever people have work to
> finish or a product to get out: a computer, a
> dinner, a term paper, an automobile, a book. We
> want to get it done and out to the people who will
> use it, eat it, read it. But no object ever fully
> embodies its makers' conception of what it could
> have been.
> *Howard Becker* [1]

> The art of writing does, in fact, give to those who
> have long practised it habits of mind unfavourable
> to the conduct of affairs. It makes them subject to
> the logic of ideas … It gives a taste for what is
> delicate, fine, ingenious and original, whereas the
> veriest commonplaces rule the world.
> *Alexis de Tocqueville* [2]

Down the ages dispassionate observers have long com-
plained that intellectuals are diffident, unbusiness-like
types. They are happy to start projects but reluctant to finish
them. Interested in books and ideas and potentialities, they are
perfectionists who cannot close a deal, cannot say 'this is good
enough', cannot easily make a sale or cut a compromise. It is a
familiar and discomforting stereotype, which unfortunately has
a large measure of truth (certainly in my case). If writing is psychologically difficult as a form of commitment, how much
more troubling is the letting go involved in ceasing to work on

a project, recognizing that its imperfections and deficiencies (so intimately familiar to the author) have just to be lived with, tolerated, perhaps never remedied or improved upon?

An apt parallel for writing a PhD is taking part in an amateur dramatics society's production of a play. In the early days there are apparently endless casting meetings and leisurely orientation sessions. The actors, the director, the producer and the art director endlessly swap differing visions of the play's period and setting, its visual 'look and feel', the characters' motivations and the significance of different scenes and plot developments. The early rehearsals are wracked by personality conflicts and tensions about who is more important than whom, and what overall emotional or dramatic style should be achieved. But as the actual performances get nearer and nearer suddenly the motivations of actors and director coarsen up in a miraculous way. The actors worry more about remembering their lines and not looking a fool on stage, getting through all right rather than being the star of the whole show. And the director becomes more accommodating, grateful for any scene or performance that passes half-way professionally rather than stumbling into disorder. Finally the curtain opens on a production that everyone involved knows would benefit hugely from another four weeks of rehearsal, another stab at this or that. Except that it would never have got this focused this quickly without that curtain opening. If we put back the start of the show, everyone involved would simply adjust their time-scale to reach much the same condition of preparedness/unpreparedness four weeks further on, rather than now.

Getting to a first draft of your entire thesis is a very important milestone in your work. At this point your priority shifts away from doing more research or adding new bits to your text mountain and towards finishing things off, having done with it, putting it behind you, moving on to other topics and other projects. This is not an easy transition to make. There comes a point in the life of any book or thesis project where the 'fear and loathing' factor tends to top out on your other enthusiasms and your original motivation. This is an infallible sign that enough is enough, and that the time to enter the completion phase has arrived. Ending is not simple, however. Your first challenge will usually be to upgrade a patchy draft text into a fully integrated thesis, unified by a clear intellectual direction and looking like an 'industrial standard' product, with all the necessary bits present and working. The second aspect is less visible but still important, and involves formally submitting the thesis for examination. The final challenge is for you to be prepared in most cases for a 'viva' or oral examination.

From a first full draft to your final text

> The last thing one settles in writing a book is what to put in first.
> *Blaise Pascal* [3]

The process of producing and banking chapter drafts is always a slightly inconclusive one, because what you put in a subsequently written chapter may always have implications for already settled text. Later text may not live up to promises made early on, requiring an important change of tone. Or it may cut across the themes and structure of what has already been written so as to create the need for revisions and reallocation of materials between chapters. In the worst cases later text may contradict earlier chapters, showing no relationship where you expected to see one, or suggesting a quite different story-line or interpretation. Just as current developments often produce a change in how we see established historical events, you can never be sure that a chapter banked early on will not need radical alterations at a later stage.

So it is a magic moment when you can for the first time spread out all your chapters on the floor and physically hold and review all the elements of the thesis as a whole. From here on your task should be consolidation, rather than producing new elements to add into the picture. Only in very unlucky circumstances will reviewing the chapter first drafts as a whole lead you to conclude that the thesis is not in fact complete and you must go back to primary research to fill a major hole in the analysis. This problem is most likely to occur if your chapter drafts taken together greatly under-shoot the thesis word norm (80,000 words for a 'big book' thesis, and perhaps 60,000 for a papers model dissertation). Otherwise a genuinely complete first draft signals that from here on the elements of your thesis are pretty fixed.

The best organization and presentation of these elements is not fixed, however. Instead there will normally be a period of three to six months after getting a complete first draft during which you must reorganize the elements you have so as to produce a much stronger and more integrated final text. Drawing out the intellectual themes of your work is a key focus of your effort at this stage. You need consistent themes that run all the way through the thesis, synthesizing your arguments, setting up and framing your research conclusions, and putting the thesis value-added into sharp focus. Figure 8.1 shows that this is not a matter of mechanical reiteration or repetition, but rather of flexibly creating and enhancing linkages across five key elements: the thesis title; the abstract; the first chapter (plus any other lead-in chapter); the conclusion sections of the middle chapters; and the final chapter.

The thesis title

Your title should introduce the central analytic concepts used or the major argument themes developed. Normally thesis titles have a colon in the middle, which authors use to separate out thematic, analytic or theoretical ambitions on the one hand, and empirical references or limiting features on the other.

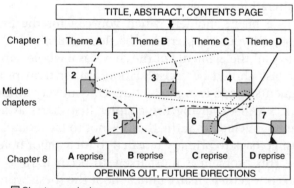

Figure 8.1   Integrating themes

Theoretically ambitious authors will usually put thematic or analytic key words together before the colon, and then indicate their empirical reference and any limits on the analysis after the colon. People who see their work as more empirical or descriptive usually put a statement of what their thesis does before the colon, and then indicate the secondary analytic or theoretical themes after the colon. For example:

Example of a theoretical thesis	Suppressing the Diversity of 'the Other': The literary treatment of servants in English and American novels from Jane Austen to *Gone with the Wind*
Example of an empirical thesis	The Decay of European Rule in Central Africa, 1930–58: Self-determination, democratization and race-thinking

Sometimes the 'colon'-ization effect can be achieved in other ways, for instance by posing theoretical issues in a general question first and then giving the empirical specification afterwards. Once a word has made it into your title you had better be sure that it is genuinely important to the analysis. Readers will definitely expect to see all the title words being carefully defined, frequently used and doing a great deal of analytic work in the main text chapters.

The bureaucracy of getting your PhD examined is always a pain, but it can be positively helpful in this particular respect. Many universities require you to send in a form with your final thesis title and an associated abstract (of 300 words or so) around six months ahead of when you plan to submit the final thesis. Once your title's form of words is formally entered and approved as satisfactory it is often very hard to change. You will have to speak to this title in your oral exam (if you have one). And you will live with having your research labelled this way on your résumé or curriculum vitae for the rest of your career. So defining the final title is not to be done lightly or quickly. You need to look very intensively and self-critically at your inherited ideas for describing the thesis, which usually date back to your first year of research:

♦ Does the current title really capture what you have done in your draft chapters?

- ♦ Does it define *exactly* the central research question which you have answered? Does it avoid drawing attention to any gaps or deficiencies in your research?
- ♦ Does your title's vocabulary include the main theoretical concepts or innovations or themes that run through your research, which are used in the chapter texts and do an important job of work there? Does it signal your line of argument in a reasonably substantive way? Are the words used ones that you will want to talk about and explain at length, in your oral exam?
- ♦ Does the title make clear the empirical referents of your research, and the necessary limitations you have set for its scope and approach?

Before answering 'Yes, of course' to all these questions, think laterally about how the thesis will really look to readers seeing it for the first time, and what your research has fundamentally achieved. Choose title words that capture these aspects in an effective way. You should also ask explicitly how your project, your discipline and the wider intellectual world have changed since the original working title was firmed up in your first year. Is the current title going to have the same fashionable connotations it once did? Is it going to stand up in future? Remember your title will be an important element of selling your work to potential university employers. Appointment committees often short-list people for interview on the basis of quite sparse information in the papers in front of them. So during your early career years, the thesis title you choose will largely define what kind of intellectual species you are seen as.

These issues are not easy to think through on your own. It may be hard for you to be self-critical about an inherited title that you have lived with for a long time. But this is the last-chance saloon, so you should set aside a whole session with your supervisor to brainstorm about the full range of possible title wordings and how they might be interpreted by outside audiences. Construct an 'alternatives' sheet containing all the feasible key terms and their combinations, paying particular attention to placing material before and after any colon in the title. Do not just look at your established title in isolation. If you compare what you already have only with a blank slate, the status quo will always seem preferable. Instead consider its strengths and weakness compared with a large number of possible alternative wordings (say, ten or twelve), each triggering different combinations of thematics or major concepts. Even where you are happy about what the key word elements in your title will be, try juggling around how they are combined.

In the social sciences if your thesis is concerned with reasonably current events you must make an explicit decision about the cut-off date when your story ends, and stick with it, writing the whole thesis in the past tense. Trying to finish a thesis about events that are still going on or are not yet capable of being evaluated is an effort doomed to failure, a genuine 'never-ending story'. With any empirical research covering an over-time period it is normally a good idea to include the date limits of the analysis somewhere in the thesis title. Try to pick start and end dates for your research which you can justify on analytic or theoretical grounds, as critical, important or 'natural' breakpoints.

The abstract

The final version of your abstract comes immediately after the title page in the bound version of your thesis. It consists of an especially intensive summary in around 300 words of what the thesis is about. The abstract is a key opportunity for you to set out the core of your argument in a helpful way for readers. Later on when your thesis sits in the university's library, the title and the abstract will also be the primary elements advertising its contents to the outside world, and the only information included in Internet bibliographies or published directories of PhD research. People deciding whether to try and secure sight of a copy of your thesis via inter-library loans will rely heavily on the abstract. So it is well worth taking the time and trouble to write it well. In practice most PhD abstracts are very badly written. Often authors devote more words to summarizing the previous state of the literature or the routine methods which they have used than to explaining their own substantive arguments, key findings or new propositions. Although abstracts are the culmination of a long process of research, students normally only write them in a hectic final rush to get finished. Some treat them as just another boring piece of university bureaucracy to be got out of the way as painlessly as possible. Other people toil over producing this short nugget of text in an unguided and not very effective way.

A well-written abstract should be about 300 words or so long. Its structure should closely follow this sequence:

◆ Start with either one or (at most) two sentences summarizing the state of the literature to which your thesis contributes, constructed so as to frame, and highlight, the value-added which your research has achieved. Be careful, though, to keep your characterization of the literature fairly broad-brush and defensible.

◆ Next add two or three sentences characterizing the theoretical contribution made by your work. They should pick up any key innovations you have made or the main theme or theory concepts from the title. You should make clear the central thrust of your argument in a substantive way. Do not write purely formalistic stuff at this point.

◆ Devote one sentence to setting out as briefly as possible the methods you followed. Standard methods are not worth expounding at length in the abstract. Only if your original contribution lies especially in methodology should you say much more than this. By now you should have covered all the material included in the lead-in chapter(s) of the thesis and you can put a paragraph break in your abstract here.

◆ Next go through the arguments of each of your more substantive chapters (usually chapters 3 to 7 in an eight-chapter thesis). Assign *one* sentence to summarize the 'bottom line' import of each chapter for the overall argument of the thesis. Do not write: 'Chapter 4 argues that ...', because an abstract is a condensation of your whole argument and not a guide to your chapter structure. Instead with each new sentence in the abstract just go straight into what the relevant chapter shows.

◆ Finish the second paragraph of the abstract with two sentences crystallizing the bottom-line conclusions of your final chapter. These points should return to the main theory or theme concepts used in the thesis title and covered also in the first paragraph of the abstract. But now your content should focus on evaluating the worth or applicability of these concepts, or showing how far your theoretical innovations or expectations are supported by the empirical findings or applied analysis of the middle chapters.

♦ Check that you are using the same language in your abstract as in the thesis title, and that both of them match up or mesh with the language of your chapter headings. (Bear in mind the point from pp. 91–2 above, that your chapter headings should work within the thesis title, rather than simply repeating elements of it exactly.) Danger signs to look out for occur where the conceptual or thematic elements triggered in the overall title, the abstract and the chapter headings do not match up. The three elements should not suggest different intellectual problematics or ways of looking at issues.

It is best to try and define your abstract early in the rewriting and text revision process. In Britain and Europe university regulations often provide a helpful stimulus in this respect, because they require you to submit an early version of the abstract at the same time that you formally register the thesis title. This first version is not binding and it is used only to help faculty boards decide who should examine your thesis.

The first chapter (plus any other lead-in chapter)

As Figure 8.1 shows, the opening chapter is critically important in defining the overall theoretical frame for the doctorate. It should set out a small number of intellectual themes stemming from the central question of the thesis. Themes are guiding ideas to which you will return. They could consist of theoretical positions, methodological innovations or empirical research findings, depending on your findings. Generally two, three or four themes are more than enough to try and handle. If you find that you have six or seven themes going on, then you need to reduce their number. Consider if you can perhaps nest some of them inside one another, so that one top-level theme includes two or more subthemes. Each theme needs to be handled in the opening chapters chiefly in a framing way, summarizing what other authors have already said about them and establishing or *anticipating* what might be said about them later on. But do not give any form of potted version of your later arguments in the lead-in chapter, lest you crudely travesty your major points to come. Instead linkages must be set up, which then need to connect with your research in the rest of the thesis.

The conclusion sections of the middle chapters

Each of the substantive chapters (that is, those numbered 2 or 3 through to 7 in an eight-chapter PhD) should be flexibly linked via their conclusions to the themes from the opening chapter(s). The conclusions (note, not the chapter openings) should pick up on at least one or two of the themes developed in the lead-in chapter, but in a variable-geometry way. The theme that each conclusion links to should be wholly relevant to the specific materials in that chapter and also adapted to the role which the chapter plays in the thesis as a whole. Do not try to cover *all* the thesis themes in the conclusions to *every* chapter. Such an approach can easily look mechanistic and inauthentic, as if you are running a kind of intellectual bookkeeping operation, rather than using genuinely relevant key ideas for analysing what that chapter has shown. The job of the conclusions section is to pull the focus away from the research detail, to bring out the chapter's key findings in a stand-back mode. You can make some small sideways links to other middle chapters relevant to the same theme(s), especially those chapters which have just been covered or are the next to be covered. But you should not make comparative comments at these points, nor begin discussing material from other middle chapters in any substantive way.

Refocusing the middle chapters and sharpening up their conclusions is also an opportunity to make some crucial checks that your work is structurally well founded. Each of your chapters should do a discrete and distinctive job, well signalled from its start, and effectively building the thesis. If there are overlaps in chapter 'jurisdictions', now is the time to simplify them. Assign one function to each chapter, and make sure that this role does not overlap with those of its neighbours. Think through how you can reach a 'say it once, say it right' pattern of chapter organization. If you still have a methods chapter embedded in the main sequence of your chapters, consider whether it is really necessary, or whether some or all of its material might be better handled in a Research Methods Appendix. Try to ensure that your sequence of chapters makes sense in a designed way, and does not just follow a 'What I did in my PhD' pattern. Check carefully that the 'need to know' criterion is being met in terms of the order of chapters so that contextual information arrives in the right sequence for readers to follow the analysis at all points.

The final chapter

The end of the thesis needs to have a clear character. It cannot just be a 'tell 'em what you've told 'em' section that only repeats points already made. It must first of all reprise each of the same themes or theory ideas used to structure the first chapter (and any other lead-in chapter). But this time the discussion of each theme should be grounded securely in the experience of the middle chapters. The focus should be on establishing clearly what has been shown by your research, and how it is relevant to your central thesis question and the themes set out at the start. The last chapter should answer the twin questions: What has been achieved by your research? How much has your thesis moved professional discussion along? Its discussion should not go again into detailed accounts from the middle chapters. Instead it should compare across those chapters, pulling together their themes and connecting up their key messages. As you move towards a close, use the second part of the final chapter to group its themes together under broader labels or higher-order issues. From there you can open out into a discussion of relevant wider professional debates and controversies. It is often useful to conclude this closing 'debate' section by considering some viable directions in which future research might go from where your work leaves off.

There are a few final checks to make at this stage also. You must ensure that your overall main text is still the right length, around four-fifths of any formal university limit, that is 80,000 words with a 100,000 limit. The formal limit is inclusive of everything except the bibliography, so your notes, appendices, preface, acknowledgements and so on must all be able to fit within the remaining fifth of the word limit. It is very common for people who thought that they were comfortably inside the word limit to find out that they have run over not just the four-fifths rule, but even the formal thesis limit by 10 to 20 per cent. Often the problem occurs because they are repeating similar material at different places in different chapters, or they are overdoing the level of detail that readers need to know. When you are pressing to reach closure on the thesis this can be a depressing realization to make, since it may mean that you must spend extra weeks or even months just cutting away text which took you so long to write in the first place. But bear in mind Robert Browning's famous dictum: 'Less is more'.[4] Any text can be fairly painlessly cut by around 10 per cent, and this operation almost always improves its overall look and feel, sometimes out of all recognition. Considered as a single problem of cutting, say, 12,000 words from the entire thesis, this order of cuts will always seem daunting. But try thinking about it instead as cutting 30 out of 330 words on each page of your A4 typescript, which may be easier to do. If you have greatly overwritten, by more than 10 per cent, then you will almost certainly have to find a bulk cut by losing one of the chapters, appendices or other sections. If you can, try to make more cuts in the lead-in chapters and to safeguard the thesis core. If you are over your limit, bear in mind that you can now very easily put data and other bulky materials on a CD bound in to the covers of your thesis, instead of having to get them printed up as text. Most university regulations about length still assume paper-only theses, and so as yet say nothing about CDs.

Normally the closing months and weeks of writing up make a surprising amount of difference to PhD theses. You may find yourself moving materials that have been stuck in a given sequence for two or three years into radically different configurations. You may drop concepts that have long been important in your research in favour of new themes, of which you were only dimly aware before you could look at your first draft as a whole. This burst of rethinking and remodelling is quite usual and predictable. It does not show (as many students worry) that your research plan was badly flawed all along, or that you did not previously know what you were doing. Instead it reflects the intellectual developments and advances which you can often only make once all the building blocks of the thesis have come into being. Redefining the thesis title and abstract in closure mode, and redoing the opening and final chapters in an integrating way, all create a crucially important opportunity for you to adjust your intellectual focus squarely back on to your central thesis question. Even if you have faithfully maintained a rolling synopsis throughout the period since your first year of PhD studies, the chances are that you will have a lot of catch-up activity to do. Inherently you could not recognize any earlier than this what has worked in the thesis and what has not, and what you have achieved or missed achieving. And if the theoretical literature in your field has also moved on substantially since you started the thesis, you should expect to make some revisions of important terminology and to rescind some intellectual judgements made early on. At this late stage, however, it is also very important to 'keep faith' with what you have done. Do not lapse into an overcritical mode characterized by regret at what you did not attempt, or what you tried but that did not work.

Nor should you fall prey to the illusion that another three-month push on a new aspect of your topic would sort things out. You must not try at this late stage to add yet another building block to the thesis, unless you have the clearest possible steer from your supervisors or advisers that the dissertation is not viable without it. Recognize that, for better or worse, your work is now in its final configuration and that there are good reasons for that. Focus on defining the boundaries of your thesis appropriately and restrict new research efforts only to essential infilling activity needed to get a viable boundary. There will be other writings and other research projects in your life, especially if you become a professional academic. Perhaps in future you may return productively to these problems and themes after an interregnum.

Submitting the thesis and choosing examiners

> I used to be indecisive, but now I'm not so sure.
> *Boscoe Pertwee* [5]

To 'submit' your doctorate is to initiate its final evaluation. This stage is marked off by various university bureaucratic procedures, which will vary from one place to another. Check that you know what you are required to do in your particular faculty and university well before you are close to finishing, ideally a year ahead of when you plan to submit. And you should discuss the timings involved with your supervisor, because they can be quite lengthy. The general format of submission procedures is that you may have to formally register a thesis title (usually accompanied by an interim abstract) around six months ahead of when you plan to be examined. You then need to produce a complete text printed perfectly in strict conformity with any university requirements on formatting. All the charts and tables must be in the right places, where they are referred to and not at the ends of chapters. All the references and the bibliography must be fully complete, along with all the appendices. And the whole thing needs to be numbered in a single page order from start to finish. If all these conditions are met then you may be ready to get the thesis bound for the examiners to read. Some universities will let you use spiral binding at the examination stage, reserving the full cloth-bound version for later when you submit to the library a final version of the thesis incorporating any revisions which the examiners have asked for. Other universities insist on a cloth-bound version for the examiners or dissertation committee, which then has to be broken up and rebound in a revised version if the examiners find that changes are needed. Along with your full text, universities normally require you and your supervisors or advisers to sign off on a number of forms, usually certifying that the work is original, fits within the required work limits, and has been approved for submission by your advisers.

Getting examined is often a very slow-moving process at PhD level. Once the examiners have copies of the thesis it will take them from six weeks to three months to read it and for your supervisor or the university to fix a date for an oral examination (where necessary). You should also remember that in most countries the time window for submitting is quite restricted in the summer terms or second semesters of the academic year, because your supervisors and examiners will normally be away on holiday, conferences or research trips throughout the long summer vacations. In Britain the blanked-out space where you cannot usually get your thesis examined runs from mid-June to the end of September, and in the USA from May to the end of August. Thus the PhD examining 'year' runs de facto for only eight months. In addition it is obviously a bad idea to plan on submitting in the last two months of this northern hemisphere 'year' (after Easter). If your timetable slips you may not get your manuscript finished early enough to allow sufficient reading time for the examiners before the long summer limbo is imminent.

The formality and typical slow pace of the submission and examination process reflects its importance and irreversibility. In many universities you can make only two attempts to be granted a doctorate. If you fail once you are 'referred' by the examiners. You then have a last chance to make changes and to resubmit within a specified time period (usually 18 months or two years). If you are referred a second time this is the end of the line for your doctoral hopes. In other universities there may be a theoretical possibility of having more than two attempts to get your thesis accepted as a doctorate. But in practice examiners will very rarely accept an open-ended process, so the effect is the same. Sometimes universities can offer a 'consolation' lower rank degree (usually called an M.Phil. in Britain) to candidates whose work just cannot make the PhD standard.

Because you have only two bites at the cherry, it is very important that you do not submit before your supervisors advise that you have a good chance of passing. Some university regulations allow PhD candidates to submit whether or not their supervisors believe that they are ready, but it would normally be foolish to do so. Very rarely supervisors may for some reason try to hold you back from submitting a thesis that is in fact already viable. But this happens only where personal relations between the student and her supervisors have deteriorated badly, and you should always be able to find alternative sources of advice in your department. An equally rare problem might occur if your supervisor or head of department tries to pressure you into submitting too early, before you feel ready. Some government funding bodies around the world require that PhDs which they fund are submitted within a specified time (usually four years), and levy penalties on departments which fail to comply. Theoretically such rules (or internal university performance indicators) might lead departments to pressure lagging students to submit theses prematurely or to chance their arm with theses which are in fact marginal. On the other hand, some students also fall into the trap of unrealistic perfectionism, over-postponing the time when they should submit. The optimal position to aim for is one where you and your supervisors are both happy for submission to go ahead.

In the United States and other countries which use a committee system of supervision there is really no separate examination stage here. Your advisers and dissertation committee are also the examiners who have to sign off the doctorate as worthy of entering the cannon of certified academic research. One or more of them may have difficulties or hang-ups about reaching 'closure' on your project. This may require you to work more closely with the most sympathetic members of the committee, to ensure that you are constructively meeting any misgivings of the other members. But the personalities involved are all very familiar to you in this system and you should be able to fine-tune when you should produce a finished text for their consideration.

In British-style and Commonwealth university systems and some European countries, however, PhD examiners are by definition senior people in your discipline who have *not* previously been involved in advising you in any way. Their sole task is to decide independently if your work meets the doctoral criteria or not. Here you need to think ahead about choosing people to be examiners, or at least trying to influence whom your supervisor or the university's faculty board choose. The point of asking you ahead of time to specify a title and an abstract is so that when your thesis is finally submitted the faculty board already has examiners appointed who have agreed to read the thesis and to conduct an oral exam (where this is necessary, as it usually is). University regulations require two or more people to sit in judgement, one an internal examiner from your own university and one or more an external examiner from a completely different university. Normally both the external and the internal examiners must not have advised you or been associated with your work beforehand. (In the University of London the concern for impartiality is carried so far that even the internal examiner is normally required to come from another college of the university.) Very zealous universities (like London) will debar as examiners people who have worked or published with you, and may even rule out people who have worked alongside your supervisor in the past or co-published with her. The key principle underlying all these requirements is maintaining academic independence. By working with you over several years your supervisors will inevitably have accumulated dozens of links and personal obligations to you, which must to some degree distort their objectivity. Separate examiners, not bound to you by personal ties, are supposed to be capable of giving dispassionate judgements about the quality of your work and how it fits with the doctoral standards prevailing in your discipline. The external examiner is there to ensure that institutional loyalties do not colour the internal examiner's judgements, and that your university sticks to the standards prevailing in the wider discipline in your country.

Some European countries have systems of PhD examining which combine aspects of the American and the British models; they use a large committee or 'collegium' of six to ten examiners, including several of your supervisors, plus senior members of your own department who have not supervised you, plus an external examiner from another university. In the European Union the external is now often drawn from a university in another EU country.

In both the British and the European models you should always try to have a hand in who gets to be appointed as separate examiners (those people who will sit in judgement on the thesis but are not already your supervisors). In theory examiners are always appointed by a faculty board or committee of your university, on the advice of your supervisor. In practice, it is usually so difficult to get people to examine PhDs, especially external examiners, that university administrators rely heavily on the names that your supervisor suggests. It is not a good idea to simply assume that your supervisor has this aspect all in hand and so give her a free hand in nominating examiners, for various reasons. You will always know a great deal more about your thesis, its strengths and weaknesses, than your supervisor. And it will be you and not your supervisor who has to sit through the oral exam (where there is one), and to handle the examiners at a personal level. Sometimes your supervisor may have close ties to senior figures in the profession, but the same relationship may not extend to you as well, especially with quirky senior people. Above all it is you who has to live with the outcomes in terms of the examiners' judgements and making any revisions to the thesis which they may require.

So what should you (and your supervisors) look for in an examiner? In addition to relevant expertise and some seniority, the key element is non-neuroticism. The ideal examiner should have a cheerful personality and strong confidence in herself. She must not feel threatened or challenged by new entrants crowding into her area of expertise, nor affronted by upstart youngsters in the field who take a different view from hers. She should be open to new ideas. She must be able to work constructively with her fellow examiner(s), rather than pursuing hobbyhorses or fixed ideas of her own as if they were all-important. A person of this kind will have a realistic grip on the mechanics of doing research in your discipline. She will be able to appreciate the hours of work it takes to stand up a piece of data analysis, the collection of documentary materials, or the production of a carefully argued piece of text. She will also know very well at least a substantial aspect of your thesis topic, so that she is confident about recognizing original work and identifying additions to knowledge in the field. Finally the ideal examiner should come from a university department at which a reasonable number of doctoral students are being supervised and graduating every year, so that she has an accurate current feel for where the doctoral standard lies.

Finding two or more examiners who fully meet this demanding brief is often difficult. Younger academics are often more cheerful (less ground-down and cynical) and more accessible than senior people. They also have more recent experience of PhD work and are more open to new ideas. But younger staff may be overinfluenced by their own recent PhD experience and they will know less than senior staff about the diversity of other people's topics and approaches. For instance, they will have had less opportunity to act as supervisor to other people. In any event, your faculty board will probably restrict the choice of PhD examiners to senior staff such as full professors (or readers or senior lecturers in the UK). Senior academics should be more familiar with looking at PhD work, and may have other advantages. Their advice on how to generate journal articles (or even a book publication) from your research may be more valuable. If your PhD is a strong piece of work then senior examiners can often be more helpful to you in getting it published, or even in recommending that you be considered for jobs. Their favourable opinions will carry more weight with publishers or appointing committees than those of junior staff.

But senior people in academia have often also acquired mildly neurotic traits along with their eminence. They may have intellectual hang-ups or blind spots, things they cannot tolerate, friendship or referencing circles they cannot abide being criticized, and a degree of closure to ideas which have arrived later than their personal 'defining moment' as a researcher. Usually these inevitable personality quirks do not matter much. Their presence often briefly enlivens conversations or seminar and conference debates. Academics normally moderate how far they expose their hang-ups in the normal ebbs and flows of interactions with colleagues (who all have different quirks of their own). But PhD examining is one of three contexts in academic life where these aspects of people's personalities can cause serious problems or be decisive. (The other two contexts, incidentally, are making academic appointments, and deciding upon promotions.)

The best way to help ensure that you end up with suitable examiners is to get out into your profession at an early stage in your research. Go on the conference circuit and try to sit in on sessions where you can see fairly senior people who might be potential examiners in action. It can be worthwhile trying to ask them a question in the session or to talk to them individually afterwards to see how open they are and how they might react to your ideas or approach. In the bars and tea rooms at conferences, quiz your fellow research students and people at other universities about possible examiners, their reputations and behaviour traits. And for possible internal examiners from your own university, make sure that you similarly know about them from students whom they supervise and that you get to see them in action. If you identify people who seem sympathetic and viable examiners, take care not to blow their independence or eligibility to serve later on by sending them chapters from your thesis and seeking comments from them.

It is permissible for your examiners to have read and even commented on conference papers or journal articles that you have written, because these are materials in the public domain. But if they have had prior sight of anything from your thesis in chapter form they might become disqualified, certainly in British- and Commonwealth-style university systems, which place a strong premium on independent examining.

You need to discuss possible permutations of examiners with your supervisor quite early on, to make sure that you have some chance of finding out about people on your 'possibles' list. In a four-year PhD, midway in your third year may be a good time to have this preliminary discussion, so that you can begin to plan ahead. But of course the actual choice of people to ask hinges completely on when you finish, because many possible examiners may be ruled out at the relevant time by sabbaticals, research trips overseas or other commitments. Bear in mind also that you will usually need a combination of examiners with different skills. Almost all doctoral theses span across subdisciplinary boundaries in some way. Thus any one examiner will normally cover only part of your thesis topic. For example, she may have the right kind of theoretical expertise but know little about the country or other context in which you are applying a given approach. So getting the whole thesis examined may mean that you have to balance an internal examiner who knows about aspect A with an external examiner who knows about aspect B. If your first preference as external examiner proves unavailable, you may have to switch around who does what, picking a second-choice external who knows about A, and looking for a different internal who knows about aspect B to balance them. In many theses you may need two examiners with different subject backgrounds, only one from your 'home' discipline and the other from a neighbouring area. Be especially careful in this case because the standards of what counts as a doctorate vary a lot between different disciplines. It must be crystal clear in your thesis which discipline's standards you are seeking to be judged by. Try and make sure that the people involved will be reasonably balanced personalities. Having a tough-minded examiner from another discipline who then personally dominates the examiner(s) from your home discipline often leads to trouble.

The final oral examination (viva)

Life-changing events often need to be marked by a rite of passage, and so it is with the doctorate where it is traditional for the final examination to be an oral one. In Britain and the Commonwealth this occasion is often called a 'viva' (from the Latin phrase 'viva voce', meaning literally 'with the living voice'). Many research students find that the prospect of a viva or an oral session with two or three examiners or their whole dissertation committee looms large in their thinking well before the time when it will actually take place. When you are writing the final draft you will inevitably think ahead about how this or that passage will play with the examiners or the dissertation committee, or how you would defend this decision or answer a question about that gap or deficiency. In some ways this anticipation is helpful. It can push you to tighten things up, chop out hostages to fortune or corrosive passages that have survived too long, and go the extra mile to clear up muddles or eliminate small weaknesses. But it is also very easy to overdo things at this stage, slipping into the overly defensive 'thesis paranoia' that can make your work unpublishably long and dense.

The importance and unpredictability of the oral examination varies a good deal across university systems. In the United States the final oral examination is never just a formality, but it is a semi-public occasion which most frequently occurs only when your dissertation committee have been coaxed by your main adviser into pretty well signing off on your doctorate in a prior private session. Thus you are always able to plan and prepare carefully for the exam, and unless your dissertation committee is racked by feuding you should go to the oral session with a high measure of certainty that you will pass. You will additionally know well by then the personalities and foibles of the members of your committee.

In European examining committees there is often an impressive, ritualized and lengthy 'public defence' of the thesis, where the doctoral candidate explains their research findings and approach in a public session, open to all comers. This may sound terrifying, but it is pretty similar to the US approach. Supervisors sit on the examining committee, along with other

218 of AUTHORING A PHD

members of the department, although there will always be at least one external examiner whom the student may not know. But most of the public audience at these occasions is actually made up of the student's friends and proud relations. They can safely attend because the whole examining committee again normally reaches agreement in private that the doctorate is acceptable before the public defence is organized.

So it is perhaps in British- and Commonwealth-influenced university systems that the oral exam or viva normally plays the most significant part in determining whether or not someone gains a doctorate. Most of the lessons appropriate for this tough oral exam system, with two or three independent examiners, also apply in scaled-down forms to other public defence systems. The famous *Monty Python* sketch has it that: 'Nobody expects the Spanish Inquisition.'[6] Yet this is what PhD students almost universally expect in their oral exam. They foresee a very text-focused session, with detailed questioning about the minutiae of what they have said. In fact under normal circumstances a viva is mostly a rather high-level but also quite general conversation amongst three, four or more people in a discipline. If things have gone well with your thesis there may not be much close 'examination' of it. The examiners will be diligent readers, and often come armed with long lists of 'literals' – spelling mistakes, grammatical infelicities, glitches in statistics or charts, or sentences that might profitably be rewritten. You will want to keep their list as short as possible, and it is certainly prudent to avoid annoying them by leaving evidence of carelessness. But unless you are very slipshod, or have made a mistake in your choices of examiners and ended up with a neurotic after all, the examiners will rarely want to nag on about these things, still less take time discussing them. They will simply pass over their list and expect to see the corrections implemented as a matter of course in minor revisions.

Normally examiners come to the oral exam with much more fundamental doubts and anxieties that they want to assuage. Your work will be unfamiliar to them in some aspects, and hence difficult for them to grasp or assess at least in part. They will worry about whether it is innovative in a worthwhile way or simply a misguided dead-end. Having lived with your research for several years, both you and your supervisors will easily understand many research decisions and issues which strangers to the work will find difficult. Examiners also often worry about doing their duty by the profession in the right way, acting as proper guardians of the 'pool' of accepted original research. In a vague, background way they may be concerned that they could make a mistake for which they might later be held responsible – such as not identifying plagiarism or the use of fraudulent data, or accepting as valid some argument or proof which later inspection somehow establishes as spurious. They may be concerned about what happens next in your career, and whether granting you a doctorate will lead to adverse consequences – such as your getting a job teaching error-laden materials to new generations of students. In the classical model PhD, the examiners may worry that your thesis work is too narrow or too specialized a preparation to enter the discipline, and doubt that you have enough grip on wider professional debates to function effectively in teaching students or researching other topics. Normally the fact that you have been supervised at a decent university by a fellow professional of accepted status and judgement means that these concerns are very slight. But they are always still there. Separate examiners are partly there to check up on your supervisor, to make sure that her standards are still in touch with those of the profession as a whole. The examiners' role is to avoid any granting of doctorates to people who are just intellectual clones of the supervisor, or people to whom she is obligated as a friend, lover or fellow worker in the university's research labs.

The opportunity for the examiners to meet you in person for around an hour and a half and to talk face-to-face, can sort out all these kinds of problems more easily and speedily than anything else. When they can ask questions and hear you explain things in your own words, your thesis text will become much easier for them to understand. They will be able to rework their existing categories to fit you and your work into them and they will better appreciate why you have made the decisions you did. They will see what makes you tick and gain a much better sense of your capabilities and expertise than is possible from poring over your text in isolation. And normally all the latent, background doubts they may have had about granting you the doctorate easily drop away over the course of this specialized conversation. The examiners recognize that you are an independent professional in your own right, fully capable of standing on your own in academic argument and debate, and not someone who lives just in your supervisor's shadow. Even where they may disagree with you, they appreciate that you are not a student making errors, but a fellow professional with well-grounded reasons for the choices you have made and the conclusions you have drawn. They also see that you are someone with a good overall grip on your discipline and a commitment to its academic and moral values. If you go out into the wider academic environment with the title of 'Dr' no one is going to hold that judgement against them as examiners, or see it as in any way insecurely based. These reasons are why many research students are surprised to find that much of their oral exams or vivas turn out to be pretty general conversations, only loosely tethered to professional topics grouped around your text, rather than working through most of it in great detail.

Of course, at some stage every oral exam will come to specifics, to points which make one or more of the examiners doubtful or anxious, or where you (and your supervisors) may have made a mistake. This intensification of the discussion usually indicates that the examiners will insist on you making revisions, which are of two kinds: minor (which are no problem) or major (which are fairly fatal). Normally university regulations allow for 'minor revisions' to be made within a brief period (around six weeks to three months): these changes are completely consistent with the thesis passing first time. With the advent of word processors the barrier for 'minor' revisions has effectively been lowered, so that examiners now commonly demand fairly extensive alterations as a matter of course. They may often smuggle in a requirement for quite substantial changes to the thesis argument or coverage under this heading. But at least the examiners congratulate you at the end of the oral exam that you have gained the doctorate, subject to making their revisions, which the regulations mean that you must do right away. In British-style systems around four in every five PhDs now will be accepted with minor revisions. Very few theses make it through without any changes at all. (In Europe or

America these revisions are rarely a problem, because the examining or dissertation committee has insisted on all the changes its members require before the thesis comes to a public examination.)

In more serious cases the examiners have major reservations about all or much of your analysis and do not feel that the thesis overall has made the doctoral standard. In these cases they 'refer' the thesis, refusing you the doctorate at that time, but writing a full report setting out its failings and what you would need to do in order to overcome them. You then have around 18 months to make these changes so that the text will meet the requirements. This can be a pretty tall order because the examiners may have refused to accept key methods that you have used, or asked for the study to be greatly reorientated, or demanded a great deal more new work from you. Referral is often seen by research students as complete failure, and it certainly will be if it happens twice in a row. But in fact many theses which are referred do get accepted within a year or 18 months, because the examiners' report on why you were refused the doctorate provides a crucial ladder back. The report is an unbreakable and unalterable contract with you. It must set out in detail what you need to do to reach the required standard of work, and the examiners cannot subsequently add new demands or change their conditions. So if you do get referred, it is important not to fall into despair. Instead consult very intensively with your supervisors on what you need to do to meet the examiners' requirements, and then set out to fully deliver what has been asked for. If you consistently follow their brief for changes then they are almost bound to accept your thesis at the second time of asking.

There are some strategies which you can follow in the oral exam and which may help dissuade the examiners from asking for genuine minor revisions, or for larger and more substantive changes short of referral, or even from concluding that a referral is necessary. In all your initial responses you must 'keep faith' with what you have done. Give a committed defence of your research, responding as flexibly and creatively as you can to any critical arguments. Listen carefully to what the examiners say, and think hard about it. But then set out to show why their counterpoints do not hold and how your research makes a substantial, value-added contribution to knowledge. This advice does not mean that you should adopt a completely inflexible or mindless insistence that all is well with your analysis. If the examiners have serious doubts after several interactions then a stubborn perseverance on your part can aggravate things. It could make things worse by appearing perverse to an unsympathetic examiner, and elicit a similar hard line from them in return. So beyond keeping the faith you need also to practice 'Defence in depth'.

This approach recognizes that most academics want to teach something and to modify other people's thinking. They want to have their input registered and get their viewpoint accepted or at least recognized. Senior professionals who have agreed to be a PhD examiner will give up a week to reading and commenting on your text, and perhaps another day to travelling across country to listen to you in person. They are by no means immune to these motivations, even if subconsciously. The examiners are not there for the money or the fun of it, but in pursuit of a concept of professional duty. So their own position in the profession is obviously important to them. And that provides you with an opportunity to deflect potentially destructive criticism or demands for difficult revisions into new pathways. Defence in depth has several main elements.

- Check before you print your final text that your thesis will not unnecessarily annoy your examiners. They must have some relevant expertise, or otherwise why are they examiners? And it is only natural for them to want to see their work (or their school of thought's work) recognized in new research. Incorporate some of their publications into the bibliography and try to refer to them subtly and non-controversially in the opening chapter at least. This does not have to be an artificial thing, since many general points can be referenced in multiple different ways. Think also about their referencing circle, and be careful that you are not gratuitously attacking a school of thought with which one of the examiners is closely identified.
- Where an examiner is critical of your work in the oral exam, acknowledge that she has made a good point which will henceforward be a stimulus to your thinking. But see if you

can get her to put it into a different, less threatening perspective. Try to adapt and absorb a hostile argument in ways that deflect it from being a criticism of what you have done: 'That's an interesting point. I hadn't thought of it in quite that way before. And of course if one went further down that avenue, one might look also at X and Y. But, you see, the reasons I approached it differently in this particular study were ...' Sometimes it may help to link an examiner's points to arguments or responses given at conference or seminar presentations, and to show that you have already tried to respond to them.

♦ Make clear also that your research is a PhD thesis carried out with minimal resources and not a large-scale funded research project. This difference is one that senior examiners (a long way past their own thesis studies) can too easily lose sight of. 'Your point is obviously an important one for a fully-fledged, confirmatory study. If I had had the resources to do A or follow up B, then I agree that this is a line that I would have liked to develop. But, of course, in a modest, exploratory study like mine, the same kind of approach was unfortunately not feasible.' Subtly make clear that you have achieved a great deal on a shoestring, largely thanks to the heroic amount of work effort you have put in.

♦ Refer to the possibility of publishing your work in journal articles or a possible book. If an examiner persists with a point which they obviously believe is important, make clear that you will have to think it through but that it will be fully incorporated in any publications arising from the thesis. Sincerely meant, and put across strongly, this concession is often enough to satisfy an unhappy examiner. They know perfectly well that very few people are likely to read a thesis buried on a university library's shelves. If they are convinced that an error or misdirection which they see in your work will be corrected before it reaches the public domain, they may not persist in demanding revisions of the thesis text itself. This aspect of defence in depth obviously works best if you can come across as a competent author defending a strong thesis that is likely to be published, in whole or part.

◆ Danger signs to look out for occur when an examiner is unusually insistent on certain points, returning to them repeatedly. She may show evident scepticism about your responses, and perhaps even follow up her initial points in ways that strengthen her original criticism and seem to enlarge the gulf between your two positions. Here you may have to acknowledge the force of a repeated criticism, but you should still try to pare down the scope of the changes the examiners are set on demanding. If both examiners join in voicing criticisms, be especially careful to acknowledge the importance of what they are saying and to give a flexible response to the points made.

Your supervisor can be an important help to you in preparing an effective defence in depth. Nowadays it is worth asking them to phone or e-mail the examiners informally a few days before the oral exam, in order to sound them out on any major issues which they have. If your supervisor calls too early the chances are the examiners may not have read the thesis yet. But equally, ringing the night before the exam is not much help, because then you have too little time to think through or research a response. Some very traditional examiners still believe that a doctoral candidate should enter their oral exam completely 'cold', and should then have to respond to whatever issues get thrown at them, 'thinking on your feet'. However, most modern examiners can see the value of alerting doctoral candidates to any main problems or points of concern they have, so that you can anticipate a rough agenda for the oral exam and think through some considered responses to the key issues. Some very conscientious examiners may even release to your supervisor (never to you directly) a copy of their preliminary report on the thesis, to give you time to prepare a fully-fledged 'defence' case. But this is still a very rare occurrence. Once your supervisor has some intelligence about the examiners' reactions, you should meet with her to discuss what the possible problems are and how they can best be handled. Again this is most useful a day or so before the oral exam rather than on the morning itself.

After an oral exam is over and things have gone well, as they normally do, most examiners will congratulate you immediately on getting the doctorate. But in many cases where you have actually passed satisfactorily, as well as in the minority of cases where a referral is possible, they may postpone telling you the outcome until they have talked things over for a while with your supervisor. In these post-viva conversations a skilful supervisor can be very helpful to you, in persuading the examiners to keep their demands for 'minor' revisions down to a minimum. The supervisor's role is also crucial after a referral, in ensuring that you are asked only for a clear and achievable set of changes. Make sure then that your supervisor will be around on the day of the oral exam and free to carry out this key role. In some universities supervisors are also permitted to sit in on the oral exam itself, but not to say anything. This is never a good idea in a British-style system, because it simply undermines your status as an independent professional.

Conclusions

Just as in athletics or a professional sport, finishing a thesis well usually requires a lot of advance preparation. In earlier chapters I have touched on many different logistical issues which if left unaddressed can cause you days or weeks of delay at the final version stage. These issues are time-bombs, which may lie apparently dormant only to explode under your feet as you rush to complete. Poor style, long sentences, complex grammar, padded writing and repetitions left alone at an earlier stage all have to be fixed. Hard-to-justify research 'methods' or odd choices of research strategy can require complex explanation later on to try and disguise them or explain them away. Interview quotations have to be firmed up and attributed exactly, and weak methods of evidencing will show up more prominently in the referencing (or lack of it) at key points. Poor-quality charts, diagrams and tables, often left unscrutinized in separate pages at the ends of draft chapters, will now look ragged if incorporated into your text. Partial bibliographic entries have to be filled in. The most common problems are Web references that prove evanescent and cannot be recaptured for checking; source documents in far-away archives that cannot be revisited; and newspaper or magazine clippings where you recorded inadequately source details at the outset. If you are using notes, significant 'version control' problems between the notes and bibliography can become apparent at this stage.

Even the suggestions made in this chapter mostly cannot be last-minute operations. Many require you to do things almost from the first stages of your research. For instance, if you are to participate in nominating examiners, or to be able to handle a general professional conversation well in an oral exam, or to choose useful ('sales pitch') words for your thesis title, you cannot switch on these capabilities overnight, or even in your last year. You need to get out into your discipline's conference circuit at least two or three years ahead of time – so that you know the personalities of possible examiners, and have a good sense of where the profession has been so far and is going now. Planning ahead for a smooth end-game is something you always need to keep an eye on. The comforting thing is that these efforts at professional orientation will also be of benefit to you beyond the submission and examination process.

A doctorate is more than just a pile of words, or a smartly bound thesis with your name on the front in gold letters. It is a process of change, and the crystallization of a substantial slice of your intellectual life. So ending a doctorate is not as simple as just completing the mandatory submission and examination stages. These mark the bureaucratically defined terminus of your apprenticeship. But they do not in themselves give meaning to three or four years of intense effort. For a more lasting way of getting your research acknowledged, you need to get it published and into print, to which I turn in the next chapter.

9

Publishing Your Research

> What good is a good idea if no one ever hears it?
> *AT & T advert* [1]

Publishing your work is the key way in which you can insert it into the slipstream of academic ideas, and so avoid your thesis becoming just 'shelf-bending' research, sitting in your university library and slowly bending a shelf over the years. The main route is to submit papers to professional journals. More rarely you can reshape your whole thesis into book form and get it accepted by a publisher as a monograph. Neither form of publication is quick or straightforward. They can protract your end-game long past the formal date at which your title metamorphoses into Dr.

Writing and submitting journal papers

> How odd it is that anyone should not see that all observation must be for or against some view if it is to be of any service.
> *Charles Darwin* [2]

A journal paper is an apparently simple-looking artefact, but it is not shaped just by the author. The professional community as a whole influences what is published, by fixing the norms and conventions of learned journals. And the editors and referees of a journal normally set specific conditions for each article. To be effective in publishing papers you need first to

228 AUTHORING A PHD

understand the journals market in your discipline and form a clear idea of what gets published in the discipline's journals, and what does not. Only then can you begin to effectively target an appropriate journal and to get your material accepted and into print.

Understanding the journals market

Academics arrange orthodox print journals into a rough hierarchy of excellent, above average, average, below average, and marginal journals. There are four major influences on journals' long-run reputations: their methods of refereeing; their citation scores; the journal's type and its circulation (which are closely interrelated); and the overall time lag from first submitting a paper through to its eventual publication.

Refereeing systems. Peer group review is the central quality-assurance process in the academic world, and how well it is handled is crucial for a journal's standing. A top-rank journal will send your paper to four diverse and well-qualified referees, and reach an editors' decision on the basis of three verdicts – quite a demanding threshold to surmount. It will be able to secure the involvement of senior members of the profession in reviewing papers. In each discipline as you go down the hierarchy of journals the publication requirements will get progressively less strict. A somewhat less prestigious journal may seek views from two or three outside referees and go on two positives. It may not be able to attract the same quality of people to look at prospective articles, bearing in mind that referees are not paid for their efforts.

Lower down in the hierarchy in most professions are those journals which do not run proper independent refereeing. Instead they may serve mainly as a vehicle for a 'referencing circle' around a particular clique in the profession. Similarly, more 'ideological' journals may single-mindedly plug a particular viewpoint, without ever publishing critical work undertaken from divergent positions. Some journals may referee internally only amongst an editorial team, or perhaps the editors may somewhat 'rig' who gets to write the references, so as to attract positive responses from their referees for material they want to accept.

This is especially the case if the journal positively needs copy just to keep its pages filled, or is struggling to keep alive the apparent level of interest in their viewpoint or their subfield. However, there are important exceptions to this general pattern. In many humanities, arts and social science disciplines there are still quite prestigious journals with large circulations, which none the less do not operate on the basis of professional-standard peer group refereeing.

In addition to the number of opinions that editors seek, there are also important differences in the conditions under which refereeing takes place. The best journals tend to use a 'double-blind' system of refereeing. Here anything that would identify the author is removed before the paper goes to referees. The referee then writes an anonymous comment, which normally comes back to you. (To comply with this approach, you usually need to have two title pages on a paper you submit. The first shows all the author names, their university affiliations and any other identifying elements, such as a note of thanks. The journal removes this page before sending the paper out to referees. The second page is retained and shows only the article title without any author-identifying elements.) This system is supposed to protect new authors from being rejected just because they are unknown. It is meant to put them more on an even plane with established authors. It is also supposed to prevent rivalries between academic personalities colouring what referees write, and to prevent any automatic 'taking sides' by referees. At the same time referees' anonymity ensures that they can be frank and say what they really think, without worrying that adverse professional consequences might attach to them in future if they comment unfavourably. Some journals now use 'single-blind' refereeing, where referees know who authors are but can still comment anonymously. The final option is an 'open' approach where referees know who authors are and authors know who has commented on their work. Some editors feel that double-blind refereeing is fake, because experienced referees can usually scan the literature references and work out who authors are. Equally, sheltering behind the cloak of anonymity, unaccountable referees may be overly critical or negative in their reviews. But most professional association journals still abide by the double-blind system, and in my view its value for new authors is still considerable.

Citation scores. Every year the ISI 'Web of Knowledge' bibliometric system counts how much articles published in each of the journals it indexes are referenced across all its journals in the social sciences and in the humanities.[3] (These systems used to be known as the Social Science Citation Index and the Humanities Citation Index, but have been rebranded.) The Web of Knowledge's coverage is heavily biased towards the United States and towards English-language journals more generally. It is very patchy in some particular fields like law, where most UK or other overseas journals are not covered. Despite these limitations, as in other walks of life, partial or inadequate data like these are widely seen as preferable to no data at all. Every serious academic wants to be noticed, and so *faute de mieux*, the Web of Knowledge's scores influence where the academic 'stars' send their papers. They also are key ways in which journals try to measure how well they are doing against their competitors.

Despite all the elaborate arrangements for sifting and improving academic papers most current evidence shows that the median journal article is referred to by nobody in the five years after it is published, and very few articles have a referencing life longer than this. In major bibliometric analyses (like the ISI indices) the leading journals in most disciplines are those which manage to achieve an impact score over or reasonably close to 1. This means that on average each of their published papers is referred to at least once in five years by some other paper in one of the journals included in the analysis. Any journal with an average citation score of more than 0.5 is also doing relatively well. Many perfectly reputable journals may have citation scores of below 0.25, meaning that papers there have a less than one-in-four chance of being referenced by anyone else.

Circulation and journal type. The chances of anyone else noticing your work partly depend upon how many people even get to eyeball the journal where it has appeared. Large-circulation journals are often those which are longest-lived in a particular discipline. Having reached good world-wide library access long ago (around 2000 to 3000 copies or above), they can to some extent rely on inertial ordering and librarians' concern for continuity to shield them from current market forces. Often these are 'omnibus' journals with rather a broad mission to cover a whole discipline, especially those run by prestigious professional associations.

By contrast, most recent start-up journals (in the last thirty years) have been specialist journals with much more focused markets and editorial statements of intent. The actual paying circulation of many new or specialized journals, even those which have been running for a decade, may be counted in the tens or at best low hundreds. Commercial publishers have kept on starting new specialist journals, even since the late 1990s when the academic market has been shrinking. Some of the circulations for these titles are so low that there is a real risk to the academics who submit papers – initially that very few people will ever get sight of the journal. In the longer term there may be some degree of risk that a small, newish journal may fold and its materials become even less accessible.

Time lags. Journal publishing is a game of many parts. First the editors send your paper out to their required number of referees. These people then sit on it for a certain period before responding, usually taking six weeks to three months, even for an efficiently run journal. In many fields responses can drag on much longer, up to four to six months, because scrupulous editors have to collect in sufficient comments to make a decision, which always takes longer than a single reference. Next the editors have to work though their in-tray of refereed submissions and decide how to respond to your paper in the light of the comments and scores, which usually takes several weeks, adding perhaps another month. Once your article is accepted without further substantive revisions, then it goes into a publication queue. Time lags from acceptance to publication in journals are almost always at least 6 months, and probably average around 12 months. Good journals will also publish their statistics in an annual report, either on their Web site or in the journal pages itself. Most reputable journals now indicate when papers were accepted, and some will give details of how long the editorial process took.

The main trouble is that journal editors and publishers are often risk-averse people who like to maintain a 'bank' of accepted articles as a safeguard against running out of copy. Some editors accept many more articles than they can feasibly publish, and so create a backlog problem. In some pathological cases the editors of highly prestigious journals can create a time lag from acceptance to publication which is up to 30 months or even three years. This approach makes a complete mockery of any journal's role to provide swift, lively and contemporaneous feedback to their academic profession. At the other extreme there are hand-to-mouth journals which only get by through their editors constantly living on their wits, acquiring papers at conferences, and so on. Here the copy for the very next issue may be problematic, so if your paper arrives at an opportune moment the editors may bend over backwards to accept it and publish it quickly. This might seem a good result for you, but only if the journal has a significant circulation and has maintained its quality reputation despite copy shortages.

In addition to these major influences on the long-run standing of journals, there are a further four shorter-term or less important influences on how journals are seen by the profession. These factors may not matter so much for the most-cited journals. But for all other titles they are worth considering because they help to differentiate the middle mass of journals one from another.

The reputation of the editors (or editorial teams) and the editorial board. Despite the importance of refereeing systems, changes of editor can have an important influence on how journals develop within their long-run market niches. Academics love speculating about what different editors' priorities are, especially for the bigger omnibus journals. Editing a journal is a thankless task, but one which tends to attract senior academics at a certain stage in their careers. A good editor is someone who is well known in the discipline, intellectually respected but not closed-minded, and who can project a strong and distinctive style for her journal. The editors who become best known often have a 'project' for changing their journal's appeal in a particular direction. Good editors are also often interested in new ideas and in bringing on younger people in their discipline via helpful and supportive refereeing. They are always committed to encouraging good writing, strong scholarship and improved standards of professional communication. The conference circuit gossip machine is often the best guide on where different journals stand in terms of the editors' orientation – yet another reason for getting out there and plugging in.

Editorial boards (sometimes also called advisory boards) are a much more distant influence on what journals do than are the editors. But the extent to which a journal has well-known and senior people on its editorial board can provide a fair indication of where it stands in the international profession. If it has no one well known involved as a board member it may have only a very small circulation, or there may be some problem in its approach to refereeing.

Professional ownership versus commercial ownership. In general, journals run by professional bodies in each of the disciplines have higher prestige than those which are chiefly set up by commercial publishers and entrepreneurial academics to earn a major buck. Professional journals are normally supplied free to members of the professional association as part of their overall subscription, which tends to mean that far more individual readers in at least its home country will routinely notice that your paper has been published. There are far fewer individual subscriptions to commercial journals, and so readers mainly have to come across your paper in the library or look it up directly. The chief reasons why people find your material are because they regularly search particular journals' electronic contents; because a colleague or the journal's e-mail alerting service draws their attention to it; or because they are starting a new article or research project of their own and hence are doing a systematic literature trawl.

Survey responses. Most of the key professional groups in the major countries survey their members each year on how they rate their discipline's journals. These responses often provide invaluable guidance about which journals are actually being read by academics and students in the different fields. Articles in prestigious journals are quite frequently unreadably dense or too esoteric for most professional readers. Their high level of citations can be sustained at any one time by a small group of elite academics citing each other but not necessarily being read or followed more widely. Sometimes a cohesive referencing circle of lesser authors can also achieve high (mutual) citation scores.

Quality of production. Journals vary greatly in their 'look and feel'. Older journals, and those run by professional bodies, often have a cramped, unattractive appearance. Indeed some misguided editors deliberately cultivate a 'classical' (that is, unreadable) format for their journals, under the illusion that this makes them look more academically 'respectable'. From an author's point of view this approach is a liability. You want your journal offprints to look prestigious and presentable to appointment and promotion committees for a long time ahead, not nondescript and old-fashioned within a few years. Other things being equal, it is always best to go for journals that have a stylish and simple modern design and clear, uncluttered layouts, incorporating appropriate amounts of white space around your text. Good handling of equations, graphics, charts and tables is important in the social sciences.

All these points of comparison above assume that you are considering publishing in an orthodox journal that essentially sells paper copies as the basis of its subscriptions. Even these journals have responded extensively to the growth of the Internet by expanding their electronic presence. Virtually all titles are available electronically via major contents aggregator sites (like Ingenta or JStor) and some journals also have electronic-only subscriptions.[4] In addition to the paper circulation of journals it may be worth learning about your possible target journal's electronic readerships, including the number of times articles were downloaded. Some journals will also publish articles in enhanced form electronically, such as using colourized versions instead of being confined to the black-and-white of the normal print version. Other print titles do 'advance on publication', putting up forthcoming articles for on-line access on their Web sites as soon as they are accepted, rather than waiting for the relevant journal issue to be printed. This way your article is officially seen as published six months earlier than otherwise, which can be important when you are looking for an academic job.

A further way to curtail the acceptance-to-publication delay is to publish in a Web-only journal, which is published electronically but not in print. Such titles are common now in the physical sciences, and they are beginning to spring up too in parts of the humanities and social sciences, especially in areas like information science, informatics and business studies. Where they have become established some refereed Web-only journals are starting to be quite successful and well read.

But this is still a developing area, and across most of the humanities and social sciences Web-only articles are not yet seen as full publications.

Appreciating what gets published

When you have identified the hierarchy of journals in your discipline you next need to consider what material they see as publishable. One kind of insight can be gained from looking at Figure 9.1, which shows an example of the forms for grading papers which many journals send out to their referees. Editors ask reviewers to score the paper they are assessing against seven or eight specific criteria, mainly to help firm up what can otherwise often be rather vague or specific qualitative comments from referees, and to assist editors to compare the strength of different referees' feelings. The most-used criteria are:

♦ *Originality or novelty of approach.* Any material submitted to a journal should be original and not have been published in a journal before. A paper that just replicates many previous papers is less likely to secure acceptance.

♦ *Scholarship and accuracy.* A paper should accurately and comprehensively summarize the current research literature bearing directly upon its central questions. Incomplete coverage of key material, or partial referencing, or misrepresentations of previous literature, are likely to attract criticisms from referees and to be seen by them as warning signs of deeper intellectual failings.

♦ *Quality of writing.* Journals want to publish readable material, if they can get any which meets their many other requirements. Obvious grammatical infelicities and a dull overall expository style will often push referees towards rejection.

♦ *Research methods used.* Journals place a lot of emphasis upon publishing work that uses a self-conscious methodological approach, preferably advancing it in certain respects. A paper which simply expresses your intellectual standpoint in an assertive way, without generating substantial supporting evidence, is unlikely to seem

Figure 9.1 An example of a journal article evaluation form

Please circle a score for the paper you have evaluated on each of the criteria below.
You may find it helpful to refer to these criteria also in commenting on the paper.

	Poor	Below average	Average, competent	Good, above average	Excellent, outstanding
Originality or novelty of approach:	1	2	3	4	5
Scholarship/accuracy:	1	2	3	4	5
Quality of writing:	1	2	3	4	5
Research methods used:	1	2	3	4	5
Theoretical interest:	1	2	3	4	5
Interest and importance for a professional readership:	1	2	3	4	5
Relevance for the journal's mission:	1	2	3	4	5
Interest for a wider audience:	1	2	3	4	5

What is your overall judgement of the paper?

☐ Accept   ☐ Accept subject to minor revisions   ☐ Revise and resubmit

☐ Reject but suggest major revisions and journal reconsider   ☐ Reject

professionally competent. There are some exceptions in parts of the humanities, a few solely theoretical areas that may place a premium on *not* having an empirical base, such as philosophy, and some modern literary theory and cultural theory.

◆ *Theoretical interest.* Of the one in ten articles which make genuine advances, quite a few are purely theoretical pieces, calling for a reconceptualization of a particular topic, or advancing propositions which might (several years from now) inspire an empirical research agenda. But genuine theoretical advances in the humanities, arts and social sciences are harder to achieve than it might appear from the outside. When acting as journal referees, senior people are notoriously hostile to specious theoretical advances, especially those which rest on nothing more than neologisms (inventing a new word to label an already known phenomenon or point of view). In empirically orientated disciplines, referees and editors may be sceptical that innovations which are purely theoretical and unaccompanied by evidence will have any application in practice.

◆ *Interest and importance to a professional readership.* Material can be original and novel, but still be boring or of only minor interest to most people in a discipline if the topic covered is not seen as important. This criterion is especially relevant for 'omnibus' journals that aspire to carry material from right across a discipline. Their editors will be especially resistant to publishing papers which may meet most of the other criteria in this list, but are unlikely to be widely read or seen as significant or interesting across a substantial section of their discipline.

◆ *Relevance for the journal's mission.* The editors of specialist journals, which aim only to tap a readership within a particular subfield of a discipline, will resist publishing material that is 'non-core' for them or even lies close to the boundaries of their field. They may fear that such material could blur the identity of their journal.

◆ *Interest for a wider audience.* Across the humanities and social sciences some of the biggest-selling journals are long-established titles which manage to bridge across between a purely academic readership and a more general readership in professionally related fields. Editors of this kind of journal will not want to run material that only people with PhDs in the discipline care about or can understand.

A typical journal will use most but not all of the criteria shown in Figure 9.1. So to this extent my composite form may overstate the difficulty of getting your work published. But on the other hand, top journals in each field are likely to require that a paper be judged 'good, above average' or 'outstanding' on around half their editorial criteria, and without attracting any 'poor' scores. Getting agreement on this from four, three or even two referees is often a challenge.

Yet despite the elaborate refereeing procedures most academics will readily acknowledge that contemporary journals contain a lot of routine papers. How great this proportion actually is will no doubt vary from subject to subject. And perhaps there may be difficulty in securing agreement about which papers fall into this category. One now rather dated but still interesting attempt at systematically assessing the value of journal papers looked at those dealing with the psychology of memory and verbal learning. The authors (E. Tulving and S. A. Madigan) found that two thirds of papers were 'inconsequential'.[5] They then classified a further quarter of their sample of papers as ' "run-of-the-mill", they represent technically competent variations on well-known themes'. The routine and unimportant papers usually offered 'one or more of the following conclusions:

(a)   variable X has an effect on variable Y;
(b)   the findings do not appear to be entirely inconsistent with the ABC theory;
(c)   the findings suggest a need for revising the ABC theory (although no inkling is provided as to how);
(d)   processes under study are extremely complex and cannot be readily understood;
(e)   the experiment clearly demonstrates the need for further research on this problem;
(f)   the experiment shows that the method used is useful for doing experiments of this type;
(g)   the results do not support the hypothesis, but the experiment now appears to be an inadequate test of it.'

Of most papers they looked at the evaluation team concluded that: 'their main purpose lies in providing redundancy and assurance to those readers whose faith in the orderliness of nature ... needs strengthening'. This meant that in their judgement fewer than one in ten papers in the area genuinely advanced learning.

The leading American psychologist Robert J. Sternberg suggested that in his field the papers evaluated as out-of-the-ordinary and particularly useful do one or more of the following:

- report results whose findings can be unambiguously interpreted;
- report experiments with a particularly clever design, which can be used as a pattern or 'paradigm' by other researchers;
- report surprising findings which none the less make sense in some theoretical context;
- debunk some previously held presupposition;
- present a fresh way of looking at an old problem;
- report results of major theoretical or practical significance; or
- 'integrate into a new, simpler framework, data that previously required a complex, possibly unwieldy framework'.[6]

The features in this list need changing a bit and extending for other disciplines, where experiments may be unknown and even systematic data may be scarce. In most of the social sciences it is very difficult to publish case study material, but easier to get journals to accept papers including quantitative data relating to more general theories or controversies. In arts and humanities subjects, papers are often more thematic or theoretical, and their 'usefulness' may depend on their interpretative impact. More of a premium tends to be placed on good writing and style, plus the pursuit of scholarly norms, such as originality, novelty, full referencing, new sources etc. And, unlike the social sciences, journals in some humanities disciplines (like history) are more likely to accept case study material. But Sternberg's criteria above still provide a helpful first checklist of questions to ask in assessing how worthwhile your own particular paper will be. And the contrast with the previous list of things that routine papers typically conclude provides quite a helpful sieve, which may help you sort out which of your chapters is worth 'paperizing' and which is not.

So far I have focused solely on main articles in journals, which are the primary means for advancing professional knowledge, and the chief 'product' you can hope to get from one or more of your thesis chapters. But, especially when you are starting out on publishing, it is useful to bear in mind also that many journals also print shorter pieces, which have lower-quality thresholds for publication and may be easier to achieve:

- *Research notes* are usually around 4000 words maximum and they report a specific empirical finding in an uncluttered way, without being surrounded by an elaborate theoretical or literature review apparatus or other lead-in material. It is usually much better to submit a straightforward piece of empirical reportage as a strong research note than to inflate it into a weak or anaemic main article.

- *Comments* are similar shorter pieces, of around 2000 to 4000 words in length, which pick up on and contest, criticize or analyse a point in the existing literature, especially a piece that the journal concerned has recently published. Most journal editors want to encourage debates and controversies in their journal and hence look kindly on balanced, concise and good quality comments.

- *Short-article journals* exist in many fields (like philosophy, geography and political science) which are dedicated to publishing only pieces up to around 3000 words long. Many of these journals have good reputations and are particularly interested in helping younger members of the profession.

- *Review articles* are published by many journals. They take a particular subfield of a discipline's literature and discuss its intellectual themes and development as a whole, drawing out commonalities between authors, identifying promising research avenues, and so on. Review articles should also have a distinctive critical angle or value-added argument of their own. They are normally around 6000 words long. Obviously they do not need elaborate methodologies or original empirical materials, and hence they are quicker to undertake.

However, most published review articles are actually commissioned by journal editors from senior figures in the discipline, with an established publications record. So if you have an idea for such a piece, send a letter to the journal editor you are targeting before you begin work. Give a brief outline of what you propose and the treatment you will use, and make clear that the length will be strictly 5000 to 6000 words. Check that the journal has not published a review article on this theme recently, because the editor will not want to repeat such a piece within three or four years. The editor may then either write back putting you off the project (which avoids your spending time on it abortively), or they may say that they cannot commit themselves to accept it but that it sounds interesting and they would like to referee the full version in the normal way. Very rarely they may be more positive than this, in effect semi-commissioning the piece from you.

Research notes, comments, pieces in short-article journals, and review articles are all excellent ways of beginning to publish at the start of an academic career.

Getting your material published

The first barrier new authors face in publishing papers is a psychological one. Main papers in academic journals are deliberately made hard-boiled and less accessible products by what Minkin calls 'the convention of perfection in presentation and the reconstructed logic of events that accompanies it'.[7] Papers often systematically perpetuate a myth about how their authors did research. The author or research team read the existing literature and ingeniously identified a problem, seen by none or very few people before them. They then coined a new theory; or saw how to apply an existing theory in an interesting way; or generated a distinct empirical test and prediction; or devised a new method for analysing an intractable problem; or they discovered a key new source hitherto neglected; or otherwise had a brilliant research idea of their own. Next they applied this new approach in a precise, targeted fashion, going to exactly the right data, evidence or sources first time. Of course, thanks to their perceptiveness, the authors almost immediately generated interesting results, generally confirmatory of their initial starting position. They conducted their analysis clearly and incisively to show hidden layers of causation or meaning or complexity resolved by their approach. There was never any muddle or confusion in their research process, beyond that generated by the clutter or indirection of earlier researchers' misguided ideas, which was soon decisively cleared away. The authors were never at a loss for explanation, but rather had a confident understanding throughout, which led to their strong value-added conclusions. They were sure that their path-breaking work would be appreciated and would now be taken up and referred to many times by future scholars. They conclude with some modest words about the agenda for future research in the aftermath of their contribution. This research article myth is a potent beacon for professionals across all the social sciences, arts and humanities. It is what people almost always aspire to reproduce in writing a journal paper. More worryingly, it is an established pattern which most editors and referees tacitly demand should be followed religiously in the structure and format of submitted papers, if they are to be successful in getting accepted.

The reality of doing research and publishing papers is quite different, for the most senior professional academics as much as for PhD students. Most new research starts out as an itch, a vague discontent with an accepted answer or a dissatisfaction with what has already been written. Authors develop a paper driven most by a career urge to get something into print and onto their CV, or a drive to get some professional recognition, or a desire to express their differences from or belonging to some group or school of thought. After a lot of chopping and changing in its direction, the paper lurches off the ground in a highly unsatisfactory preliminary form on the author's PC. The basic idea is next given in university workshops or seminars, only to be criticized by even the author's friends. After a lot of rewriting, and many false starts, the author has something more credible and decides to devote some scarce research time or even scarcer sabbatical to the chosen theme, perhaps also searching for a grant or funding support to meet the costs involved. The actual in-depth research period proves confusing, demoralizing and difficult. The sources or evidence are not there, or the data resist all explanation, or the analysis which the author expected to stand up is bit by bit destroyed. Getting to anything but a commonplace explanation turns out to be overwhelmingly more complex than the author expected. The funded or designated period for research ends inconclusively and the author is profoundly depressed, and goes back to other things – teaching, administration, 'distracter' research. But after a while it is clear that this project remains the best bet for publication amongst the possible materials that the author has available. In time she gradually begins to see a couple of different ways for presenting things in a better light. After a lot more effort and false starts she manages to reconstruct something vaguely in the form of the necessary research myth and create a paper which can claim a little value-added, even if this is partly achieved by judiciously exaggerating or misrepresenting a previous viewpoint. After giving the paper to a sceptical audience at a professional conference and making a lot of revisions in its aftermath, the author selects a journal and sends the paper off.

After a long pause the editor writes back rejecting the paper outright and enclosing two or three comments from anonymous referees which make strong and devastating criticisms, in the process judiciously exaggerating or misrepresenting what the author is trying to do. The author is again a bit depressed at this reception. But after a while she picks up the piece again, tones it down, reworks it to avoid the misinterpretations of the previous referees, adds more references to deflect possible criticisms, and submits it to another less good journal, lower down the profession's 'pecking order' of academic journals. After a further long pause the editor writes back grudgingly conceding that perhaps they might publish it, but only if the author cuts the length by a quarter and makes revisions to accommodate all the comments of two more anonymous referees which are attached. The author struggles to regard this as a success, especially when it becomes apparent that the two referees want contradictory things and that the editor has opted out of explaining how they can be reconciled. Eventually though the author tones down anything that obviously annoyed either referee and obfuscates any other points that seem controversial. She achieves the cuts asked for by radically underexplaining the methods and the evidence or data findings, making them more difficult and inaccessible. The article is resubmitted, the editor at last writes back accepting it, and after a very long further wait it duly appears in print. In due course the article is referenced five or six times in other articles or publications in the field over the next five years, including three times by its own author in other papers. After five years the paper is scarcely ever referred to again. You might think that this account is pretty cynical and extreme. But in fact the sketch above is a very moderate one and not at all unusual. It captures my typical pre-publication experience quite well, for example. And I have already noted above the low citation rates of journal papers in general (although, of course, I fondly believe that this aspect is *not* typical of my own work).

Research students are often perplexed to find that meeting the requirements for originality in the doctorate does not in itself guarantee the publishability of their material. You might ask, if a reputable university and (in Europe and British/ Commonwealth systems) independent examiners have accepted that a research work is a substantive contribution to knowledge, then surely professional journals in the same discipline must recognize the same qualities? This matching up of criteria might seem even closer for a papers model dissertation, where the chapters are supposed to be potentially independently publishable. But in practice a great deal of material in PhD dissertations may not be journal-publishable. In 'big book' theses the lead-in and lead-out chapters are chiefly there to frame the thesis core, and so they cannot usually be translated into stand-alone journal articles. In many theses some of the densest and most research-intensive core chapters may not be independently publishable, because they consist of very detailed case study or applications research at a micro-level. In addition they are often much too long to fit within the normal paper length (8000 words or less). Universities and examiners will accept such detailed or micro-level work as perfectly valid scholarship, and the kind of exploratory or observational contribution that can be appropriately done by a PhD student. But that does not necessarily mean that any journal wishes to broadcast news of these discoveries, unless it is relevant for broader professional debates.

As the Darwin epigraph to this section stresses (p. 227), all such case material or detailed evidence has to be analysed and interpreted in a context where other scholars can grasp it as significant for some controversy or debate in their discipline. Almost the first question that journal referees ask of authors with case studies is: 'What is your case study a case of? And why should we care?' For a PhD intrinsic interest can play a larger role in justifying case analysis, but professional readers are much more sceptical when it comes to journal publication. Similarly a piece of text may be accepted as meeting the doctoral standard, without being inherently well written or appealing. Acceptable doctorates can be worthy and dull, unexceptional, micro-focused, ponderous, over-referenced, hyper-cautious, overly methodological, and so on, without being failed. But none of these qualities are recommendations for publication in a journal.

Start by identifying which chapter of your thesis has most potential to become a paper. Think about how your possible paper is likely to score on the criteria considered in Figure 9.1 and then do your market research. In the library, look carefully at the various journals you might submit to, so that you are thoroughly familiar with what they accept and are sure that your paper will fit their established pattern. Get your supervisors' advice on what changes are needed and which are the possible outlets that you might send it to. As in every other walk of life, choosing a journal involves trade-offs. If you go for a very prestigious journal with your first serious publication and are successful then you will scoop more prestige points. But you are also far more likely to wait quite a long time (three to six months) only to be eventually rejected. You may also get rather strong criticism of your piece, which can be demoralizing. Or a top journal may reject the paper in its current form but leave half-open a possible door back, if very time-consuming demands for changes are met. Even if you make these revisions a 'sniffy' editor may still not accept that the piece is sufficiently changed, which is invariably very demotivating.

To lose half a year to a whole year on abortive efforts to publish like this can seriously jeopardize your overall work rhythms, so there is really no point in pitching your material higher than it is likely to be accepted. Journals rarely change their spots, so do not let the idea that your paper is particularly path-breaking or novel affect your judgements here. Opt for a journal which publishes the same kind of material as your paper, and has a good but not necessarily a top reputation in your field, ideally one with fairly low time lags and an approach of encouraging new authors. Again the conference circuit is your best guide to the state of play across the main journals in your discipline. But it is always worth 'triangulating' two or three views of each journal, to control for the potent misinformation capabilities of professional rumour machines.

Once you have a clear target journal in view, amend your chapter to fit its requirements, both small and large. Try to make sure that everything conforms exactly to the journal's style guide, and that the references are in the required format. Editors are notoriously hostile to authors who submit material in the wrong style format. But the single most important change to put a chapter into paper format is always to get the length down. Journal papers should *never* be more than 8000 words long – only academic superstars will be accepted above this length in most fields. Be careful to split up long chapters into manageable paper-length components before trying to get them published. Squeezing the length down even further to 7000 or even 6000 words will usually greatly boost your chances of getting a main article published. If you go much below this length, however, there is a danger that the editor or referees may not see your piece as a proper main article but as an over-length research note. They could then ask for a 5000 word paper to be cut further, to fit within the normal 3000 to 4000 word limit for research notes.

Journal papers also need to be written in a different style from chapters. They must be completely self-standing and independently intelligible, with no references to material in other chapters. Papers also need to be written to do just one job, to hit a single target well – whereas PhD chapters often handle several aspects, a key reason why they are longer. You need a fast and preferably high-impact start to your paper, devoid of any waffle, which gets to the key issues quickly. Cut out long literature reviews or set-up components, because your readers are experts with busy professional lives. Try and reference other recent synoptic literature reviews to avoid running over more familiar territory yourself. But make sure that you make sufficient appropriate genuflections to previous scholarship in the area, since the authors of relevant work are likely to be your referees. Get long data or methodology sections out of the main line of the text argument and put them into annexes, leaving the key 'bottom line' results appropriately established and framed in the main text. Many journals now are developing a terser style and putting data and other annexes onto the Web only, a trend that will probably develop further. Remember that the 'need to know' criterion can be easily adapted to meeting the needs of a professional readership. Applying the 'Say it once, say it right' maxim can also help keep length minimal.

Because of the long time lags in papers being processed by journals it is always a good idea to try and anticipate any criticisms before you send the paper off, rather than afterwards. Show your 'paperized' version of your chapter to your supervisor and fellow students, and try to get a wider range of comments by giving it at seminars and a conference. Much as it is painful to do so, you should religiously note down and carefully reflect upon the critical or bored/uncomprehending comments that you get from these audiences and readers, and then adjust your text to try and pre-empt or counter them. This kind of feedback can also sometimes be helpful in reappraising which is the best journal to send your work to.

Once you have submitted the piece and borne the frustrations of waiting for a response, you need to be able to deal with the referees' and editors' comments that you will get back. It is best to anticipate that your paper will not be straightforwardly accepted without any revisions, a rare achievement even for senior academics. Instead you should expect to receive an editor's letter which is either some kind of tentative acceptance or a not complete rejection or a flat no. An attitude of making changes to respond to all criticisms (recommended above) can stand you in good stead again here. Any journal's referees are likely to make some criticisms of your work that will be unsympathetic or misguided in some respects. But however infuriating and unjustified some criticisms may seem, the referees normally could not have made them without *something* problematic in your analysis to latch onto. Constructively handled, these pointers can help you make improvements in your work.

So if the journal comes back with an 'acceptance subject to revisions' letter, you should congratulate yourself on having made it past the worst hurdle and not let yourself be put down by also receiving some criticisms. This kind of letter may seem tentatively phrased, but it is still an implied contract that if you do your bit the journal will publish. But you need to close that contract quickly while it still 'holds'. Make it a top priority to meet *all* of the journal's conditions for acceptance and to return the paper in fully revised form within a definite short period, like three months. When you send it back give the editor a brief covering letter explaining exactly where and how you have met her requirements for changes to the text. This 'refresher' guidance will simplify her job in giving you a firm acceptance.

If the journal instead gives you a response saying 'revise, resubmit and we will referee the new version', this often seems very off-putting. The referees' comments in this case will be more serious and entail more changes to meet them, and you may well feel that even if you do a lot more work the publication prospects are not assured. But it is still worthwhile doing what the journal asks and kicking back the paper in fully revised form. Editors who have requested changes may have been careful not to commit themselves to publish any revised piece, but they will become morally obligated to you the more work you do, and the more you tell them about what you have done in an accompanying letter. If there are some changes you really cannot accept or cannot make, use your covering letter to explain why not, in very cool and dispassionate language. Many editors will give you the benefit of the doubt here, especially where you have done everything else that they and the referees asked for. In addition if the editor can see strong signs that you have changed things to meet the journal's previous reservations, she may send your revised paper out to fewer referees than with the first draft – perhaps only to the most critical referee last time. So the success rate for resubmissions is actually much better than for initial submissions. After receiving a 'rejection' letter, therefore, be very careful not to withdraw your paper in a fit of pique, nor to send it anywhere else, until you are crystal clear that the journal concerned is not going to publish it.

Even if a journal rejects your paper outright, you should still look carefully at the referees' comments and try to work out why it failed. Again discuss these reactions with your supervisor and other experienced colleagues. Next make sure that you revise the paper to prevent the same criticisms recurring elsewhere. Then pick a journal lower down the professional hierarchy and submit the revised paper to them.

While you are working on your thesis it is usually a good idea not to try and start work on any paper which does not derive from and form part of your thesis. Writing one of the shorter pieces discussed above may not be too serious a diversion from your main work. But working on a full paper on a topic different from your thesis is definitely to be avoided, because of the long time lags and concentrated effort entailed, and the potential for encountering demoralizing rejections or criticisms along the way. So stick to trying to 'paperize' your best and most original thesis chapters. It is a good idea to work on a single paper at a time. But because of the lengthy process, once you have one paper under submission, it can also be helpful to start straightaway on another one, so as to get a small 'production line' of papers progressively under way. It is better to have several publication efforts at different stages of development at any one time, as most established academics do, rather than having a single, lonely effort out there on which all your hopes rest. The chances are high that one paper, like one lottery ticket, may not progress.

In addition, many universities now expect research students with a completed doctorate (or one that is near-finished) to have at least one or two short pieces published if they are to consider them for appointment, a trend strongly reinforced in Britain by the government's research assessment exercise (RAE) process. The RAE effectively requires all academic staff to publish at least four pieces of research every five or six years, or risk being categorized as 'research inactive'. So departments are very reluctant to appoint anyone who has not shown concrete publishing capability. Similar approaches have been introduced or are being considered by governments in some other countries. So having a small portfolio of publications already in place when you graduate is becoming more important for PhD students than in previous periods.

New authors are often not aware that there is a very strong norm against submitting the same paper to more than one journal at a time. Academic journals are by and large still voluntary operations. Referees give their services free, solely out of a sense of professional commitment or obligation. And most editors draw only a modest honorarium or get no payment at all. It is consequently seen as a major abuse of trust to get free advice and guidance from journals' referees and editors while sending out the same paper to different journals at the same time. If editors find that you have made multiple submissions they will mostly react by immediately rejecting your paper and possibly blackballing you for any future consideration of your work. Academic networks are closer than you might think, and editors and referees gossip heavily about mistakes like this. If you make multiple submissions they will quickly be detected and give you an unfavourable reputation. So this potentially serious mistake must be scrupulously avoided. If you have a paper under consideration by one journal which has taken ages considering it, you still need to notify the editor formally that you are withdrawing the paper from consideration with them before sending it on to a different journal.

Some PhD students each year also make mistakes about the conventions on 'dual publication' of material. As soon your material has been accepted in one academic journal it cannot be considered, let alone republished, in any other journal. If you were to succeed in reprinting large amounts of the same material in a second article then the journal involved would be breaching the first journal's copyright. It could perhaps have to pulp its whole issue. The personal consequences for you would also be severe. Your reputation within the academic community would be damaged, since by 'plagiarizing yourself' you would seem to be inflating your curriculum vitae or résumé by underhand means. So this is a quick route to professional suicide.

However, it is not only permissible but perfectly acceptable for you to republish a journal article (usually in a somewhat revised form) later on in a book. This could be either as a component of your whole thesis if you can get this accepted by a publisher (see below), or as a chapter in an edited book. Journals take the copyright of any paper which they publish, so if you want to reuse your article material in your book or in an edited collection you need to get the journal publisher's permission to do so, and to include an acknowledgement of where it first appeared. Journal editors and publishers always give authors such permissions to reproduce their own materials without any copyright fee; for if they did not do so, their supply of copy would soon dry up. Journals always need to first-publish material, however. They make their money by getting original research into print, and their scholarly reputation would suffer if they seem to be duplicating or reprinting material which is already out in book form. The journal could also run into copyright difficulties if the book version of your paper by any chance comes out before the journal version, a not unlikely event given the long time lags in journals publishing, and one to strictly guard against.

So long as you keep these timings in sync there is no problem in publishing material in a journal article and then later in a book. Many of the best organized senior academics regularly generate one or several articles on different aspects of their current research project, each of which 'trails' or refers to their forthcoming book. Then they publish the full connected version of the research as a book, varying from six months to a year or two years later on. This approach delivers repeat messages to the academic community about the research, and is the best way of ensuring that the work gets noticed at all. It would also work for a student finishing her PhD, although it is a very demanding 'dissemination strategy', viable only for the best or most original doctorates.

Re-working your thesis as a book

> *Interviewer*:   What came first, the lyrics or the music?
> *George Gershwin*:   What came first was the contract. [8]

Some theses become books, of a particular kind called research monographs. A monograph, as its name implies, is a detailed study of one particular topic. It stands at the opposite extreme in publishing terms from a best-selling textbook, which may cover all or many topics in a discipline. The worldwide sales for English-language monographs are usually measured in the low hundreds, say between 300 and 600 copies. So although a contract between author and publisher is still a necessary basis for publication, it is rarely necessary to spend much time worrying about the division of the spoils, for they are often non-existent.

If 'the contract' is not the reason for wanting to get your thesis published as a monograph, there are none the less three substantial reasons why it is worth doing. The first and most important incentive is just to get the message of your research out into the wider academic community. A book, any book, is a surprisingly long-lived and multi-accessible artefact. The chances of other people learning about and drawing from your research are much greater if you can write a good book, which then makes it onto the shelves of at least the major research libraries in your own country and overseas. A second incentive is to build your résumé or curriculum vitae and to establish your bona fides as a fully fledged academic researcher. In some social science disciplines (like economics) people now rarely write books to communicate research. In these areas journal papers are the main research medium, and most published books are student texts written by senior academics, sometimes penned by authors who are no longer operating innovatively at the research frontiers. But across the more text-based social sciences, and in all the humanities and arts disciplines, books still count for a lot. A third reason for producing a monograph is a composite of the previous two. Books are usually much more cited than journal articles. They are a good way of amassing a large pile of citations on the Web of Knowledge. You will also find a larger stock of Web pages referring to a book on the best Web search engines (such as the world leader in most dimensions, www.google.com).[9] Books generate name recognition. A good book may be reviewed several times in academic journals with review sections, and it is still much more likely to be cited in bibliographies or included in student reading lists than are journal articles.

However, as the academic publishing industry has been consolidated into larger and more commercially orientated global corporations, the number of major firms that actually handle academic monographs has sharply declined since the 1980s. So your options of publishers to try are unlikely to be great and the chances of success are not high. Before you start a perhaps difficult, time-consuming and demoralizing book publishing process, you need to get clear whether there is a reasonable chance of success for your doctoral research. You should take advice on this issue from your supervisors or advisers, and from departmental colleagues and your examiners. If they are sceptical or not encouraging, it is probably not worth pushing things. Your topic may just be unsuitable or the publishing climate may be very unfavourable in your discipline for academic monographs.

Assuming that you have surmounted this first hurdle, your next step should be to consider possible companies to approach with a book proposition. Monograph publishers are arranged in a rough order of general academic prestige that is also something of an order of difficulty in getting an acceptance. It runs as follows:

◆ *Major university presses* are at top of the hierarchy, such as those for Oxford and Cambridge in the UK or for leading Ivy League universities in the United States. These companies still publish key works of scholarship as part of their overall academic mission. There is often some bias towards their own alumni's doctorates, but they also have some general sense of responsibility to academia more widely. They are typically only interested in the cream of works, however. And even they may specialize in areas where they already have a well-established list and a reputation, or a series into which your PhD might fit. These kinds of publishing houses are very prestigious because they will carefully referee your book and suggest changes before accepting it (usually taking at least six to nine months doing so). If they like your text, they may not worry overmuch about asking you to make large-scale length reductions. Then they will painstakingly sub-edit your text to a high standard and produce it well, often taking a year to 18 months doing so. The main drawback here then is that (after you have added in time for you to make changes), the complete publication process may stretch up to three years. And beyond that the publicity for your book may be rather skeletal – you should bank on doing most of the promotion work yourself.

◆ *Major commercial publishers with monograph lists* still exist, although they are a rapidly diminishing species. If you can find one or several in your field then they may offer the most attractive option open to you. These firms tend to be quicker off the mark than university presses, more insistent on reasonable length (70,000 word) books, better at dissemination, and more commercial in their approach. They make their money by having a large catalogue of titles and producing relatively small runs of copies at fairly high prices. The limit for first-print runs has come down from (say) 300 or 400 copies ten years ago to below 100 copies now. And 'warehouse' publishing can take place with digital printing machines technology that can cost-effectively generate single hardback copies of books from the publisher's formatted text database in response to individual orders. This 'publish on demand' approach means that your book may never go 'out of print'. In some ways this is a plus point for you, since your text remains available so long as people go directly to the publisher, and you do not need to worry about it being remaindered. On the debit side, the publisher can retain the copyright for its full term (now 70 years) without many real copies ever getting into circulation. And bookshops and major retailers like www.amazon.com may still robustly list your book as unavailable, whatever its notional status.

◆ *Less well-known university presses* also have some commitment to monographs, but usually a highly selective one, focusing on only a few fields or on their own doctoral students. If your university has its own press it is always well worth trying them, even if they do not have a big list in your field. You may also try another university press that happens to have a good list in your topic area or subdiscipline. Because they do fewer books these presses may produce your work faster than the top-rank university presses. But their big drawback is that their catalogues usually have a much lesser circulation, so the chances of your work being noticed in the profession are much smaller. Sometimes their books are also less prestigiously produced. And because the smaller university presses do less work in this line, they may ask for shorter manuscripts to keep their risk exposure down.

◆ *Smaller or lesser-known commercial publishers* have more specialist lists, smaller internet-and-mail-only marketing operations, and often higher prices and shorter print runs. But they are otherwise similar operations to the bigger firms. They are distinguished from vanity presses by being commercially reliant on achieving sales and they still sign contracts with their authors. In practice, the payment of author fees is usually either completely nominal or (in view of the non-commercial character of monograph publishing) the firm may ask that it be waived entirely. Some commercial publishers may also look for a partial subsidy to help finance the costs of issuing monographs. It is well worth exploring whether some form of limited subsidy may be available to help secure book publication of your research. Potential sources are your own department or university, where little-known funds often lurk for years without anyone bidding to them for assistance; national or regional-level professional associations in your discipline; and some kinds of foundations or charities. Ask your advisers and departmental colleagues if they have any suggestions here: this kind of information is often hard for graduate students to find out unaided.

Included in the category of smaller commercial publishers with monograph lists there are a diverse range of companies. Some of them are medium-sized firms, well known and long established. Others are reputable or well-regarded companies, but quite newly formed. There are also many start-up companies with an unproven track record and potentially uncertain futures. Try to find out as much as you can about companies before getting involved with them, and be reasonably sceptical about promises from smaller outfits. Make sure that you get sight of previous books and catalogues that the firm has produced, and check out the company Web site and its facilities. It is very important for your career track purposes that your book should be properly edited, designed and printed to a good standard, and that it should be effectively distributed and publicized so that potential readers get to hear about it.

♦ *Vanity publishers* are not really publishers at all. Essentially they ask authors to pay for the publication of their own manuscript. They are not worth considering because a book issued by them cannot build your résumé or CV in any

worthwhile way. In addition once issued by such presses
your thesis does not become any more accessible than
sitting on the shelf in your university library. Vanity press
titles are not taken seriously either by the reviews editors of
journals or by university librarians doing book ordering.
And such operations typically have no marketing operations
to speak of. If a company writes to you offering to publish
your thesis sight unseen, or without any independent
refereeing process, you should be highly sceptical.

With a small set of target publishers in view, your next task
is to come up with a book proposal that will seem viable. A PhD
thesis can only very rarely be published as a book without
substantial alterations. Your first priority should be to keep the
length of your proposed book manuscript down. A 100,000-
word piece of text will simply be too long and expensive for
publishers to even begin to look at, however academically
meritorious it may be. Your chances of publication are much
better if your actual thesis text is no more than 80,000 words,
which is why this has been the recommended main text length
of even a 'big book' dissertation throughout these pages. But to
make book publishing feasible even this restrained length will
need editing down a bit further. A manuscript of 60,000 to
70,000 words is widely quoted by publishers as the ideal book
length. There is rarely any incentive to go lower than this, however. Academic books of much less than 60,000 words may look
'short weight' and appear poor value for money to reviewers,
libraries or potential professional readers.

A second important change is to make a book version much
more accessible than your original thesis. Cut out all the 'boring
bits' if you possibly can. Once your doctorate has been awarded
and the full PhD text is available in your university library, you
can refer readers to it to explain the most esoteric or routine
points of methodology, or data, or other evidence. So there is no
need to reproduce such material again. Similarly you can economize a good deal on the referencing of materials. If you have
not done so already, switch to Harvard referencing and get rid as
far as possible of all but the most important endnotes.

Next consider whether your doctorate can be reshaped in
some way to enhance its potential readership and hence sales

appeal. Are there parts of the thesis which are off-putting for readers and that can be hived off to a separate journal article? A prime candidate here is an overlong literature review chapter, some of which might be spun off to form a review article in a journal. You can then simply reference the article in a shorter set-up chapter for the main core of the book. (In rare cases a very strong PhD may best be published in the form of two shorter books, one handling the literature review elements more as a student-orientated book, and the other handling the original research.)

Before you approach publishers you should also examine whether there are elements that could be *added* to the book, to extend your thesis analysis and to make it more attractive for potential purchasers. In the social sciences if the period covered by your thesis ends some years ago, then publishers often want it brought right up to date. Similarly publishers may be interested in additional sections or chapters which put a thesis analysis in a wider context, or make it less narrowly focused, and perhaps boost the book's usability for advanced students as well as professional readers. Of course, any such additions come at a high price. You have to make space for them by achieving greater cuts in the wordage allocated to your original thesis chapters. New writing then takes extra time to accomplish, and you may also have to do new research to cope with the extensions.

Only when you have formed a plan for achieving a marketable, fully 'book-ified' version of your thesis should you approach publishers. You need to write a book proposal which meets these points:

- *Set out the academic rationale for the book.* Explain the intellectual reasons why your book is valuable for your discipline or broad research area. It can be very helpful to attach at this point positive references about your PhD thesis from distinguished and well-known examiners, who can stress its suitability for publication and wide interest in the profession. A brief supportive reference from your supervisors might also be useful, if they are well-known people. Make clear, though, that what you are proposing is a thoroughly reworked book version of original, high-quality research, and not the direct publication of an unchanged

PhD thesis itself (or even large bits of it). Even the few publishers who still look carefully at academic monograph books may well shy away from the prospect of issuing your PhD thesis, sending you a premature standard letter of rejection if you leave any room for doubt.

✦ *Specify the book's structure.*   Give the overall length of the text, chapter and maybe section headings, and each chapter's length.

✦ *Describe the book's contents.*   Write about half a page per chapter, concentrating on giving a substantive account of the book's key value-added contribution.

✦ *Give a market rationale for the book.*   You need to specify who the readers will be and make a properly justified and realistic estimate of the sales prospects for a hardback edition. Such books are expensive, especially from British or European publishers. They sell mostly to university libraries (but perhaps also to a business market in disciplines like management or information technology). You can also estimate some sales (50 to 100 copies) to professional academics in your particular subfield. In some circumstances it may be feasible to anticipate some public library sales. A reasonable minimum number of sales to aim for is 500 copies worldwide for a US-based publisher, although this may prove very optimistic if you are writing to a British or European firm producing very high-priced hardcover monographs. In this latter case 300 sales may seem more feasible. You should also include a case for a paperback edition, if you can estimate at least 1000 sales. Explain how the market would broaden out if lower-cost copies were available. Publishers will very rarely publish a paperback version of a monograph immediately, preferring to wait and see how many hardcover sales are achieved, so the paperback case is mostly nominal. But it may help to include one, so long as you can make a credible case.

✦ *Include a very brief suggested marketing strategy.*   Try to identify journals and more general-purpose library or university periodicals which might review the book and generate sales. If your book is accepted the publishers will want you to fill in a detailed marketing plan questionnaire. But it can help convince them that your book has a realistic chance of achieving significant sales if you seem to know how to promote it from the outset. In your marketing bit you can assume a reasonably prominent entry in the publisher's catalogue in the year of publication, and maybe a briefer catalogue mention in the year after. But do not assume that the publisher will otherwise spend any money on advertising the book, a luxury usually dispensed with in the monograph market. The effective period for a monograph book to achieve sales is normally two years. Sales in the first year are sustained mainly by the catalogue entry. With big firms the publisher's reps bring the book to the attention of librarians and university bookshops, and promote it at academic conferences. Thereafter sales may be generated by any reviews of the book in journals. If the book has not become known to members of the profession within two years, its chances of further sales are very slim. It can be very helpful to mention that you will e-mail a long list of relevant scholars yourself or can supply specialist mailing lists to the publisher. It is also helpful to promise to write conference papers to signpost the book at key professional meetings in the first year it comes out. You might also point to one or two articles that you have had accepted in good-quality journals, which will come out well ahead of the book's publication and alert readers to its imminence. But you also need to make sure that (in the publisher's mind) this does not undermine the reasons why people will want to buy your book.

◆ *Give a timetable for delivering the final manuscript.* Build in a two- to three-month period for the publishers to send your manuscript out to referees and receive comments back. Then build in a further two to three months for you to make the changes demanded in the referees' comments. Promising to be able to deliver a complete manuscript within six to nine months is best for publishers. (Delivering more rapidly than this is not much help, because publishers' catalogues and publicity materials can rarely be redone at shorter notice.) Stress that the manuscript is your publications priority and that these timings will not slip. If you do not meet your delivery date then in theory your publisher can cancel a book contract.

• *Include a specimen chapter.* Send your best chapter for the purposes of getting the book accepted. This may not necessarily be a very detailed core chapter, nor just a literature review. It should be a well-written chapter which shows your work in a good light but which is relatively easy for a referee to get into and appreciate. Sometimes it makes sense to provide a few extra pages of lead-in or scene-setting material for the chapter, and a summary of what comes next at the end. You will need to provide a purpose-edited chapter bibliography if you are using Harvard referencing, but not if you are using endnotes. The point of the specimen chapter is to show that your work is well written, of a good professional standard, on an interesting topic, and likely to generate the sales you have promised. It should be fully 'book-ified' with no unnecessary thesis apparatus. It obviously might carry more weight with publishers if you could promise to send a fully ready manuscript immediately by return if they would like to see the whole thing. But this is rarely practicable, because you cannot invest all the effort involved in converting your entire thesis into book form without knowing how likely it is that any publisher will accept it. And it may not be crucial anyway. If a publisher is at all interested in adopting your book they will have to commission one or more academics to review your materials. It is normally much easier (and cheaper) for them to get a book outline plus specimen chapter refereed than a complete book manuscript, especially with a research monograph which demands that the readers pay close attention to detail. If you think a single sample chapter will not be enough to show what your book will be like, then send two chapters.

Assembling this package of materials is a time-consuming business, and waiting for a response also takes more time. However, unlike journals you can legitimately send your book proposal and materials to more than one publisher at once. It is not a good idea to broadcast it to a large number of publishers, however, because their commissioning editors also meet regularly at conferences and other venues and swap notes. Finding out that you have adopted a shotgun approach to seeking a publisher may lead them to take a collectively unfavourable view of your work. In addition, if you send off copies of your proposal to ten different publishers you are unlikely to have targeted the proposal sufficiently, and are more likely to receive a row of outright rejections. And if you send the first version of your proposal to all available publishers then you cannot revise it in the light of feedback you get and send it off in a different form to anyone else. So it is best to send your proposal pack to no more than the two or three publishers who offer the best chances of getting your thesis published, keeping other names in reserve for a second-round effort.

If a company comes back with an offer to publish your monograph you should virtually always close the deal. But there are just a few safeguards to keep in mind. You must have a proper contract not because you will make any significant money out of a monograph, which is highly unlikely, but in order to ensure that you are dealing with a reputable firm. The contract will specify that you supply the publisher with a clean manuscript, warranted to be free from libellous or defamatory material, of a certain length and meeting the comments of the publishers' readers, by a certain date. In return for you ceding the publisher the right to market and distribute your text (usually worldwide) for a certain period, the publisher engages to deliver a book and to sell it in their normal way. A good contract from your point of view will have royalty terms in it, usually promising you something like 10 per cent of the publisher's 'net receipts' (that is, profits). Often such sums only kick in, however, after the book has achieved a certain number of sales (say 300 or 500 or 1000 copies), which may be the maximum one might expect anyway for a high-level research monograph in hardcover. On this kind of book these royalty terms are not usually worth haggling over. You will very rarely get an advance on royalties for a monograph, but if you can extract one that is a small additional incentive for the publisher to promote your book positively.

The key thing to watch for in a monograph contract is how long it binds you to the publisher, and what counts as the publisher keeping your book in print. Holding your book on a digital server ready to print an individual copy whenever an order is received can mean that your book is never in practice available in any bookshop or really noticeable in any catalogue, but remains formally 'in print' for ever. Be on the look-out also for clauses in your contract that may commit you to offer your next book to the same publisher for consideration, before it goes to anyone else. Only if your monograph has been accepted by a very prestigious and efficient publisher is it a good idea to let such a clause stand. Otherwise you should just draw a line through this bit and initial the deletion on the contract form, asking your publisher to do the same.

Normally nothing much hangs on monograph contracts. The author stands to make little or no money and the publisher to sell pretty few copies. But once in every several hundred titles something substantial may crop up. Perhaps you may not deliver your manuscript on time, a potentially fatal mistake to make in book publishing, and the publisher may disappoint your expectations of elastic deadlines by wanting to pull out of the deal altogether. Perhaps your book may suddenly sell a lot of copies or go to paperback, in which unlikely case the contract should ensure that you get a decent royalty. Perhaps someone may sue you and the publisher, which can be personally catastrophic for you, so take the non-libel, non-defamatory, and non-plagiarization clauses in contract documents seriously. Perhaps your publisher may go bankrupt or default on their obligation to publish your text, leaving you looking for some leg to stand on in getting back control of it. Normally these are remote contingencies, and with a friendly and reputable publisher not worth worrying about overmuch. But if in doubt, ask a more experienced colleague to check over a prospective publisher's contract with you before signing up.

Conclusions

Like the rest of authoring, publishing takes a lot of time and dedicated effort. It is never easy to do. It always requires persistence and resilience in the face of rejection, criticisms or demands for further changes to text that has already taken so long to produce. You also need to look ahead, and try not to publish material that within a few years you will not particularly want to acknowledge. But publishing is the only way in which you can disseminate the messages from your doctoral research to a wider audience. It is the principal mechanism by which your ideas can shape and become part of the traditions in your discipline (the other way being teaching). The goal of all publishing is in part an acknowledgement of your creative contribution, your value-added, to the discipline's mission. To then be cited by others, to shape their further work (whether positively or in opposition to your own propositions) is to acquire a kind of 'immortality'. Milan Kundera's novel of this title makes a powerful case to have us recognize this motive as a basic human drive.[10] Perhaps, though, reflecting on such goals and motives is too heady stuff, best tempered by a degree of cynicism. A famous cartoon of Garfield the cat starts with his owner, John, confessing in a moment of introspection: 'Garfield, I'm depressed. When I'm gone, no one will care that I ever existed.'[11] The normally unsupportive Garfield seems for a moment to be acting out of character: 'Cheer up John', the cat thinks in the middle frame. 'They don't care now', it concludes.

Afterword

'If a thing is worth doing', said G. K. Chesterton, 'it's worth doing badly.'[1] His brilliant reversal of common sense captures an important truth. Something intrinsically worthwhile for us to accomplish remains worthwhile, however imperfectly we carry it through. This thought has sustained me in writing these pages, which in the end have done so much less than I initially hoped they might. In closing I want to stress again the message of the Preface that none of the advice given here should necessarily be applied, still less adopted, in a mechanical or 'handbook' way. This book offers only suggestions, to be considered, evaluated, perhaps tried out, amended or discarded, as seems useful for your own situation and purposes. As Nietzche recognized: 'Ultimately, no one can extract from things, books included, more than he [or she] already knows. What one has no access to through experience one has no ear for.'[2]

There is a final danger, a risk of misconstruction that I want to underscore. This book tries to partially condense a set of practices which to a large extent must still be lived to be fully appreciated. It is, in short, a 'crib' book, of which Michael Oakeshott once remarked: 'Now the character of a crib is that its author must have an educated man's [or woman's] knowledge of the language, that he must prostitute his genius (if he has any) as a translator, and that it is powerless to save the ignorant reader from all possibility of mistake.'[3] Most of us will know the sinking feeling of making a transition from the apparent simplicities of a phrase book to an actual conversation in a foreign language. So let me stress that moving between these pages and your own doctoral work will entail a similar amount of heroic commitment on your part, a wholesale and necessary reconstruction. You must not, ever, construe a gap between the apparent straightforwardness of this text and the messiness or difficulty of your own authoring experience as reflecting adversely upon your authorial competences. Reading so far has been the easy bit. Doing authoring remains, for all of us, every time, a considerable trial.

In case this seems too sickeningly modest a view on which to end, let me mention that the object of Oakeshott's condescension about crib books was actually Niccolò Machiavelli's *The Prince*, a book so original, widely read and influential that it gave English (and many another language) a new complex word ('machiavellian'). In my own view a new 'crib' book is as valid as any other book, helping us to consolidate an established body of knowledge, to systematize it and then immediately to begin to change and reimprove it. How else, in our text-based civilization, can we make progress? The really important thing for any book is how readers approach it and what they seek to do in using it. As A. D. Sertillanges once wrote: 'A book is a signal, a stimulant, a helper, an initiator – it is not a substitute and it is not a chain.'[4]

Glossary of Maxims, Terms and Phrases

> All good maxims are in the world. We only need to apply them.
> *Blaise Pascal* [1]

The maxims included here are general suggestions for effective authoring, referred to at several points in the book. They are shown in grey-shaded boxes below. The terms or phrases included here are those which are not part of common parlance but are used widely in the book. The glossary does not include some specialist terms that are defined and used only at a single point in the main text. Words highlighted in *italics* denote other entries in the glossary below. Numbers in square brackets show page numbers for relevant sections in the main text.

ABD – an acronym for 'all but dissertationed', denoting a student in the *taught PhD model* who has passed her general examination but is still working on completing her dissertation.

analytic structure – a way of organizing a piece of text by chunking it up into logical or typological categories devised by the author. The categories fragment the materials, allowing them to be handled more easily, with materials in one category unified by some common characteristic. For instance, an analytic structure might look at necessary and sufficient causes; long-run and short-run influences; or the economic, political, cultural or other aspects of a single set of phenomena. [pp. 68–70]

archetypal singular – a stylistic mistake where an author describes the behaviour of a group or collectivity through an abstract, stereotyped and actually non-existent individual (for instance, 'the writer'). Using the archetypal singular form opens up a broad pathway to writing nonsense. [p. 119]

argumentative structure – a way of organizing a piece of text by pre-senting in turn two or more viewpoints identified by the author, such as competing theories, alternate sides in a controversy, or differing empirical interpretations. The case for one viewpoint is given in full, then the case for one or more alternative views, for example, in a 'for and against' or 'pros and cons' pattern. [pp. 70–4]

authoring – the complete process of producing a finished piece of text, that is: envisaging what to write, planning it in outline, drafting pas-sages, writing the whole thing, revising and *remodelling text*, and fin-ishing it in an appropriate form, together with publishing all or parts of the text. [p. 1]

bibliography – an exhaustive list of all the articles, books and other works cited in a thesis or book. A bibliography should always be set out completely in one sequence arranged by alphabetical order of authors' main names. Bibliographies should never be segmented (for instance, into separate lists for primary and secondary sources), because that would violate the *one-stop look-up* criterion. Every thesis needs a bibli-ography, whatever referencing or notes system is used. [pp. 122–33]

'big book' thesis – a very long dissertation (usually limited to a maxi-mum of 100,000 words) and the normal end product of a *classical model PhD*. It is constructed in an integrated, book form, with all the chapters closely linked to each other, and an overall introduction and conclusion. [pp. 5–11]

body – the major part of a paragraph, coming after the *topic sentence* and before the *wrap sentence*. [pp. 112–13]

body text – in word processors this term describes the main part of a piece of text, that which has not been identified as a heading or sub-heading in the 'organizer' part of the software. [p. 267]

classical model PhD – traditional British, Commonwealth and European model of the doctorate, in which the student works for a long period (usually three to five years) on producing a *'big book' thesis*, supervised either by one or two *supervisors* (in the British or Commonwealth model) or by a collegium of staff members (in the European model). [pp. 5–11]

compromise model – an intermediate approach to the overall struc-turing of a PhD thesis, which seeks to combine features of the *focus down model* and the *opening out model*. [pp. 60–1]

data reduction – techniques for screening out superfluous, unneces-sary or unwanted detail in numerical information. Key steps include: using charts or graphs instead of tables; cutting or rounding numbers in tables; reducing or eliminating decimal places; following the *three or* *four effective digits* maxim below; and using exploratory data analysis methods. [pp. 185–92]

descriptive structure – a way of organizing a piece of text by presenting the materials in a sequence given outside the author or fixed externally – for instance, following a chronology or narrative sequence; a 'guidebook' pattern; a sequence in which the author accessed materials; or a random, 'shopping list' approach. [pp. 63–8]

dissertation – the final stage of a PhD in the *taught PhD model*, a long and connected piece of text setting out an original analysis. More generally I use dissertation and PhD thesis interchangeably.

dissertation committee – a set of four, or five or more academics who oversee a research student in the dissertation stage of the *taught PhD model*. The committee always includes the student's *main adviser* and *minor adviser* plus other senior staff who do not work closely with the student. The committee members read the student's work at several stages, but especially carefully when the dissertation is complete, and they conduct the *dissertation defence* or *final oral examination*. Normally a dissertation cannot be accepted without either all members of the committee agreeing, or without all bar one member agreeing. [pp. 5–15]

dissertation defence – a common name for the *final oral examination* in the *taught PhD model*. [p. 217]

double-blind refereeing – a system where author identification details are removed before papers go to referees, and the referees make comments anonymously. The system is supposed to put all authors on a par for publication, and to allow reviewers to give frank comments. [p. 229]

dual publication – publishing material twice, first in a journal article and later in a book, a recognized and legitimate practice. Note, however, that the material must always be published first in the journal, and that material can never be published twice in different journals. [pp. 250–1]

effective digits – the numerals which vary from one number in a table to the next. See the *three or four effective digits* maxim.

emergency stop test – a check on how well your text is organized and signposted. If I interrupt a reader in mid-flow in your chapter or paper, can they give a clear account of its overall structure, what has been covered and what is still to come? [pp. 98–100]

endnotes – system of notes where all the referencing materials and other elements come in a single bloc at the end of the chapter or book, not broken up across the foot of each page. [pp. 130–3]

examiner – in the *classical model PhD* a senior person not otherwise involved with a student's research who decides whether their work reaches doctoral standard or not. In the UK variant two or three examiners read the research student's thesis, hold the *final oral examination* or *viva* with her, and then either grant the doctorate or issue a *referral*. There is always an external examiner (from another university) and an internal examiner (from the same university as the student). In the European variant, the examiners are all the members of a five- or six-person committee, who read the student's thesis, determine whether it can be accepted or not, and hold an examination in public. The supervisors will form part of this committee, and at least one member will be from another university or country. In the *taught PhD model* the members of the *dissertation committee* are the examiners of the final thesis, although they are not called by this name. [pp. 209–26]

(final) oral examination – the stage when either the *examiners* (in Britain, Commonwealth countries or Europe) or the *dissertation committee* (in the United States) formally discuss a student's thesis with them, raising issues and problems and testing their ability to defend their argument and to discuss relevant questions in the academic discipline. Commonly called the *viva* in British-influenced systems, where it is held in private, and the *dissertation defence* in the United States, where most of the session is held in public. [pp. 216–26]

first-order subheading – the heading for a main section inside a chapter or paper. It is more prominent than a second-order subheading in terms of font and location on the page. [p. 78]

focus down model – a sequence for organizing a thesis that begins with a long literature review, covering several chapters, during which the scope of the study is progressively reduced, followed by set-up material. The main analysis or evidence chapters thus arrive late on within the thesis, and are typically followed by only a very brief analysis and conclusions chapter. [pp. 53–9]

footnotes – system of notes where the referencing materials and other elements are given at the foot of the page where a note number occurs, and not in a single bloc at the end of the chapter or book. [pp. 132–3]

Get it down, then get it organized – write a quick first draft, without worrying too much about how it is structured, concentrating instead upon setting out your materials, stating arguments and expressing points. Then at the revision and upgrading stages focus hard on re-arranging your materials into a single, clear argument sequence, grouping together and linking up closely related points. [pp. 136–9]

Harvard referencing – a system for citing, where the author name and date are given in the main text at the reference point, and can be looked up in a single *bibliography* at the end of the work. Notes are not needed in this approach. [pp. 125–30]

high impact start – a dramatic or attention-grabbing way of beginning a chapter or a main section; for example, by using a starting quotation or a particularly vivid or compelling piece of evidence, or stating a paradox or a problem in clear terms. High impact starts should be carefully written. [pp. 92–5]

High impact start, Lead-in materials, Signposts – a suggested sequence for material needed in the introductory part of a chapter (or possibly of a long section). A *high impact start* engages readers' attention (see above). It is followed by any framing or set-up text, *lead-in material* needed to situate the analysis to come. The *signposts* briefly point forward to the sequence of topics in the main sections of the chapter (or in the body of a large section). [pp. 91–7]

Keep the faith – at a late stage in your doctorate maintain confidence and belief in what you have done in your research. Do not be tempted to overextend or overprolong your research or to launch out on brand new paths. Do not lightly abandon a major part of the work you have done. Instead find a way of defining and framing your research, consistent with the maxim *You define the question, you deliver the answer.* Be prepared to defend what you have done convincingly in the *final oral examination.* [pp. 221–2]

---

lead-in materials – text which provides a frame for what is to come next, for instance, which gives set-up information, a context, a background description, or other elements necessary for understanding a core piece of analysis. [pp. 49–51]

lead-out materials – text which puts a piece of analysis into clearer focus, drawing out conclusions and implications, and setting them in the wider context of a body of literature, a subfield or a discipline. [pp. 49–51]

Lead-out materials, Thematics, Links forward – a suggested sequence for material needed to finish off a chapter (or a main section) effectively. *Lead-out materials* draw out the conclusions of a piece of analysis and their implications. *Thematics* link back from this chapter to the opening chapter, and possibly to other preceding chapters. *Links forward* connect this chapter to the next one in sequence. [pp. 97–8]

Less is more – at the final draft stage of a thesis, finding economical ways of expressing your arguments creates a more professional feel for your text, especially getting rid of repetitions or thematic fragmentation (see the *Say it once, say it right* maxim). This principle should not be confused with a general style bias towards *parsimony*, which can sometimes improve your writing and sometimes make it less accessible. [p. 208]

Link, Frame, Deliver – a suggested sequence for organizing materials within sentences. Start with words or other elements already familiar to readers from previous text, establishing linkages. Try to get qualifying or subordinate clauses out of the way next. These elements normally frame the core proposition of the sentence, which is delivered last. See also the *Subject, Verb, Object* maxim. But good style also depends on some variation between sentences, and avoiding a mechanical repetition of any single form. [pp. 114–17]

main adviser – the staff member who principally guides a PhD student completing the dissertation in the *taught PhD model*. The main adviser is akin to the principal supervisor in the *classical model PhD*, except that the main adviser also forms part of the dissertation committee which determines whether the student gains a doctorate or not. [pp. 8–9]

Manage readers' expectations – the central task of an author. Do not create expectations on the part of readers that you will not fulfil, for instance, by over-promising or signposting in a misleading way. Aim for a controlled release of information, which always follows the *'need to know' criterion*. Make sure that readers appreciate the importance of what you have found out by framing it and situating it appropriately within a professional literature. [pp. 11–16]

minor adviser – a staff member who works with research students in the *taught PhD model*, but less intensively than the *main adviser*. Some universities stipulate that the minor adviser comes from an area of the discipline different from that which the student's dissertation is in. The minor adviser is a member of the *dissertation committee*. [pp. 8–9]

'Need to know' criterion – a key principle to use in determining how much detail or information to include in your text. Ask: 'What do readers need to know in order to follow and appreciate my argument?' Provide only enough set-up or background information to meet this need. [pp. 52–3]

For data numbers included in the main text give enough details to meet readers' needs, but do not overburden them. For instance, use charts instead of tables, round up data appropriately or employ other *data-reduction* methods. Present full information for the specialist readers and the examiners in appendices or on a CD bound in with the thesis. [pp. 159–65]

numerical progression – data which has been organized in either a descending sequence (highest to lowest numbers) or an ascending sequence (lowest to highest numbers). See the maxim: *Put data in a numerical progression.* [pp. 168–9]

One-stop look-up – a key principle for referencing. To find the source of a quotation or the full details of a reference for a book or paper, readers should need to look in only one place in your text. They should never have to go to two locations to find full referencing or source details. [pp. 121–2]

open refereeing – a system of peer review for journals, where author's details go to referees, and where referees' names and comments are disclosed to authors. [p. 229]

opening out model – a sequence for organizing a thesis in which there is a short lead-in or set-up chapter, followed immediately by the main analysis or evidence chapters. The discussion then 'opens out' into an analysis of what has been found, and from there into a wider consideration of issues in the existing literature or the discipline. [pp. 59–60]

oral examination – see *final oral examination, dissertation defence* and *viva.*

organizers – the complete apparatus of devices by which authors (and publishers' editors) allow readers to orientate themselves within a piece of text. Organizers include prefaces and introductions, headings and subheadings, *signposts*, author promises, running heads, conclusions, and so on. [p. 78]

papers model dissertation – a medium-length thesis (of around 50,000 to 60,000 words), which normally forms the second part of the *taught PhD model.* The thesis is written as four or five journal papers, of publishable quality. It will not necessarily have the integrated form of the *'big book' thesis.* [pp. 8–11]

paragraph – a unit of thought, usually around 100 to 200 words long. In English texts, the paragraph is a key organizing device. Its start is indicated by a blank line above or by an inset (tabbed) beginning. See *Topic, Body, Wrap.* [pp. 111–14]

parsimony – a general stylistic bias in favour of saying things in the shortest possible amount of words. Useful in avoiding repetitions and encouraging concise and efficient exposition, this attitude can also often produce rather hard-boiled or inaccessible text. See the *'Less is more' maxim*. [p. 108]

> **Print, Edit, Revise, Upgrade, Go public** – a suggested sequence for revising text. Always print out your writings and edit them on paper. Do not just do on-screen editing, which will be too confined to a verbal level and simple corrections. Once you have cleaned up the text, ask how it can be strengthened, extended, clarified, better-evidenced, and so on. Make revisions and then write or paste in upgrade materials. Go public with a draft to collect commentaries and ideas for changes. See also *remodelling text*. [p. 138]

problematic – an intellectual paradox or set of issues which provides the central research question(s) of the thesis. See the maxim, *Structure your thesis around a paradox, not around a gap*. [pp. 18–26]

> **Put data in a numerical progression** – a key principle for presenting tables and charts. Numbers and bars should be arranged in clear descending or ascending sequences wherever feasible. Numerical data in tables should never be presented in a way that creates a jumbled appearance down rows or across columns. Bar charts should have rows or columns arranged in a sequence which gives an up or down numerical progression. Never use data arranged in an alphabetical, geographic, random, official or customary sequence where a numerical progression is feasible. Only over-time data, some categorical data and a few other specialized uses are exempt from this rule. [pp. 168–9 and 181–2]

> **Put the story in the heading** – so far as possible your headings should express your substantive findings or conclusions, the 'bottom line' message of your text. Never use headings that are formalistic, vacuous, vague or obscure. [pp. 84–5]

referencing circle – a group of academics who regularly cite each other's works in a mutual back-scratching way. [p. 222]

referral – a refusal by the *examiners* to accept a PhD thesis. They will impose and list a set of major changes that must be made as a requirement for the thesis to be *submitted* again. A thesis that is referred twice is a failed doctorate. [p. 221]

remodelling text – an intensive way of evaluating and usually changing how a chapter or paper is organized. Number and list each paragraph in sequence with a one-line statement of its key message, interspersed with headings and subheadings. Devise one alternate sequence and repackage paragraphs by number under it. If it looks promising, cut and paste the paragraphs on word processor into the new sequence. If this looks convincing tidy up inter-paragraph linkages. Check the final structure for evenly spaced subheadings and adequate organization. [pp. 143–8]

> **Say it once, say it right** – a principle for structuring your text's argument. Do not fragment similar material and scatter it around your text in lots of little bits. Try to pull all the similar material together and deliver it in a single compelling bloc. This approach avoids repetitions and fragmentation. It helps you build a clearer argument, made up of fewer, larger blocs. [p. 109]

second-order heading – the heading for a subsection, inside a main section of a chapter or paper. It is less prominent in terms of font and placing than a *first-order heading*. [pp. 77–92]

shelf-bending research – produces a text that is read by only a handful of people. The work sits on a shelf, and over a period of years its only real-world effect is to slowly bend the shelf in a minuscule way. Because it is not published the research does not feed into broader professional debates in any way, and normally cannot be referenced or consulted by other authors. The two biggest categories of shelf-bending work are PhD theses sitting in university libraries, and applied research reports produced by academics or consultants for government agencies or companies. [pp. 12–13]

signposts – elements in the main text which point forward to the structure of a chapter or a main section. Signposts are always very brief and indicate strictly the sequence of topics to be handled. They should not summarize the substantive argument or be miniature advance guidebooks for your analysis or conclusions. [pp. 95–7]

single-blind refereeing – a system of peer review where referees know who has written the papers they look at, but they can still preserve their own anonymity. It is less restrictive than *double-blind refereeing*. [p. 229]

> **Structure your thesis around a paradox, not around a gap** – a principle for clarifying the central research question or *problematic* of your thesis. You should aim to explain a non-obvious puzzle in an original way, not just to produce the first description of something not already (extensively) studied. [pp. 18–26]

Subject, Verb, Object – a core principle of English grammar in constructing sentences. Do not separate a subject from the main verb or the verb from its object. Qualifying or subordinate clauses should come at the beginnings or ends of sentences but not in the middle. And such clauses should never come between subject, verb and object. [pp. 114–17]

submit – formally send a completed doctoral thesis or dissertation to the university for it to be assessed. The thesis must be in an acceptable final form. There may be limits on how many times you can submit a thesis, often two times only. [pp. 209–16]

supervisor – in the *classical model PhD* the individual staff member (or one of two members) accepting prime responsibility for a research student completing a *'big book' thesis*. In the UK or Commonwealth model the supervisor does not serve as *examiner* of the PhD, but is otherwise equivalent to the American *main adviser*. In the European model the supervisor may be a member of the collegium of examiners. [pp. 1–11]

taught PhD model – a two-part doctoral qualification. It is composed first of coursework assessed by a general examination (usually after two or three years); and secondly of a medium-length *papers model dissertation* undertaken for a further two to four years and assessed by a *dissertation committee*. [pp. 5–11]

themes – main argument strands or theory elements in a dissertation, especially those which recur and structure the thesis as a whole. Themes especially link the opening and closing chapters, usually via the conclusions of intermediate chapters. [pp. 199–209]

Three (or four) effective digits – a rule of thumb for how much numerical detail should be presented in tables. Only three or four *effective digits* or numbers should vary from one data point to the next. The other elements of numbers should be rounded up or cut or rebased to achieve this effect. For example, with three effective digits the number 1,346,899 would become 1,350,000 or 1.35 million. With four effective digits it would become 1,347,000. [p. 275]

topic sentence – the first sentence of a paragraph, which communicates what issue or subject it covers. It is followed by the *body* of the paragraph. See the *Topic, Body, Wrap* maxim. [pp. 112–13]

Topic, Body, Wrap – a suggested sequence of material within paragraphs. The first *topic sentence* makes clear what issue the paragraph addresses, what its focus is on. The main *body* of the paragraph

> comes next, giving reasoning, justification, elaboration, analysis or evidence. The final *wrap sentence* makes clear the bottom line message of the paragraph, the conclusion reached. A very common and serious authoring mistake is to misplace the wrap sentence, so that it misleadingly appears as the topic sentence of the next paragraph. [pp. 112–13]

version control problem – a discrepancy between different versions of something at two different points: for instance, how something is described in the text and in a diagram, or how a source is referenced in footnotes and in a bibliography. Readers get two versions and do not know which to believe. [p. 127]

viva – the commonly used name for the *final oral examination* in British-influenced systems. It is a shortened form of the medieval Latin term 'viva voce' (literally meaning 'with the living voice'). Vivas involve usually two or three examiners talking for around an hour or two to the research student about her thesis. Sometimes supervisors can sit in on vivas (without speaking), but they are otherwise private sessions. [pp. 216–26]

wrap sentence – the final sentence of a paragraph, which sums up its key message. It follows the *body* of the paragraph. See the *Topic, Body, Wrap* maxim. [pp. 112–13]

> **You define the question, you deliver the answer** – a central principle of the doctorate, making clear how it differs from earlier stages of education where other people define the questions and you deliver the answer. The principle also emphasizes the importance of choosing and framing your central research question so as to mesh closely with what your research will accomplish. Do not include any elements in your research question that will not be addressed in substantive and (hopefully) original ways by your analysis. Do not have elements of your research analysis or evidence that are not covered by the statement of your key research question. [pp. 18–26]

Notes

Opening epigraph

'All rules for study...', Friedrich Wilhem Joseph von Schelling, *On University Studies* (Athens, OH: Ohio University Press, 1966), translated by E. S. Morgan, edited with an Introduction by N. Guterman, p. 34.

Preface

1. Michael Oakeshott, 'The study of "politics" in a university: An essay in appropriateness', in his *Rationalism in Politics and Other Essays* (Indianapolis: Liberty Fund, 1991), p. 194. Originally published 1962.
2. John Stuart Mill, *On Liberty*, Ch. 3, from the volume J. S. Mill, *Utilitarianism, Liberty and Representative Government* (London: Dent, 1968), p. 123. Originally published 1859.
3. Max Weber discussed bureaucratization most clearly in *The Theory of Social and Economic Organization* (London: William Hodge, 1947), pp. 302–12. It was originally written in 1913.
4. Friedrich Wilhem Joseph von Schelling, *On University Studies* (Athens, Ohio: Ohio University Press, 1966), translated by E. S. Morgan, edited with an Introduction by N. Guterman; Francis Bacon, *The Advancement of Learning* (London: Dent, 1861), edited by G. W. Kitchen.
5. Von Schelling, *On University Studies*, p. 34.
6. I thank especially my supervisees who have completed doctorates: Kate Ascher, Françoise Boucek, Ian Emsley, Raquel Galliego-Calderon, Stephen Griggs, Gunnar Gunnarsson, Stephanie Hoopes, Jaejuhn Joo, Won-Taek Kang, Tom Ioannou, Leo Keliher, Kuang-Wu

277

Koai, Helen Margetts, Andrew Massey, Rosa Mule, Mark Patterson, John Peterson, Yvonne Rydin, Richard Sandlant, James Stanyer, Helen Thompson, Carol Vielba, John Xavier, Andrew Webster, Daniel Wincott and Spencer Zifcak. I am grateful also to Kiyoko Iwasaki, Gita Subrahmanyam and Pieter Vanhuysse, whose doctorates were still ongoing at the time of writing. I learnt a lot also from: Davina Cooper, Penny Law, Abigail Melville and Anne Meyel. Amongst LSE people who were not my supervisees, I benefited from conversations with Richard Heffernan, Andrew Hindmoor, Rolf Hoijer and Oliver James.

7. I thank especially: Martin Bulmer (now at the University of Southampton), Keith Dowding, George Gaskell, Michael Hebbert (now at the University of Manchester), George Jones, Paul Kelly, Peter Loizos, Helen Margetts (now at the School of Public Policy, University College, London), Brendan O'Leary (now at the University of Pennsylvania), Anne Power, James Putzel and Yvonne Rydin. I am especially indebted to Liz Barnett and her supportive staff in the LSE's Teaching and Learning Development Office for their extended help and assistance. I thank also Andy Northedge (Open University).

8. Plato quoted in Ernest Dimnet, *Art of Thinking* (London: Cape, 1929), p. 95.

Chapter 1   Becoming an author

1. Alain de Botton, *The Consolations of Philosophy* (London: Penguin, 2000), pp. 58–9.
2. C. Wright Mills, *The Sociological Imagination* (New York: Oxford University Press, 1959), p. 243.
3. Michael Oakeshott, from his inaugural lecture at LSE, 'Political Education', p. 15, quoted in W. J. M. Mackenzie, *Explorations in Government* (London: Macmillan, now Palgrave Macmillan, 1975), p. 24.
4. Ernest Dimnet, *The Art of Thinking* (London: Cape, 1929), p. 151.
5. Thomas Gray, 'Elegy in a country churchyard':

   Full many a rose is born to blush unseen
   And waste its sweetness on the desert air.

6. Charles Caleb Colton (1780–1832). Colton was a British clergyman who coined aphorisms now popular on US religious Web sites. This quote was given to me by a student, and I have been unable to trace it to a source.

Chapter 2 Envisioning the thesis as a whole

1. W. B. Yeats included this line, attributed to 'Old Play', in the frontispiece of his poetry volume *Responsibilities*, first published in 1914. See W. B. Yeats, *Collected Poems* (London: Vintage, 1992), edited by Augustine Martine, p. 95.
2. Quoted in *Great Writings of Goethe*, edited by Stephen Spender (New York: Meridian, 1958), p. 272.
3. Quoted in A. A. Schuessler, *A Logic of Expressive Choice* (Princeton, NJ: Princeton University Press, 2000), p. 29.
4. Robert Nozick, *The Nature of Rationality* (Princeton, NJ: Princeton University Press, 1993), p. 164.
5. G. K. Chesterton, an untraced quote from one of his less well known 'Father Brown' stories.
6. Nozick, *The Nature of Rationality*, p. 165.
7. John Stuart Mill, *On Liberty*, Chapter 3, from John Stuart Mill, *Utilitarianism, Liberty and Representative Government* (London: Dent, 1968), p. 123. Originally published 1859.
8. A. D. Sertillanges, *The Intellectual Life: Its Spirits, Conditions and Methods* (Dublin: Mercier Press, 1978), translated by Mary Ryan, p. 145.
9. PhD regulations of London University, as printed in London School of Economics and Political Science, *Calendar 2001–2001* (London: London School of Economics, 2000), p. 228.
10. Quoted in Sertillanges, *The Intellectual Life*, p. 173.
11. Arthur Schopenhauer's *Paralipomena*, quoted (vaguely) in E. Dimnet, *The Art of Thinking* (London: Cape, 1929), p. 163.
12. Ivan Illich, *Tools for Conviviality* (London: Fontana, 1973), p. 101.
13. Johanne Goethe, 'On Originality' from *Great Writings of Goethe*, edited by Stephen Spender (New York: Meridian, 1958), p. 45.
14. Quoted in Patrick Hughes and George Brecht, *Vicious Circles and Infinity: An Anthology of Paradoxes* (Harmondsworth: Penguin, 1978), p. 60.
15. Robert Oppenheimer, 'A science of change', reprinted in E. Blair Bolles (ed.), *Galileo's Commandment: An Anthology of Great Science Writing* (London: Abacus, 2000), p. 298–9.
16. Blaise Pascal, *Pensées* (London: Dent, 1932), p. 106, Thought number 395.
17. J. K. Galbraith, *The Affluent Society* (Harmondsworth: Penguin, 1958), pp. 18–20. Galbraith uses the phrase 'conventional wisdom' to describe 'ideas which are esteemed at any time for their acceptability, and ... predictability'.
18. Quoted in C. Rose and M. J. Nicoholl, *Accelerated Learning for the 21st Century* (London: Piatkus, 1997), p. 193.

19. Quoted in Rose and Nicoholl, *Accelerated Learning*, p. 195.
20. Quoted in Sertillanges, *The Intellectual Life*, p. 223.
21. Quoted in G. G. Neil Wright, *Teach Yourself to Study* (London: English Universities Press, 1945), p. 123, from Shaw's play, *Major Barbara*, Act III.
22. *Sunday Times Magazine*, 28 January 2001, p. 25. Eddie Izzard is a well-known British comedian.
23. Quoted in L. Minkin, *Exits and Entrances: Political Research as a Creative Art* (Sheffield: Sheffield Hallam University Press, 1997), p. iv.
24. G. A. Miller, 'The magical number seven, plus or minus two: Some limits on our capacity for processing information', *Psychological Review*, (1956), vol. 63, no.1, pp. 81–97.
25. Quoted in Rose and Nicoholl, *Accelerated Learning*, p. 198. Linus Pauling won the Nobel Prize for chemistry.
26. Quoted in Minkin, *Exits and Entrances*, p. 10.
27. Michel de Montaigne, (1533–92), quoted in Sertillanges, *The Intellectual Life*, p. 186. Sertillanges goes on: 'Notes are a sort of external memory.'
28. Blaise Pascal, *Pensées* (London: Dent, 1932), p. 101, Thought number 370.
29. Minkin, *Exits and Entrances*, p. 298.
30. Quoted by Lewis Wolpert, *The Unnatural Nature of Science* (London: Faber, 1992), p. 81. This quote was a favourite of Alexander Fleming (1881–1955), the discoverer of penicillin. In the Hollywood film, *Under Siege 2: Dark Territory* a shortened version ('fortune favours the prepared mind') was also the motto of the arch-villain, a terrorist plotting to blow up the world by triggering earthquakes from space satellites.
31. Virginia Woolf, *A Room of One's Own* (Frogmore, St Albans, Herts: Granada Publishing, 1983), p. 32.
32. Alexander Hamilton (1755–1804), one of the 'founding fathers' of the US constitution. The singer John Mellencamp uses an almost identical formulation in the anthem *You've got to stand*, from his CD *Scarecrow* (New York: Polygram, 1985).
33. Teilhard de Chardin, *The Phenomenon of Man* (London: HarperCollins, 1975), p. 323.
34. Albert Hirschman, in his paper 'The Hiding Hand', quoted in J. Elster, *Sour Grapes: Studies in the Subversion of Rationality* (Cambridge: Cambridge University Press, 1983), p. 158.
35. Elster, *Sour Grapes*, p. 158.
36. Quoted in Dimnet, *The Art of Thinking*, p. 95.
37. A character in Robertson Davies's novel, *The Lyre of Orpheus* (London: Penguin, 1989), p. 212.

38. Louis Pasteur, quoted in many websites.
39. Quoted in Minkin, *Exits and Entrances*, p. 58.
40. Minkin, *Exits and Entrances*.
41. Quoted in Minkin, *Exits and Entrances*, p. 48.
42. Minkin, *Exits and Entrances*, p. 15.
43. Quoted in Francis Wheen, *Karl Marx* (London: Fourth Estate, 1999), p. 311.

Chapter 3 Planning an integrated thesis: the macro-structure

1. Vladimir Nabokov, quoted in *The Guardian*, 23 December 1999, G2 section, p. 3.
2. Neil Young from 'Crime in the City' on his CD *Freedom* (New York: Reprise Records, 1989).
3. Jean-Jacques Rousseau, quoted in S. and K. Baker, *The Idiot's Guide to Project Management* (Indianapolis: Macmillan, 2000), 2nd edn, p. 359.
4. C. Wright Mills, *The Sociological Imagination* (New York: Oxford University Press, 1959), p. 245.
5. Randall Collins, *The Sociology of Philosophies: A Global Theory of Intellectual Change* (Cambridge, MA: Belknap/Harvard, 1999), p. 52.
6. T. S. Eliot, 'The Hollow Men', in his *Collected Poems, 1909–1962* (London: Faber, 1974), pp. 89–92, quote from p. 92; originally published 1925.
7. The science fiction writer Poul Anderson, quoted in Arthur Koestler, *The Ghost in the Machine* (London: Hutchinson, 1967). See also www.quotationspage.com/quotes/poul_anderson/
8. The distinction between descriptive, analytic, argumentative and matrix patterns was first made in P. Dunleavy, *Studying for a Degree in the Humanities and Social Sciences* (Basingstoke: Macmillan, now Palgrave Macmillan, 1987), pp. 86–97.

Chapter 4 Organizing a chapter or paper: the micro-structure

1. Jerome K. Jerome, *Three Men in a Boat*, ch. 3.
2. Stanislaw Lem, *Solaris* (London: Faber, 1970), p. 120.
3. Henry Ford, unsourced quotation from a 'thought pyramid' in the office of a Ford salesperson who sold me a Mondeo car in Milton Keynes, June 2002.

4. Robert J. Sternberg, *The Psychologist's Companion: A Guide to Scientific Writing for Students and Researchers* (Cambridge: Cambridge University Press and British Psychological Society, 1988), p. 58.

5. The *Sun's* headline synopsis of the quiet revolution in Czechoslovakia was: 'Commies Czech Out'.

6. Michelangelo quoted in A. D. Sertillanges, *The Intellectual Life: Its Spirits, Conditions and Methods* (Dublin: Mercier Press, 1978), translated by Mary Ryan, p. 222.

7. Johanne Wolfgang von Goethe, quoted in R. Andrews, *The Routledge Dictionary of Quotations* (London: Routledge, 1987), p. 292. The same quotation from Faust is also rendered as: 'When ideas fail, words come in very handy', in L. D. Eigen and J. P. Siegel, *Dictionary of Political Quotations* (London: Robert Hale, 1994), p. 466.

8. Michel Foucault, *Discipline and Punish: The Birth of the Prison* (Harmondsworth: Penguin, 1979), translated by Alan Sheridan.

Chapter 5   Writing clearly: style and referencing issues

1. Robert Sternberg, *The Psychologist's Companion: A Guide to Scientific Writing for Students and Researchers* (Cambridge: Cambridge University Press and British Psychological Society, 1988), p. 3.

2. Alain de Botton, *The Consolations of Philosophy* (London: Penguin, 2000), pp. 158–9.

3. Howard S. Becker, *Writing for Social Scientists* (Chicago: University of Chicago Press, 1986), p. 81.

4. Quoted in R. Andrews, *The Routledge Dictionary of Quotations* (London: Routledge, 1987), p. 250.

5. Quoted in *The Observer, More Sayings of the Week* (London: The Observer, 1983), p. 60.

6. Blaise Pascal, *Pensées* (London: Dent, 1932), p. 45, Thought number 145.

7. Pascal, *Pensées*, p. 7, Thought number 23.

8. Pascal, *Pensées*, p. 45, Thought number 145.

9. Quoted by Antoine Laurent Lavoisier in his Preface to *The Elements of Chemistry* (1789), reprinted in E. Blair Bolles (ed.), *Galileo's Commandment: An Anthology of Great Science Writing* (London: Abacus, 2000), pp. 379–88, quote on p. 380.

10. G. K. Chesterton, *The Everlasting Man* (London: Hodder and Stoughton, 1925), p. 161.

11. Anatole France (1844–1924), quoted in Andrews, *The Routledge Dictionary of Quotations*, p. 218. Of course, by 'copy it' here France means quote and acknowledge it, not plagiarize it!

12. Joseph Gubaldi, *MLA Style Manual and Guide to Scholarly Publishing* (New York: Modern Languages Association, 1998), 2nd edn.

13. For Endnote see www.endnote.com.

Chapter 6 Developing your text and managing the writing process

1. I have not been able to trace this quotation. For Nietzsche generally, see Laurence Gane and Kitty Chan, *Introducing Nietzsche* (Cambridge: Icon Books, 1999).

2. John Fowles, *Mantissa* (London: Triad/Panther, 1984), p. 117.

3. The Emperor in George Lucas's film *The Return of the Jedi*. Shooting script on http://corky.net/scripts/returnOfTheJedi.html

4. Howard S. Becker, *Writing for Social Scientists* (Chicago: University of Chicago Press, 1986), Chapter 3.

5. James Thurber quoted in Lewis Minkin, *Exits and Entrances: Political Research as a Creative Art* (Sheffield: Sheffield Hallam University Press, 1997), p. 100.

6. Becker, *Writing for Social Scientists*, p. 60.

7. Umberto Eco, *Kant and the Platypus: Essays on Language and Cognition* (London: Verso, 1997), translated by Alastair McEwan, p. 4.

8. Bernard Lonergan, *Insight* (London: Ward Lock, 1978), p. 174. Originally published 1958.

9. Francis Bacon quoted in E. Dimnet, *The Art of Thinking* (London: Cape, 1929), p. 108.

10. Eco, *Kant and the Platypus*, p. 4.

11. A leading example is *Nudist*, a package designed for systematic analysis and handling of large amounts of qualitative data. It includes split-screen editing facilities, which some people have found useful.

12. Quoted in Minkin, *Exits and Entrances*, p. 313.

13. Quoted in Minkin, *Exits and Entrances*, p. 313.

14. Sir Phillip Sidney (1554–86), originally from *Astrophe and Stella* (1519), Sonnet 1, and quoted in different forms in *The Concise Oxford Dictionary of Quotations* (Oxford: Oxford University Press, 1981), p. 241, and R. Andrews, *The Routledge Book of Quotations* (London: Routledge, 1987), p. 292.

15. Quoted in *The Observer, More Sayings of the Week* (London: The Observer, 1983), p. 60.

16. The next few paragraphs draw on the useful discussion in Eviatar Zerubavel, *The Clockwork Muse: A Practical Guide to Writing Theses,*

Dissertations and Books (Cambridge, MA: Harvard University Press, 1999). Zerubavel offers detailed guidance on how to timetable writing sessions.

17. Quoted in A. D. Sertillanges, *The Intellectual Life: Its Spirits, Conditions and Methods* (Dublin: Mercier Press, 1978), translated by Mary Ryan, p. 220.
18. Zerubavel, *The Clockwork Muse*, chs 4–5.
19. James Gleick, *Faster: The Acceleration of Just about Everything* (London: Abacus, 2000).
20. St Thomas Aquinas, *Summa Theologica: A Concise Translation* (London: Methuen, 1991), edited by T. McDermott, p. 439.
21. Blaise Pascal, quoted in Sertillanges, *The Intellectual Life*, p. 216.
22. Immanuel Kant, *The Critique of Pure Reason* (Basingstoke: Macmillan, 1986), p. 338.
23. Johanne Wolfgang von Goethe, *Great Writings of Goethe* (New York: Meridian, 1958), edited by Stephen Spender, p. 272.
24. W. H. Auden, quoted in S. and K. Baker, *The Idiot's Guide to Project Management* (Indianapolis: Macmillan, 2000), second edition, p. 142.
25. F. Scott Fitzgerald, quoted in Baker and Baker, *The Idiot's Guide to Project Management*, p. 272.
26. Neil Simon, quoted in Minkin, *Exits and Entrances*, p. 102.
27. John Dewey, *Democracy and Education* (New York: Macmillan, 1916), p. 140.

Chapter 7 Handling attention points: data, charts and graphics

1. National Audit Office, *Presenting Data in Reports* (London: National Audit Office, 1998), p. 1.
2. Radiohead, 'Karma Police' from their CD *OK Computer* (London: Parlophone, 1997).
3. Quoted in L. D. Eigen and J. P. Siegel, *Dictionary of Political Quotations* (London: Robert Hale, 1994), p. 470.
4. National Audit Office, *Presenting Data in Reports* (London: NAO, 1999), p. 10.
5. See A. S. C. Ehrenberg, *A Primer in Data Reduction* (Chichester: Wiley, 1982) for a full set of examples).
6. Greg Evans in his science fiction novel *Diaspora* (London, Orion Books, 1997), p. 36. Evans's original quotation is in the past tense, but I have rephrased it in the present tense. The quote describes how virtual entities called 'citizens' in future electronic communities called polises (that is, identities 'born' from computer images of original human personalities), learn maths.

7. My favourite sources are now dated but still useful works, such as Catherine Marsh, *Exploring Data: An Introduction to Data Analysis for Social Scientists* (Cambridge: Polity, 1988); Ehrenberg, *A Primer in Data Reduction*; B. H. Erickson and T. A. Nozanchuk, *Understanding Data: An Introduction to Exploratory and Confirmatory Data Analysis for Students in the Social Sciences* (Milton Keynes: Open University Press, 1979); John W. Tukey, *Exploratory Data Analysis* (Reading, MA: Addison-Wesley, 1977); and Frederick Mosteller and John W. Tukey, *Data Analysis and Regression: A Second Course in Statistics* (Reading, MA: Addison-Wesley, 1977).

8. See Tukey, *Exploratory Data Analysis*, pp. 221–2.

9. Umberto Eco, *Kant and the Platypus: Essays on Language and Cognition* (London: Verso, 1997), translated by Alastair McEwan, p. 83.

Chapter 8   The end-game: finishing your doctorate

1. Howard S. Becker, *Writing for Social Scientists* (Chicago: University of Chicago Press, 1986), p. 122.

2. Alexis de Tocqueville, quoted in J. P. Mayer, *Prophet of the Mass Age* (London: Dent, 1939), p. 123.

3. Blaise Pascal, *Pensées* (London: Dent, 1932), p. 7, Thought number 19.

4. Robert Browning, from his poem 'Andrea del Sarto (called "The Faultless Poet")', line 78: 'Well, less is more Lucrezi, I am judged'. For the complete poem, see: www.libraryutoronto.ca/intel/rp/poems/browning12.html. The catchphrase 'less is more' was picked up and made famous as a motto of modernist architecture by Mies van der Rohe, in the *New York Herald Tribune*, 28 June 1959. The architect Robert Venturi famously retorted: 'Less is a bore.'

5. Boscoe Pertwee, quoted in Umberto Eco, *Kant and the Platypus: Essays on Language and Cognition* (London: Verso, 1997), translated by Alastair McEwan, p. 2.

6. Monty Python. The full script can be found at: www.ai.mit.edu/people/paulfitz/spanish/script.html

Chapter 9   Publishing your research

1. AT&T poster advertisement, autumn 2000. The company is an American phone giant.

2. Quoted in G. G. Neil Wright, *Teach Yourself to Study* (London: English Universities Press, 1945), p. 96.

3. ISI Web of Knowledge is at www.isinet.com and includes the Social Science Citation Index and Arts and Humanities Citation Index.
4. See www.ingenta.com and www.jstor.org It is best to access them via your university library, where it should be free.
5. E. Tulving and S. A. Madigan wrote their piece in 1970, and are quoted in Robert J. Sternberg, *The Psychologist's Companion: A Guide to Scientific Writing for Students and Researchers* (Cambridge: Cambridge University Press and British Psychological Society, 1988), pp. 166–7.
6. Sternberg, *The Psychologist's Companion*, pp. 179–83.
7. Quoted by Minkin, *Exits and Entrances*, p. 15.
8. Quoted by Minkin, *Exits and Entrances*, p. 90.
9. Other useful search engines include: www.alltheweb.com; www.teoma.com; www.vivisimo.com (which gives nicely clustered results); www.wisenut.com; and even www.search.msn.com. For articles in magazines try www.findarticles.com.
10. Milan Kundera, *Immortality* (London: Faber, 1991).
11. Garfield is written and drawn by Jim Davis and published in New York by Ballantine Books, see www.randomhouse.com/BB/.

Afterword

1. G. K. Chesterton quoted in *The Concise Oxford Dictionary of Quotations* (Oxford: Oxford University Press, 1981), p. 70. The original source was his essay 'Folly and female education', Iv. 14.
2. Quoted I. Gane and K. Chan, *Introducing Nietzsche* (Duxford, Cambridge: Icon Books, 1998), p. 40.
3. Michael Oakeshott, 'Rationalism in politics', in his *Rationalism in Politics and Other Essays* (Indianapolis: Liberty Fund, 1991), pp. 29–30. Originally published 1947.
4. A. D. Sertillanges, *The Intellectual Life: Its Spirits, Conditions and Methods* (Dublin: Mercier Press, 1978), translated by Mary Ryan, p. 172.

Glossary

1. Blaise Pascal, *Pensées* (London: Dent, 1932), p. 103, Thought number 380.

Further Reading

Many people have written useful or inspiring things about authoring in professional contexts and about being creative about research. But these ideas are mainly small snippets in works on diverse topics. Tracking down these bits and pieces was worthwhile for me, and the sources involved are shown in the Notes (starting on p. 277). But I would rate only a few of these works as worthwhile for readers to follow up. I give a couple of lines of commentary to explain or qualify all my recommendations, because each book is likely to be helpful for only a specific kind of reader.

General writings relevant for intellectual work

S. and K. Baker, *The Idiot's Guide to Project Management* (Indianapolis: Macmillan, 2000), second edition. A clear and self-deprecating guide to planning a large-scale piece of work, full of useful reflections but not specific to doctoral projects.

Howard S. Becker, *Writing for Social Scientists* (Chicago: University of Chicago Press, 1986). A very sympathetic discussion of the difficulties of writing and going public with your material. A 'must read' for strong-willed social scientists doing more literary research, but perhaps not for those who already feel lacking in confidence?

Howard S. Becker, *Tricks of the Trade: How to Think about Your Research While You're Doing It* (Chicago: University of Chicago Press, 1998). Not much on authoring here, but Becker offers social scientists helpful ideas on formulating problems and thinking through appropriate research methods and solutions.

Alain de Botton, *The Consolations of Philosophy* (London: Penguin, 2000). A beautifully written example of authoring, focusing on five philosophers through the ages who have a great deal of relevance for contemporary intellectuals. It is worth looking at even just as a style exemplar.

Gillian Butler and Tony Hope, *Manage Your Mind: The Mental Fitness Guide* (Oxford: Oxford University Press, 1995). Doing a PhD is a high-pressure experience and comes at a time when people's life situation is often changing radically for other reasons. This very humane book may help you review a range of common mild problems. If you feel more than very mildly stressed or depressed, do see a doctor or other expert counsellor. Despite appearances, academic work is work, and you need to be fit and well to do it effectively.

Jon Elster, *Sour Grapes: Studies in the Subversion of Rationality* (Cambridge: Cambridge University Press, 1983), Chapter IV on 'Belief, bias and ideology'. A leading social theorist considers the stimulus to thought arising from making personal commitments.

G. A. Miller, 'The magical number seven, plus or minus two: Some limits on our capacity for processing information', *Psychological Review*, (1956), vol. 63, no.1, pp. 81–97. A very old paper now, but still valuable for all authors to think through how readers will react to their work.

C. Wright Mills, *The Sociological Imagination* (New York: Oxford University Press, 1959). A key 'think piece' addressed to young sociologists, with good insights on authoring too.

L. Minkin, *Exits and Entrances: Political Research as a Creative Art* (Sheffield: Sheffield Hallam University Press, 1997). Minkin usefully synthesizes a lot of the earlier literature on creativity. He also adds his own original and helpful reflections on how to puzzle through issues and dilemmas while authoring. He is a political scientist of the old school, and so his reflections are highly relevant for historians as well.

Rebecca B. Morton, *Methods and Models: A Guide to the Empirical Analysis of Formal Models in Political Science* (Cambridge: Cambridge University Press, 1999). An insightful analysis of the research design issues in formal modelling work, using political science examples. Morton perfectly captures the often elusive 'oral wisdom' of formal modellers and she condenses the general ethos of modern social science intellectuals doing empirically orientated but 'techno' research.

Robert Nozick, *The Nature of Rationality* (Princeton, NJ: Princeton University Press, 1993), pp. 163–72 only, on 'philosophical heuristics'. A leading philosopher reflects on how intellectual problems are defined and ameliorated in his discipline. (In the remainder of this complex book his thesis is that rational beliefs are those which maximize the causal, evidential and symbolic welfare of the belief-holders. The argument has a great deal of resonance for academic work generally, but it is set out here chiefly for specialists.)

Blaise Pascal, *Pensées* (London: Dent, 1932). Some outstanding reflections on intellectual work in general are scattered throughout a mainly theological seventeenth-century text: it will interest religiously inclined people.

A. D. Sertillanges, *The Intellectual Life: Its Spirits, Conditions and Methods* (Dublin: Mercier Press, 1978), translated by Mary Ryan. Originally published in 1920. A warm but serious reflection on intellectual work infused throughout by Catholic thinking. It should be useful for religiously inclined people, but the theology will put off others.

Robert J. Sternberg, *The Psychologist's Companion: A Guide to Scientific Writing for Students and Researchers* (Cambridge: Cambridge University Press and British Psychological Society, 1988). Very specific to psychology in some parts, but with more generally relevant insights as well.

David Sternberg, *How to Complete and Survive a Doctoral Dissertation* (New York: St Martin's Griffin, 1981). A fairly general book about completing an American PhD but with plenty of insights too about managing a dissertation committee.

Eviatar Zerubavel, *The Clockwork Muse: A Practical Guide to Writing Theses, Dissertations and Books* (Cambridge, MA: Harvard University Press, 1999). A stylishly produced short book focusing on the logistics of the writing process, written by a sociologist. Zerubavel gives some detailed guidance drawn from his own experience, but reading it may give you an inferiority complex. As the title suggests, he believes in keeping to time!

Books discussing style and related issues

There are numerous general books on writing, mainly on issues around style. Most are not a great deal of help for doctoral work. Each of these books has different virtues and limitations, but they may be helpful in upgrading your writing style for the demands of writing a lot of text.

Peter Elbow, *Writing with Power: Techniques for Mastering the Writing Process* (New York: Oxford University Press, 1998), second edition. A substantial collection of advice, orientated towards literary and cultural areas and lower-level courses. But it is helpful on quite a range of issues and for people whose first language is not English

Albert Joseph, *Put it in Writing: Learn How to Write Clearly, Quickly and Persuasively* (New York: McGraw Hill, 1998). A business-orientated treatment and not at all academic, but it provides a useful guide to modern, 'generally accepted standards' of good communication. The book does not overclaim and it is very well presented.

Theodore A. Rees Cheney, *Writing Creative NonFiction: How to Use Fiction Techniques to Make Your Nonfiction More Interesting, Dramatic and Vivid* (Berkeley, CA: Ten Speed Press, 1991). The advice here is orientated towards journalism and general-interest non-fiction writing, but it could apply also to literary and cultural studies areas. The emphasis is on actively trying to interest readers.

Joseph M. Williams, *Style: Towards Clarity and Grace* (Chicago: University of Chicago Press, 1995). I find this the most useful book on style issues, with systematically based and modern-looking advice. There are a lot of carefully worked examples, but also a useful focus on the intellectual purposes that you are trying to achieve.

Index